THE COMPLETE IDIOT'S GUIDE® TO

Discovering Your Past Lives

Second Edition

by Michael R. Hathaway, D.C.H.

ALPHA

A member of Penguin Group (USA) Inc.

ALPHA BOOKS

Published by the Penguin Group

Penguin Group (USA) Inc., 375 Hudson Street, New York, New York 10014, USA

Penguin Group (Canada), 90 Eglinton Avenue East, Suite 700, Toronto, Ontario M4P 2Y3, Canada (a division of Pearson Penguin Canada Inc.)

Penguin Books Ltd., 80 Strand, London WC2R 0RL, England

Penguin Ireland, 25 St. Stephen's Green, Dublin 2, Ireland (a division of Penguin Books Ltd.)

Penguin Group (Australia), 250 Camberwell Road, Camberwell, Victoria 3124, Australia (a division of Pearson Australia Group Pty. Ltd.)

Penguin Books India Pvt. Ltd., 11 Community Centre, Panchsheel Park, New Delhi—110 017, India

Penguin Group (NZ), 67 Apollo Drive, Rosedale, North Shore, Auckland 1311, New Zealand (a division of Pearson New Zealand Ltd.)

Penguin Books (South Africa) (Pty.) Ltd., 24 Sturdee Avenue, Rosebank, Johannesburg 2196, South Africa

Penguin Books Ltd., Registered Offices: 80 Strand, London WC2R 0RL, England

International Standard Book Number: 978-1-61564-098-0
Library of Congress Catalog Card Number: 2010915381

13 12 11   8 7 6 5 4 3 2 1

Interpretation of the printing code: The rightmost number of the first series of numbers is the year of the book's printing; the rightmost number of the second series of numbers is the number of the book's printing. For example, a printing code of 11-1 shows that the first printing occurred in 2011.

Printed in the United States of America

Note: This publication contains the opinions and ideas of its author. It is intended to provide helpful and informative material on the subject matter covered. It is sold with the understanding that the author and publisher are not engaged in rendering professional services in the book. If the reader requires personal assistance or advice, a competent professional should be consulted.

The author and publisher specifically disclaim any responsibility for any liability, loss, or risk, personal or otherwise, which is incurred as a consequence, directly or indirectly, of the use and application of any of the contents of this book.

Most Alpha books are available at special quantity discounts for bulk purchases for sales promotions, premiums, fund-raising, or educational use. Special books, or book excerpts, can also be created to fit specific needs.

For details, write: Special Markets, Alpha Books, 375 Hudson Street, New York, NY 10014.

Publisher: *Marie Butler-Knight*
Associate Publisher: *Mike Sanders*
Executive Managing Editor: *Billy Fields*
Executive Editor: *Randy Ladenheim-Gil*
Development Editor: *Megan Douglass*
Production Editor: *Kayla Dugger*
Copy Editor: *Jan Zoya*

Cover Designer: *Kurt Owens*
Book Designers: *William Thomas, Rebecca Batchelor*
Indexer: *Brad Herriman*
Layout: *Ayanna Lacey*
Proofreader: *Laura Caddell*

To Penny my eternal love, Brian, Brenda, Marc, Carter, and Madison.

Contents

Part 1:   **Echoes from the Past** 1

    1   **What Do You Mean, I've Lived Before?** 3

        You Are What You Were 4

        Mental DNA: How the Mind Works 5

        You Are in a Play of Many Lifetimes 7

        Relationships: Past, Present, and Future 9

        Relax and Imagine 11

        Top Reasons to Go Backward 12

    2   **Who Was I?** **15**

        Is This All There Is? 15

        The Soul Knows 18

        Is It Real or Your Imagination? 20

        Follow Your Heart 22

        Have You Ever Been a Ghost? 24

    3   **Children Still Remember** **29**

        A Child's Wisdom 30

        From One Life to the Next 31

        Role Reversals 33

        Helping Children Keep Their Memories Alive 35

    4   **How to Create a Trance** **39**

        The Different Kinds of Trances 40

        Use Your Imagination 41

        Take a Breath and Relax 43

        Creating a Daily Practice Schedule 46

Part 2:   **Peeking Through the Veil** **49**

    5   **You Live in a Trance** **51**

        Do You Like Old Things? 52

        Feeling Comfortable in a Different Time 53

        I Think I've Done This Before 55

        Dreaming About the Past 57

6   Making Use of Your Senses 61

The Past, Future, and Present 62

Your Conscious, Unconscious, and Universal Minds 64

How Do You Rate Your Mental DNA? 65

Seeing with the Mind's Eye *65*

Can You Hear It? *66*

How Do You Feel? *67*

Let's Add Taste and Smell *69*

Making Sense of It All *70*

7   Now Get Comfortable 73

Where's Your Favorite Relaxing Place? 74

Take a Deep Breath, and Let Your Eyes Go Out
   of Focus 76

Count from Five to Zero 77

Enjoy Your Comfort Zone 79

Count Back to Reality 79

What If I Don't Have a Special Place? 80

8   A Visit to a Past Life Discovery Specialist 83

What Should You Expect? 84

Brad's Past Life Discovery Session 86

Journey to Atlantis with Stephanie 91

Dora's Panic Attacks 94

Part 3: Preparing for the Adventure 97

**9   What Is It Like to Discover Your
       Past Lives? 99**

What Will You Experience? 99

Is It Possible to Get Stuck in the Past? 102

After Your Past Life Discovery Experience 104

Experiencing or Just Imagining? 106

10   The Karma Club 111

Your Past Lives Can Catch Up with You 112

Does Your Life Run in Cycles? 114

The Connection to People, Places, and Things 117

Unexplained Fears and Phobias 117

Mysterious Aches and Pains 118

11   **Keeping Yourself Grounded**............................**121**
Travel Insurance: Understanding Your Faith....................122
Include Your Faith..125
Include Your Guides or Angels 126
A Ground-Level Exercise 128

12   **Creating a Travel Plan**..................................**133**
Where Do You Want to Go?...134
What to Look For 135
Traveling Alone or with a Partner?................................137
Tools to Bring with You...139
How Long Should You Spend There? 141

13   **What to Do When You Get There**...............**145**
Put Your Mental DNA to Use..145
Just Allow Yourself to Experience.................................148
You Can Be a Detective in Your Own Mind...................149
Study the Cast of Characters..152
Follow the Story's Theme Wherever It Goes 154

Part 4: **Going Through the Window**...........................**157**

14   **Past Life Discovery Scripts**.........................**159**
Going to the Library 160
Movies of Your Mind 163
I Saw It on TV...163
Going Backward in Time 165
Where Did That Feeling Come From? 167

15   **Back to the Past: Time for Travel** **171**
Check Your Final Preparations for Your Past Life
  Journey 172
Begin Your Trance 174
Travel Time! 177
Coming Back to the Present..179

16   **What Just Happened?**....................................**183**
Collecting Your Thoughts...183
It Can Be Confusing at First..185
Making Notes...187
Keeping a Journal..190

17   What You've Learned **193**
Sifting Through the Data...193
Was One Visit Enough?...195
Going Back Again 198
Filling in the Blanks...199
Research the Story 201

Part 5:   Updating Your Past **205**

18   Was That Really My Past Life? **207**
How Do I Know That Was Me?...................................... 207
Two or More Lives at the Same Time 209
The Collective Unconscious: Meeting All Kinds
    of People 211
Channeling and Spirit Communication 213

19   Relationships from the Past...........................**217**
I Know You from Somewhere 217
Crisscrossing Paths 218
Understanding Soul Mate Connections 221
Soul Mate Connections to Current Family....................223
The Twin Soul Connection..225

20   Resolving the Old Karma............................... **231**
Old Karma Dies Hard...232
Free Will: You Don't Have to Change 234
Healing the Past and the Present....................................236
Soul Memory Healing Exercise 239

21   Putting Past Talents to Use........................... **243**
Rediscovering Your Skills... 244
Were You an Artist?...245
Were You a Writer?... 248
Did You Have a Psychic Gift? 249
Were You Famous? 251

22   Future and Parallel Lives **253**
A Peek into the Future...253
Establish a Travel Plan...255
Create a Future Life Discovery Technique.....................258
Can Future Knowledge Help You Right Now?................ 260

In-Between Lives: Life Reviews and Sacred Contracts....261
Parallel Lifetimes 263

23   Balancing Your Lives.. 265
Using Past Positive and Negative Experiences in
    the Present...265
Get in Tune with Your Soul's Purpose...............................267
Rediscovering Lost Talents and Other Abilities................269
Continue to Use Your Ability to Discover Past Lives 270
What You Were and What You May Be 273

Appendixes

A   Glossary 277

B   Resources 285

    Index 291

Introduction

Past lives was a subject that I had little knowledge of during my childhood and young adult years. It was never part of the conversation at our dining room table and certainly not a topic in the Baptist church I attended as a teen. It didn't even come across my radar screen until I was hired to play piano for a stage hypnosis show. Then I was hooked! I had to learn this magic power! A psychologist friend, Dr. Donald Orsillo, loaned me a couple books on the subject, and I was on my way. I became very interested in ghost hunting and started using hypnosis as a tool to contact the unseen. The idea of past lives began to creep into the picture, but I was still unsure how it fit with my traditional beliefs at the time.

Then a car hit me the summer of 1989 while I was crossing the street (in a crosswalk). Even though I didn't recall going through a tunnel to the other side, I was a different person afterward. I was still alive, and I knew that there must be an assignment left for me on Earth. I began to receive insights and became aware that I had a very special team to guide me. After all, I was obsessed with walking a year before I was hurt, doing up to 10 miles a day. I believe now that I was training for the accident and my life change.

In the process of my studies of hypnosis, I learned about Edgar Cayce, and on a chance visit to the Association of Research and Enlightenment (A.R.E.) in Virginia Beach, Virginia, I had an encounter with an old man who brought me face to face with the subject of past lives. He was in the library, and it seemed that he was waiting for me. Besides telling me about the workings of the library and Cayce, he insisted that I take a small booklet by a Jesuit priest written in the early 1900s that contained reincarnation information that had been removed from the Bible by the early Catholic church. All of a sudden I knew that there was much more to life than I had thought. The hologram, or second view, in my unconscious mind had been opened. Since that time, my life has been filled with the insights that many gifted and talented psychic people bring me. In one of my ancient lifetimes I was a strong and powerful ruler who misused his abilities for self-gain. Perhaps we knew each other then.

I really believe that this book holds something special for you within its covers, which will help you if you so choose to become in tune again with a part of your soul that's waiting to be rediscovered.

How to Use This Book

The Complete Idiot's Guide to Discovering Your Past Lives, Second Edition, is divided into five parts:

Part 1, Echoes from the Past, starts your journey through this book by helping you to become aware of the echoes from your past that may already have been calling to you through your unconscious mind. As you begin to prepare for your journey back in time, you will get an overview of what different cultures believe about reincarnation, learn about Edgar Cayce, and discover how to put yourself in a relaxing image trance.

Part 2, Peeking Through the Veil, prepares you to look through the thin shroud that has thus far hidden your view into your past lives. You will learn how you naturally experience a trance, how your mind works, how to find your comfort zone, and what it is like to visit a past life discovery specialist. You will also find out how children easily remember past life experiences.

Part 3, Preparing for the Adventure, helps you learn what to expect during a past life discovery journey and how to identify karma. You will practice keeping yourself grounded using your belief and your inner and outer guidance systems. You will begin to create your past life travel plan and learn how to use your mental DNA to get the best images while you are there.

Part 4, Going Through the Window, shows you several different techniques to help you have the best past life experience possible. Then you will travel back in time and learn how to get the most out of the information you collected. You will be shown how to resolve the karma that may have accompanied you when you entered this lifetime.

Part 5, Updating Your Past, shows you how to identify and update the abilities and talents you developed during a past lifetime. You may even want to visit a future lifetime or see what it is like between lifetimes. Finally, you will see how your past can be a very important part of your present and your future.

You'll also find two helpful appendixes: a glossary and a list of resources.

Extras

In addition to the chapters and appendixes, I've included several kinds of sidebars sprinkled throughout the text that give additional information, define terms, identify potential pitfalls, and share fascinating anecdotes. Here's what you'll find:

SOUL STORIES

These sidebars contain anecdotes from case studies that will help you understand how past lives can influence people in their present lives.

DEFINITION

Check here for definitions of some of the more significant and commonly used words in the book; you'll also find these terms and more in the Glossary.

AGELESS INSIGHTS

These sidebars provide useful information and miscellaneous tidbits that will help you understand the past life discovery process.

KARMIC CAUTIONS

Check these sidebars for possible pitfalls you may encounter on your journeys into your past lives.

Acknowledgments

This book would not have been possible without the pioneers in past life discovery who have opened the doors and minds of countless people. Foremost in that group would be Edgar Cayce and the work that continues through the A.R.E. in Virginia Beach. More recently, the works of Roger Woolger, Brian Weiss, Robert Grant, Dick Sutphen, and Henry Bolduc, among others, have helped the public become aware of the value of understanding the importance of reaching into the memories of the soul.

There needs to be a great big thank you to the organizations and people behind them who are helping to advance the study of hypnosis and past life research. These include Dwight Damon and the National Guild of Hypnotists, The American Institute of Hypnotherapy, and Thelma Freedman and the Internal Board of Regression Therapy.

I would like to thank Katelynn Lacopo of BookEnds for her tireless effort and guidance representing this and other works. To author Morgan Llywelyn, who is a wonderful teacher and a source of inspiration. Also included is the work and encouragement that the editors of Alpha Books provide.

There are many friends who have encouraged the development of this book. I am surrounded by psychics, including Martha Douglass, Megan Crawford, Lisa Halpin, Ramona Garcia, and Pat and Don Bleyle (who has passed over), and they all told me about the adventures that I would have, long before they started. The Wednesday Night Metaphysical Group brings me insights that have helped stretch my mind, and Jan Weinraub, who has an incredible library of books, has provided a wealth of information for this and other works.

Then there is the team on the other side. I believe old friend Ellen Turner, someone who knew and was linked to Edgar Cayce through many of his lifetimes, heads the list. Incidentally, her grandmother was a sister to William James, who had a summer estate near where we live. Author Robert Grant had written to tell me of her passing and said she had told him that it was time to go because she had assignments on the other side. Three weeks later my first offer of a book arrived over the Internet.

I would like to thank Pastor Sean Dunker-Bendigo and the good congregation of the Madison Baptist Church for still allowing me to be a member despite my nontraditional views of religion. Finally, to my incredible and talented family, including the Whitmans, Bennetts, Davises, and Hathaways, especially son Brian, daughter Brenda, her husband Marc, and children Carter Davis and Brenda Marie (a little girl who talks to and sees her spirit guides), thanks for your support. The real proof in past lives, however, is the greatest miracle in my life, my soul mate and wife, Penny, whose abilities as an editor are incredible. Without her, this and other works would not have been possible. Thank you, my love.

Trademarks

All terms mentioned in this book that are known to be or are suspected of being trademarks or service marks have been appropriately capitalized. Alpha Books and Penguin Group (USA) Inc. cannot attest to the accuracy of this information. Use of a term in this book should not be regarded as affecting the validity of any trademark or service mark.

Echoes from the Past

Do you enjoy a good mystery? Do you like to imagine what it would be like to interview the witnesses, collect the clues, and solve the case? If you like intrigue, you are about to become a detective on a case with a fascinating scenario.

Your assignment is to put together someone's missing past. Your search may connect you with royalty, wealth, and possibly even murderers. Perhaps you will follow them in between lifetimes to see if they existed in spirit form as a ghost. You might find that the pieces of the puzzle come together easily, or you may have to search for the smallest clues.

There is a risk that goes with this case. It may develop into a passion as you find yourself going deeper and deeper into the history of your suspect's past. After all, it is yourself and your soul that you are assigned to investigate. Welcome to the adventure of discovering your past lives.

What Do You Mean, I've Lived Before?

In This Chapter

- What is it like to discover your past lives?
- Understand your conscious, unconscious, and universal minds
- The karmic connection between past and present lives
- How your past lives influence you in this life
- Know what trances really are
- What can you learn from visiting your past lives?

Do you believe that you lived before? You may have asked yourself that question from time to time. Perhaps you're particularly interested in a certain period of history. You might imagine how the people actually lived or what it felt like to wear their clothes. Whether you believe in past lives or not, you can benefit from this book.

No one can say absolutely for sure that you really lived in the past. There are many theories and no actual proof. You must judge for yourself, and it's up to you to decide. As you read this book and participate in the various exercises, you will have an opportunity to investigate the workings of your mind. No one else's mind is the same as yours. If you enjoy a good mystery, then you are about to take part in one—the search for your past lives. If you have an imagination and are willing to follow where it goes, you may be in for a fascinating adventure into the journey of your soul as you discover your past lives.

You Are What You Were

Are you comfortable living in today's world? Is there a period in history that you find absolutely fascinating? If so, do you read books about it or listen to music of that time? Do you imagine what it would be like to live back then? Do you visit places that have historical sites related to that time period?

You may wear your hair a certain way or dress in a style that was popular in a different time period. It doesn't have to be hundreds of years ago. Your interest need only go back to before you were born this time. In fact, everything you do in some way or other has the potential of relating back to a different lifetime, including the way you dress, the way you walk, the way you eat, and even the way you think. Chances are, when you were a child, you may have been much more open to past lives than you are as an adult. Society has some very narrow beliefs about reincarnation.

Your interest in different time periods can be influenced by the memories that are stored in your unconscious mind. When you're in an open frame of mind, images of your past lives can float up to the surface of your conscious mind. Once they become part of your conscious thinking, you are influenced by your memories from another time without even knowing where they came from.

A past life discovery experience is the process of going back into a previous lifetime through your unconscious mind while you are in a relaxed, self-hypnotic state. Your soul will reincarnate or experience many different lifetimes before its journey is complete. Each lifetime or incarnation adds to your soul's memories, such as an interest in the things you knew from before. The process of reincarnation happens each time a soul enters a new lifetime. When you experience a past life journey, you are actually going back to the memories of one of your previous lives.

SOUL STORIES

Paul found himself being drawn more and more to the history of the Civil War and could not forget a southern plantation that he had visited. He began to imagine how it felt to live there before the War Between the States erupted. He even got to the point where he considered moving his family to that place. He finally sought out a past life specialist to find the answers. He discovered that he had a strong connection to the plantation but didn't believe in the war. He had treated his slaves with care and compassion and only joined the ranks of the Confederacy to save face. When he came home, there was nothing left, and he died with the conflict still weighing heavily on his mind. Through the process of discovering his past life there, he was able to finally find peace.

Mental DNA: How the Mind Works

Your mind works differently from anyone else's on Earth. Just as you have a physical *DNA* that can be traced backward in your bloodline to your origins, you also have an individual mental DNA that is connected to your soul. Just as physical DNA helps determine your size, weight, coloring, and hair (among other physical characteristics), your mental DNA is shaped by past life experiences as well as your physical makeup.

Mental DNA may sound complicated, but it's really quite simple. You don't have to change a thing about yourself to understand it. In fact, it's a process you have naturally been doing your entire life. When you become aware of the way you think in terms of your sensory images, you will be helped in many aspects of your life, besides that of learning from your past lives. Let's see if we can put this into perspective and understand how your mental DNA images relate to your conscious, unconscious, and universal minds.

DEFINITION

DNA, or deoxyribonucleic acid, is a chemical found at the center of the cells of living things that controls the structure and purpose of each cell. It carries genetic information.

You have three different minds—your conscious mind, your unconscious mind, and your universal mind. The conscious mind is your analytical mind. Some of you have a very active conscious mind, and you have a hard time trying to stop thinking. It's very easy for the conscious mind to become confused. Besides handling all the momentary decision-making, thinking about the past and the future, the conscious mind also is constantly being sent messages from the unconscious mind. The conscious mind makes up only about 10 percent of your total mind.

That means that the unconscious mind makes up the difference, or 90 percent. The unconscious is your memory bank. It does the same thing as a computer. It stores the information that you send to it and brings the data back when it is requested. It keeps on file an image record of everything you have ever experienced. Your experiences also include the memories from your different lifetimes.

Your universal mind is connected through your unconscious mind to a high information source in the universe. It is an intelligence that houses all information. It can communicate through forms of energy, angels, guides, dreams, and other unexplainable ways.

Your mind works in three different tenses—the past, the present, and the future. Every time you recall a memory, you are reaching into your unconscious memory bank. Some of you may be stuck in this tense, and you constantly replay a certain memory over and over. It may be a memory you are familiar with, or it may be something that you have no idea where it came from.

When you imagine something before it actually happens, you are projecting into the future. You consciously imagine the future by using your present and past experiences. It is also possible to dream of the future in ways that are connected to neither your conscious nor unconscious minds.

AGELESS INSIGHTS

You create your memories through five different senses: seeing, hearing, feeling, tasting, and smelling. Everything you experience through your senses is recorded in your unconscious memory, and when you consciously remember, you replay the experience in one or more of your senses.

Guess what? Not everybody remembers in the same way. Have you and someone else ever compared an event you both witnessed? Did you remember it the same way? Chances are you didn't. Here's why: our five different senses—seeing, hearing, feeling, smelling, and tasting—are not processed, stored, and recalled equally by everyone's unconscious minds. The way you experience your memories is different from anyone else. It's your mental DNA for the most part that determines the difference. (You'll learn how your mental DNA makeup is determined in Chapter 6.)

You Are in a Play of Many Lifetimes

Did you know that you are participating in a play? At times you may feel like you are. Your play has many different characters and many different themes. In fact, you are in a traveling group of the same actors, and in most every production you have a changing role. Sometimes you're the main character, and sometimes you may have a supporting role. You may be the hero or you may be the victim. You may be royalty or you may be a peasant. You may be the winner or you may be the loser.

You are a member of the Karma Club Players. The script for each production has a lot of flexibility. The play begins with a basic theme, but it can change as the play continues on. Each scene fades into the next without a break.

Sometimes you're offstage a long time, and sometimes you have only a short break. You have the opportunity to make changes as the production progresses. So do all the other players you are acting with. Your actions on stage will help determine the next role you play after you have exited the current segment. You might have a similar role, or it might be very different. It all depends on how you and the other actors played your parts in the last scene.

In the Buddhist religion, *karma* represents the unfinished business that carries over into your current lifetime from one or more of your past lifetimes. Each incarnation has a specific set of lessons for the soul to work on. These lessons can vary widely from control to greed to love to relationships. You revisit the karma in order to help you progress on your soul's journey toward a higher understanding of the workings of the universe.

DEFINITION

Karma is the force produced by people's actions in one of their lives that influences what happens to them in their future lives.

In Hinduism, it is believed that your mental or physical acts will determine the conditions of your life and rebirth. That is, what you have done in the past can affect your current life, and what you do now can affect your future lives. There is both good and bad karma, meaning that you can advance or be required to improve upon the conditions you have created. This means that your play will be affected by the way you act your role.

So what's your current role in the play? Do you think you have a specific script to follow? If so, how do you know what it is? Do you believe you were born with certain karma? Do you feel life is a challenge that you must overcome in order to succeed, or do you feel you are traveling hand in hand with the universe at a rate that feels comfortable and positive?

You, the actor, have been given one more key element by the universe, that of free will. Free will means you may or may not go by the script you were given for this lifetime when you were reincarnated onto the earth plane. You have the potential to advance way beyond this life's lessons, or you could lag way behind. You make the choice whether or not you will follow your lessons, which is the opportunity of understanding your own free will.

KARMIC CAUTIONS

If you choose not to work on a karmic lesson, you may have to repeat it in another lifetime. If these are relationship lessons, how you progress as a group will determine how the characters are assigned in the next lifetime.

Free will works two ways. If a warning signal pops up relating to someone you think you have negative past life karma with, then it's a good idea to pay attention to your intuition. It's also important that both of you have the opportunity to resolve the old behavior patterns. It's very possible that positive gains can be made from the situation in this lifetime.

As you can see, you are not in this alone. Everyone is a member of the club. That is a perspective you might often forget. It's easy to feel isolated as you progress through the scenes in this lifetime. Many times the memories from before are so strong that you try to follow the same script as before. That script may be outdated now, and failure to recognize this can create potential problems that can result in more of the same karma in future lifetimes.

Relationships: Past, Present, and Future

Much of your karma in this lifetime is based on relationships from the past. Perhaps there is one or more individuals in your life who you feel you've known from somewhere before on some different plane. You may have that feeling about someone when you meet her for the first time. It's as if your relationship is as comfortable as an old pair of shoes. There seems to be some unexplainable bond— an instant connection—and it's possible that you both feel the same thing. You like and dislike the same things and find yourselves magnetically drawn together.

It's also possible that when you meet someone for the first time you have an unexplainable dislike or mistrust for him. You may go to great lengths to avoid that other person even though he's known to have the highest integrity. It's possible there is another person or persons who feel the same way about you, and it seems as if there is nothing you can do to gain their trust.

You may have friends who seem as if they should be part of your family. You may be like siblings or have more of a parent-child bond with them than with your own family. You may feel out of place in your family, almost as if you had been adopted, but you know that's impossible. It's as if you got switched in the hospital, and your real parents are out there someplace but not with your blood relatives. All these feelings may be coming from past life karma that is continuing over into this lifetime.

You may have a "fatal attraction" for someone who comes into your life. There may be such a powerful connection that you disregard all caution in the need to tighten the bond. This bond, however, may have been developed during a different lifetime where the roles were different than they are now. Sometimes it's an accumulation of karma from several lifetimes that needs to be addressed. How you address it can have a major impact not only on your life, but on the lives of others connected to you.

Knowledge of your past lives can help you get a fresh perspective on your relationships with other people. They could be anyone in your family, your friends, your business associates, or any new acquaintances you may meet in the future. Once you've become comfortable examining your past lives, what you learn from them can be a great help in dealing with your relationships.

SOUL STORIES

Carl, single and in his twenties, turned on the television one day and saw a beautiful young actress playing a role in a popular western series. He knew at that moment that he was going to marry that woman. The actress eventually left Hollywood and moved east. They met and were married as they had been in a past life. Unfortunately things were different in this life, and they were not as compatible as before. Perhaps they will try again in a future life.

Knowing how you worked with someone in the past can give you a good indication of what it would be like to be involved with the person in the future. You may get an indication of potential pitfalls or strengths and talents that someone might have just under the surface of her conscious mind. Your past life knowledge can give you an opportunity to be on the lookout for danger signals as well as an indication of a hidden talent that you might encourage.

For the fun of it, imagine each person you see every day as if they lived during a different time in history. Make notes on what you imagined. Is there a common time period or theme? Make note of their clothes, their haircut, and the way they walk and talk.

Relax and Imagine

Did you know that you've been *hypnotized* before? You have. Actually everyone experiences *hypnotic trances* many times a day. For example, have you ever driven down the highway so absorbed in your thoughts that you forgot to turn off where you wanted to? If so, you have experienced "highway hypnosis." You were driving safely and aware of the road, and yet you were absorbed in thought. You were paying attention and not paying attention at the same time. Have you ever been absorbed so deeply in reading or watching television that you failed to hear someone speak to you? If so, you were in a reading or television trance.

 DEFINITION

Hypnosis, also known as imagination or imagery, is an altered state of consciousness where the unconscious mind accepts suggestions without question. A **hypnotic trance** is an altered state of consciousness in which the unconscious mind is open to suggestion and loses its ability to make critical decisions.

You don't need to enter a deep trance in order to discover your past lives. As long as you're willing to work with your imagination and analyze what happened after the experience rather than during it, you may be amazed with the results.

Image trances can take relaxation one step further. When you are relaxed, hypnosis adds another goal to work toward. In the case of a past life discovery experience, it might be to go back to a specific time or to find a lifetime with a lesson related to this lifetime.

Your goal might be to find a connection to a current relationship or to determine why you may have a reoccurring and unexplained health problem. When a self-relaxing session is nearing its end, you can give yourself a suggestion to help you after it's over. As you go through this book, you will understand and learn how simple and natural it is to put yourself in a relaxed and positive trance.

AGELESS INSIGHTS

Relaxation is the key to experiencing self-image trances. There are many depth levels of trance. Some are very light, such as a daydream; others can be so deep that the person experiencing it could have a medical operation and not even feel it.

Could you get "stuck" in a trance? Could you wind up being trapped in a past life and forget the life you're in now? Quite a few years ago there was a television comedy called *Soap*. For a period of weeks one of the characters did get stuck in a past life. The audience watched and laughed at this poor soul as he tried to understand the modern world from the viewpoint of someone who was snatched out of a lifetime several hundred years before. Fortunately, that doesn't happen to someone experiencing self-trances. It is possible you might relax so much that you fall asleep and wake up normal and rested.

Top Reasons to Go Backward

Why would you want to discover your past lives? There are many reasons that people choose to visit a past life. Here are some of the most common:

- You may learn something from a past life that can explain how you feel about yourself in this lifetime.

- You may learn something from a past life that will help explain a relationship with someone in this lifetime.

- You may discover a hidden talent or ability in a past lifetime.

- You may gain insights into a medical condition by visiting a past life.

- You may discover how to resolve old karma.

- You may find an answer to why you have a fear or phobia in this lifetime from a past lifetime.

- You may discover the answer to certain dreams you have had or are currently having.

- You may use past life information for writing and/or research.

- You may be able to trace some of the actual lifetimes your soul has had.

You may go backward just for fun, without any other specific reason except to have an interesting and positive experience.

The Least You Need to Know

- Whether you believe in past lives or not, discovering them can help give you new insights that may be useful tools for your present life.
- Like your DNA, your mind is different than anyone else's.
- Karma can be a good thing if you allow yourself to resolve it positively; unresolved karma could follow you from life to life.
- Insights from the past may be beneficial to you in the future.
- Self-imagery trances are a natural phenomenon that you experience many times a day.
- There are many reasons why one might choose to revisit a past life.

Who Was I?

In This Chapter

- Do we live more than one lifetime?
- Bringing up the subject of reincarnation
- Your soul remembers
- Are your experiences real or imagined?
- Following what your heart tells you

As a child, you probably thought about what you wanted to be when you grew up. You might have wanted to be a doctor or a lawyer, maybe a cowboy, or an actress. You might have even imagined what it would be like to the point where your playing seemed like reality to you.

Perhaps you were acting out what you *had* been in the past. It could have been the memories of another lifetime that were coming through your unconscious mind. You were young enough to blend the realities of a past life with your imagination of what you might be in this life. The images you brought forward were transferred onto your future. Who were you, anyway?

Is This All There Is?

Have you ever wondered about who you really are? Why you even exist? It's easy to get lost in these thoughts on a clear, starry night when you gaze into the universe and see the countless possibilities for other life. Or perhaps you think that there is nothing more than being born, living, and dying. No before. No after. Is there anything to the idea that you have lived more than once, or are you just here for the duration of your lifetime?

If that were the case, would life itself have any purpose? For the premise of this book, just imagine that there is a possibility that you live during more than one lifetime and that each of your lifetimes are connected together by your soul. This approach might give you the opportunity to view life in a way that provides greater meaning.

If there is something beyond your current lifetime, then how do you know? At the moment, there is no hard, scientific proof of that. Dr. Ian Stevenson of the University of Virginia, a leading expert in the field, has done research over a 40-year span. He has compiled more than 3,000 case studies that strongly indicate the possibility of past life experiences.

For a moment, let's consider what it might have been like back in the beginning of your soul's existence. The soul is defined as the "principle of life, feeling, thought, and action in man," and is considered to be a separate part of the mental, physical, and spiritual self. It is believed to survive beyond death.

AGELESS INSIGHTS

If you would like to investigate some of Dr. Stevenson's findings, you may want to read his book, *Where Reincarnation and Biology Intersect* (see Appendix B). Published in 1997, it documents 200 stories supported by photographs and other evidence of children's past lives.

Where did you start? Perhaps if there is such a thing as a universal energy force, in the beginning you were a part of that energy. And like a mist from a cloud, you were spawned into the pure essence of knowing.

In a hypnotic trance, the great psychic Edgar Cayce was able to access the *Akashic Records* and look up the history of a soul (see Appendix B for information on Cayce and the Akashic Records). He envisioned one of the soul's early existences in the lost culture of Lemuria. There the soul had no physical form. In another lost ancient land, Atlantis, he saw souls that had evolved into a human form as well as souls that had no form. If this is true, after the soul is created it goes through an evolution to gain its physical form.

DEFINITION

The **Akashic Records** is considered to be a repository someplace in the universe that contains the records of all knowledge. Cayce would go there in his mind to look up the record of a soul.

When you were young, you may have had flying dreams. Is it possible that these dreams were actually memories of when your soul was in energy form and not weighed down by a body? Edgar Cayce was able to go to a specific address when reading a subject and often gave the temperature there. A part of him was somehow able to leave his physical body. Was this an ability he had learned early in his soul's development and continued to practice in his current life?

Each of our lifetimes brings us closer to completing the balance of knowledge and experiences. The experiences are the roles that we choose to play during each of our lifetimes. The more we progress, the more memories we carry with us that in themselves may either help or hinder us in our current life.

When you are close to the end of your soul's journey and have nearly completed your lessons, others may refer to you as an old soul. Old souls are people who just don't seem to fit in with others. They know more than they can tell anyone; if they try, they are looked at as odd or a misfit. Old souls can spend a great deal of energy trying to block the knowledge that their soul contains. Many of them would be much happier living simple lives of self-pleasure as many of their friends and families do.

When you reach the stage of old soul and have completed your lessons, you will again shed your earthly body and return to pure energy. At that time you may assist fellow actors who have not yet completed their play. Your role may be as an angel, a spirit, or just a miracle.

The Soul Knows

Consider the possibility that the universal energy that forms the makeup of your soul contains your personal code and soul map. It also has a complete record of the history of your journey to this point. This history is available to you if you allow yourself to be open to it.

The greatest block to accessing this knowledge is your ego mind. That portion of your mind seeks self-satisfaction, and you have the right to accept its wants and needs over your soul's master plan. As you learned in Chapter 1, free will is the term given to your ability to do as you want rather than follow your soul's life plan. If you choose not to follow your purpose you will have the opportunity to do it over in a future lifetime.

The ego's desires and needs sometimes greatly overshadow the soul's purpose. While on Earth, the ego is more often than not the commander of your ship. It doesn't like to listen to the communications of your soul's purpose. You knowingly or unknowingly are in the middle of the battle for control between your ego and your soul's plan.

Have you ever wanted to do something that a part of you knew was wrong for you? That was your conscience speaking to you. Perhaps you listened, and perhaps you didn't. If you didn't and forged ahead against your own advice, you may have felt very guilty later.

Many times when you give in to your ego, you create new karmas such as those you may knowingly or unknowingly be trying to resolve from a previous lifetime. The more you become aware of your ego's drive, the more opportunity you have to allow yourself to quiet your conscious mind and open to the communication of your soul.

There have been many documented stories of near-death experiences where a person's soul left his or her body. Some of them began to review their *life maps* with kindly beings. When they were brought back to life, they often felt they had been snapped back into their human body with a sensation described as hitting a brick wall.

Relaxing imagery trances can help them to go back and revisit what happened when they were suspended between life and death. In fact, it's possible to follow a person's soul from death to the other side and gain insights on how the lessons are reviewed.

DEFINITION

Imagine that somewhere in the universe there is a plan for your soul to gain the experiences to match the knowledge it already has. Each time any soul experiences a different lifetime, it has the opportunity to continue along its plan. That plan is known as a **life map.**

Sometimes you aren't ready to know or understand the information regarding the other side. What you want to know and what your soul wants you to know may be two different things. When you visit the other side through image trances, you may not go where you think you want to go. The answers you expect may not be what you actually receive.

The more you reach into your past, the greater the opportunity you will have to reach and surpass the potential of soul development that you've been given in this scene of your play.

You may want to pick a quiet place and have a conversation with your soul. If you are inside, you may want to put on some relaxing music and experience a relaxing smell by lighting a candle. Just let the muscles in your body relax and focus on your breathing. Feel the companionship of your mind, body, and soul all there together with you to help you become in tune with your whole self. As you feel this special connection, ask your soul for permission to begin to examine your past so that you may use this knowledge to help you become and stay in tune with your life map.

KARMIC CAUTIONS

Sometimes in life you face situations where you have to deal with your soul's purpose. The great equalizers are resistances by your ego. You may look at life as a challenge or an opportunity. The more you clash with your purpose, the less improvement your soul makes in this lifetime.

Is It Real or Your Imagination?

Have you ever imagined that you lived before? If you have, what did you imagine? Perhaps as a child you used to tell other family members about different lifetimes. Perhaps you have dreamed of yourself in faraway lands at different times. Perhaps you like to read stories about a specific time in history. Perhaps you can imagine what it would have been like to live then.

When you read, have you ever gotten so far into the story that it changed your perspective of where you were? When you finished, did the scenes remain so vividly in your imagination that it seemed as if you existed in a time warp? You may have been trapped between the realities of the location where you were at the time and the story that you were living in the book.

You may not need a book or movie to be able to experience another reality with your imagination. It may happen when you visit a place that is steeped in history, and all of a sudden you find yourself engulfed in an unfolding story from a different era. As you remain there soaking in the images, they get stronger and stronger and you find yourself stepping into this parallel reality, until something jerks you back to your conscious world.

These images may have been so real that they still remained with you some time after you returned. Was this your imagination, or had you tapped into a reality that existed on another plane? Was this a resonance of your soul that began to vibrate distant memories of the past when you happened to visit that location? Was this experience one that has been recorded in your soul's memory, or was it something you imagined? If you have ever had an experience like this, whom could you tell it to? If you shared this story with friends or family, how would they respond to it? Would they advise you against telling the story to anyone else out of loving fear that others would think you were crazy?

SOUL STORIES

When Carter was two, he was having lunch between his mother and grandmother when he reached out, grasped their hands, and exclaimed, "My family." Perhaps he recognized them from another life. On another occasion he nonchalantly said, "When I was a big boy, I used to like coffee." This was spoken with a knowing from another time.

Are you able to write stories that come from your mind about a different period in time? Do you imagine them vividly when you write? Can you put yourself in the story and feel the experience with all your senses? Can you write descriptions of situations as if you had been there when they actually happened? Can you imagine what it would feel like to live there and experience the emotions? Can you draw pictures of a past time from the images you have in your mind?

If you have an active, analytical conscious mind, it can get in the way of your imagination. In other words, you are always trying to find a reason for the thoughts that just pop into your head. The more you can wait to think about what you're thinking until you have finished the process, the better your "imagined" images will be.

Here's a case in point. When Rob wanted to discover his past lives, his active mind prevented him from going into a deep trance. However, he did imagine back to the Second World War and found himself flying combat in a fighter plane. At the same time as he answered the past life specialist's questions, he was also analyzing why he was imaging that particular scene.

"I've always been very interested in the Second World War," he said emphatically in the middle of the session. "I think this is just my imagination from all the reading I've done and movies I've seen on the subject." The specialist suggested that Rob just go along with his imagination as he continued to ask more questions that focused on the details.

The past life specialist was able to lead Rob deeper into his imagery and take the pilot through the crash that caused his death after his plane was seriously damaged by enemy fire. Then he brought Rob back out of his trance. "That was odd," he said as he took a moment to get his bearings back. "I know I was just making up that story, and yet when the plane was going down, I really felt dizzy."

Do you think Rob just imagined the whole thing? How do you think he became interested in World War II in the first place? Perhaps he had a soul memory that was powerful enough to lead him to his interest in that time period. Has he been experiencing a second reality originating from World War II that he was trying to resolve in this lifetime?

So what do you do with your imagination? Do you believe the echoes of your mind reminding you of your distant past life experiences in time, or do you dismiss it all as a product of your mental fantasies? You can chalk it up to imagination if you want to. You can listen to those who tell you there is nothing there. Or if you want, you can investigate further. You can become the detective of your own mind and search for clues to the identity of your past.

Follow Your Heart

Now that you've had an opportunity to consider how and where the journey of your soul began, how does it fit with your heart? Is there something inside of you that vibrates with a feeling of recognition when you think about having lived before? Have you, like Rob, been missing the clues you are giving yourself because you aren't paying attention? It's very easy to get caught up in your analytical mind instead of paying attention to the reality of your imagination.

If you do, you're not alone. Many people never have the opportunity to connect to the rich heritage of their own past lives because they are too focused on the present and the future. Your past can be a wealth of information that can help you as you move forward into the future. No one knows your soul better than you do. You just may not be aware of that yet. As you progress through this book, you will be.

You may move at a pace that is comfortable for you, and you don't need anyone else to help you if you want to explore alone. At the same time, having someone support you can be fun, and the other person may discover something about your past lives that you might miss. Either way, you will have an interesting and educational adventure.

What does your heart say to you? Have you taken the time to communicate with it? If not, let's take a little time right now. Find a comfortable place and let yourself relax. You may feel yourself breathing slowly in and out as you relax more and more. In a moment you may ask your heart and soul the following questions. The answers may not come right away, but they may surface at any time in your dreams, as a thought, or you may be reminded from an outside source.

Just a word of caution: if for any reason you experience images that are unpleasant or confusing, you can always end the exploration of your past lives by taking a deep, relaxing breath and coming back to your conscious mind.

AGELESS INSIGHTS

You may be so closely connected to your past lives that you're afraid of going back. Regardless of what you might have been, this is your life now. You can take steps to resolve the past karma and build on past strengths to update them to your current lifetime.

You may ask your soul for permission to learn of your past lives and to let your heart know the answer. Is it good for me at this time to begin to examine my past lives for the purpose of helping me use the knowledge in this lifetime? May I be aware of the past life influences that have been and are now present in my life?

You may have other questions you want to ask your soul and to feel the answer in your heart. When you have finished communicating with your soul and heart, let yourself drift back to consciousness and allow yourself to be open to the messages.

Is this the time for you to give yourself permission to explore your heritage, a heritage deep and rich with the memories of many adventures from your soul's past? A part of you already knows the answers that are inside of you, regardless of what anyone else says. You are the keeper of your soul. The resonance of the vibration that rings true and whispers to your mind can lead you down the path to great adventure as you follow your heart.

Have You Ever Been a Ghost?

If *ghosts* are spirits of humans that are somehow stuck in a dimension on the earth plane, is it possible that I could have images of being a ghost in my unconscious mind? The answer to that is "yes." Although it may not come up in your past life memories, or for that matter be recognized if it does, it is a memory that can come to the surface of one's conscious mind. So how will you know if the past life images you are getting are from a ghost or from a person?

DEFINITION

A **ghost** is the spirit of a dead person that never traveled to the other side. It may have suffered a sudden death, leaving it suspended in time, not knowing how to make the transition. Or it may be a spirit that lingers because it had unfinished business.

Carl and his wife were very close. Nearing retirement age, he built a home for them to live in during their golden years. His wife died unexpectedly on a trip to visit relatives in a southern state. The cause of her death was never completely determined. Carl took it hard. He lived the rest of his life and also died in the home he had built. Many years later, it was discovered that he was still there, waiting for his wife to return from her travels. He didn't want to go to the other side without her.

Susan experienced what it was like to be a ghost during a past life expedition. She went back in time looking for some insights into current family situations. She found herself outside an old house, and then as she moved through the lifetime, the image of the house flip-flopped back and forth between two different scenes. In one, the house was older, and she was able to experience being in the body of the person she was during that lifetime. The past life specialist moved her forward several years to see if she was still alive at a certain age, and she got a second image of the house that confused her. It had an addition attached to it, yet during the lifetime she was experiencing, its size had not been changed. Not only that, but strangers were in "her" house. She also indicated that she could not feel her physical body. She was able to watch her death scene in that life and found that she had died young with small children and without a husband. She had literally worn herself out trying to care for them. She did not want to move on and existed suspended in time as a spirit hoping to reunite with her family.

It is possible for your unconscious mind to remember the emotional experiences that you, as a ghost, felt during the time you spent before you crossed over. You could have felt sorrow, sadness, jealousy, happiness, or anger, depending on what you experienced during your time as a ghost. You might have felt upset that someone was changing or messing up your house. You may have tried to communicate with others who were still alive. These can all be soul memories of a spirit who was trapped, lost, or somehow felt the need to stay on this side.

There are people with a fear of leaving their house who discover that the source of their feeling came from a death experience in another lifetime. When people die suddenly, they may find themselves in spirit form, suspended above their body. They are confused because they don't realize they are dead. They just know that they are out of their body and can't get back inside. Eventually they move on to the other side, but they often come back to another life where they have unconsciously transferred the fear of separating from their body to being separated from their home.

AGELESS INSIGHTS

An effective way to help resolve the fear of separation is to rediscover the lifetime where the separation occurred, and after the death scene, help the spirit understand that they are now in a different life and are in a physical body again.

Here are some suggestions to help you understand some of the ghostly experiences of your soul. You may use the induction from Chapter 7 if you wish. Remember, when you visit a past life, you may always take a breath and open your eyes and come back to a full state of wakefulness, relaxed and feeling positive. If you are comfortable, allow yourself to imagine with all of your senses a story of a different time that is in the memory of your soul and held in your unconscious mind. Go with the first image that comes to you. Allow yourself to either watch the images play out in front of you, or step into them and experience what is taking place, knowing you can step back out at any time you want.

- Are you able to physically experience being there when you look through the eyes of the person you were in the past?

- Can you step back and see a picture of this person, or do you just feel that you are there?

- Is it possible to interact with others who may be in the same scene, or does it feel as if you are completely detached, with no way of communicating?

- Do you have the sense that you are somehow floating or not able to feel any physical sensations? If you experience this, then it's possible you may have been in spirit form during the time you're remembering.

- Can you experience any emotions while in this nonphysical state? If so, what are they? How intense are they?

- Are you aware of any other sensual images such as sounds, smells, or temperatures?

- If there are people or animals there, can you make contact with them? Do you feel the need to make contact?

- Where are you, and can you move to different locations? If so, how do you get there?

- Can you move backward or forward in time?

- Do others realize that you are there?

If the answers you receive indicate that you may be in spirit form, ask to see the situation that caused you to exist on this plane. If you can step out and watch, first view the scene in a dissociated state, similar to watching the images as if they were a movie. You may want to do this more than once until you are comfortable with what you're watching before you put yourself into the scene. Experience as much as you need but not to the point of being overwhelmed. As I have stated before, remember you can always take a deep breath, open your eyes, and come back to the surface of your conscious mind feeling positive and grounded.

Follow your soul memories from being alive to transitioning into spirit form. What were the conditions that caused the change? Follow your spirit form to the point where it finally migrated on to the other side. What caused it to leave the plane it was on? When you are ready, come back to your conscious mind and take some time to make notes on the experiences you had while you rediscovered those soul memories. It's very possible that once you have opened the window to your past, more and more details will become a part of your conscious memory.

SOUL STORIES

Margaret had become aware that every time she drove down a certain rural road she would have the foreboding feeling that something tragic was about to happen. The more she drove that road, the stronger the feeling became. On foggy or misty nights, she'd also had the experience of seeing a ghostly woman's figure floating in front of her vehicle. The image was only there for a brief moment, but it always snapped her into a state of high alert. With the help of a past life specialist, she journeyed back through her unconscious mind to a cottage on a lake on a similar road. She saw herself in a past life married to a man who had become so abusive that she could not bear it any longer. She had thrown herself in front of a passing car. Is there a connection between the spirit that comes to Margaret on a foggy night and the part of her soul who suffered at the hands of her abusive husband in that past life?

The Least You Need to Know

- Although there is no scientific proof, research strongly suggests that reincarnation exists.
- Your soul knows the history of your past.
- You can decide whether your past life experiences are real or imagined.
- Regardless of what anyone else tells you, you know in your heart the right answers regarding reincarnation.
- A ghost is the spirit of a dead person who has not traveled to the other side.

Children Still Remember

In This Chapter

- Children and past lives
- Acting out a past life
- Role reversals: were you the child?
- Adjusting to the present lifetime
- Helping a child keep past life memories alive

Children often carry the attributes of their past lives that can be a great benefit to this lifetime. When children are encouraged to tell the stories that are in their minds, they are much more open to sharing the memories they've brought with them from other lifetimes. Unfortunately, this isn't the case in many Western families, and any memory that could have been shared will all too soon be forgotten, as the child grows older.

The Tibetans believe that their Dalai Lama is the reincarnation of their God Kings. The current Dalai Lama, born in 1935, is the fourteenth in the known succession of this soul. After the Thirteenth Dalai Lama died, the Tibetan Regent received a vision of a three-story temple near a house that was adorned with carved gables and blue eaves.

In 1937, search parties were dispatched throughout the Chinese territories to locate the child who was the reincarnated Dalai Lama. The landmarks in the vision were found in the village of Takster.

The two-year-old boy inside the house with the blue eaves asked for the rosary around the leader's neck. Then he named everyone in the search party correctly and identified items that the group brought with them. The party saw that he had birthmarks that helped confirm he was the next Dalai Lama.

A Child's Wisdom

When you are born, you bring with your soul memories of the past. You don't have any experiences yet in this life to record in your unconscious mind, so you don't think the same way that adults do in terms of imagination. The older you get, the more information you gather for this lifetime.

Dr. Ian Stevenson, a professor of psychology at the University of Virginia, has spent much of his life studying reincarnation. His work has included field research in countries that embrace the concept of reincarnation. In more than 3,000 case studies, Dr. Stevenson has concluded that children will spontaneously remember past life experiences and report on them as soon as they are able to speak.

SOUL STORIES

Christine had always spoken a little differently than other children. Her family, classmates, and teachers could understand her, so it never became an issue until she went to college. As an intern, her supervising teacher told her that her speech impediment made it hard for the students to understand what she said in the classroom. Later on, a past life session revealed that she had experienced several lifetimes in Canada. Her speech impediment was actually a Canadian accent. It was just her natural way of talking.

Eddie was fascinated with anything connected to the military, especially the Army. As a child he spent countless hours creating elaborate battle scenes with his toys. His parents had no military background. He joined the Army ROTC in college and when he entered the service, he found he excelled at military strategy. When he investigated his past lives, he found out why. He had been a leader in battles before. The old saying "out of the mouths of babes" is definitely true in reference to a child's imagination. They can tell fantastic stories that most adults totally overlook if they're not acquainted with past life concepts. When children are old enough to talk, they can be a wealth of information if they are encouraged to let the images of their unconscious mind flow freely.

Children may use words that they didn't learn from their family's vocabulary. The words they use can be clues to their past lives. When Brian was young he referred to himself as "The Brian." He would always answer that way if you asked him what his name was. Perhaps he still remembered a title he had earned or inherited during another lifetime.

As soon as she could talk, one little girl started to call her mother "Mommy Anne." It might mean that she knew in her mind that Anne was her current mother but she had had a mother before by a different name.

Perhaps you have heard the following story, which is told in different ways. A young family had a new baby girl. A few weeks after she was born, her four-year-old brother asked to speak to her alone. From the baby monitor they heard him ask, "Can you please remind me about what God looks like? I am beginning to forget." This little story, true or not, hits the nail on the head regarding the complexity of a child's mind.

KARMIC CAUTIONS

Pay attention to what a child tells you. If you think of them as "only children," you may miss the ancient wisdoms that are part of their soul. Try thinking of them as old people with memories trapped inside a child's body.

From One Life to the Next

Many children will do more than talk about their past lives—they will try to keep living them. They will bring mannerisms, skills, and habits with them when they come to this life. They may have "natural" creative abilities or excellent rhythm and coordination.

They can do things that make you wonder where on earth they could have learned how. Here are three examples:

- Josh was really good with his hands when he was a small child. He was very interested in carving, and his mother bought him some Ivory soap to practice on. She was amazed to see the results of his work. Josh produced works of art that looked as if they had come from an ancient civilization.

- David was fascinated with items from the Revolutionary War period. One day he showed his mother a set of plans to build a musket rifle and then proceeded to tell her in great detail how to build and fire it.

- Nora used to play an interesting game with her friends when they were small children. She called it "crossing the Himalayas." She would have them line up and walk in single file along a course she had laid out. They had to climb over obstacles as they worked their way over the "vast mountain range." As an adult, Nora discovered that in a past life she had tried to lead a group of children over the Himalayas to escape from invaders of her country. Unfortunately, they were caught by a winter storm and froze to death in the mountains. Unconsciously she was trying to lead her children to safety in this lifetime.

Perhaps you remember (or your parents or other relatives told you) stories of how you acted as a child. Some of these stories may directly link you to an earlier past life that you were trying to continue to live during the first few years of this reincarnation. Perhaps you had a childhood interest that has stayed with you into your adult life.

AGELESS INSIGHTS

Sometimes your children will experience past lives through dreams or nightmares. They may try different skills or games they rediscovered in their dreams. Their ability to imagine is the key to the whole process. The more you allow them to imagine in a positive way, the more clues you will receive.

Let's look at it from a child's perspective. For a moment, imagine what it would be like for you if you suddenly woke up in a different body. This body won't do all the things you want it to do. In fact, it's very small. You know how to move, but it won't move the way you want it to. You know how to walk, but your legs just won't cooperate. Then, when you get big enough to finally do something you already know how to do, you discover that it isn't the right thing to do in this lifetime.

So there you are with all this knowledge inside of you. How are you going to use it? How are you going to tell anyone about it if they won't believe what you want to tell them? Everyone keeps telling you that you're just imagining things and it would be better if you just forgot all about them. Everyone wants to treat you as if you were a little child. Perhaps you had an experience like this when you were little.

This example may give an idea of how children might feel when they're wrestling with memories from the past. Keep this in mind when you have the opportunity to observe and/or communicate with a small child. If you want to ask someone else's child about "before," you may want to get permission from the child's parents. Not everyone is comfortable with the idea of past lives. You can really be a great help to a reincarnated child as she tries to adjust to her current earthly assignment. You also may be taught something in exchange for your kindness.

Role Reversals

As children continue to grow and communicate more effectively, they can still retain memories from their past lives. These memories can remain so close to the surface that they will shift their focus from *conscious reality* to the reality of the past. When this happens, they sometimes will blend the two realities together. They can mix up past life assignments and relationships with the present.

DEFINITION

Conscious reality is your awareness of what everyone who is in close proximity to you can experience at the same time.

Perhaps you as a child decided to take on a different role in your family. You may have tried to take care of your parents. You might have been jealous of one of your parents because you felt he or she was taking over your rightful place in the family.

Perhaps you have or know of a child who isn't comfortable with his current position in his family yet. He may reverse the role of parent and child in his mind. He may want to protect, comfort, love, worry about, or discipline his parents as if they were his children. You might have called a child "little man," or some other term that implies that the child acts much older than his age.

The child may also treat the parent as a sibling. This is a role that can continue into adulthood. You may have a child or a parent who you think of as a brother or sister. You share confidences and other interests and keep in close contact with each other. You may even look much closer in age than you really are. Your physical features may also indicate a close connection.

Just think—you might be your own great-grandmother! When Lisa was a small girl, she visited her great-grandmother's gravesite for the first time. Her great-grandmother had died before she was born. She had an overwhelming feeling of sadness and suddenly envisioned a casket being lowered into the ground. This image stayed with her into adulthood. She also recognized many of the landmarks in the town where her great-grandmother had lived. Through hypnosis, Lisa was able to go back and experience a lifetime when she was her great-grandmother.

AGELESS INSIGHTS

A child may be the reincarnation of a family member. Past lives can have very short turnarounds. Sometimes a child will remember people from a past life and greet them by name even though they have never met them before in this lifetime. You may have known someone as a child from a past life or you may know a child who has this ability.

Watching a child play can give you clues to relationships that may have started in the past. Pay attention to the names they give their dolls. Do they have imaginary friends who have names of deceased relatives? If so, how did they know them?

Like Lisa, they may recognize family landmarks when they visit them the first time. They may tell you stories about your relationships with them in a past life. They may comb their hair or want to wear their clothes in a style of a deceased family member. They may even grow to look like a relative who has died. They might have the same birthmark or a scar that relates to an injury of the person they are reincarnating from.

Helping Children Keep Their Memories Alive

One of the greatest gifts parents can give their children is a sense of their heritage. The more they learn about family genealogy, the more they have the opportunity to appreciate relatives who have gone on before them. At a young age this may start with stories about Grandfather or Grandmother or others who have passed on.

Now that you know children can be a wealth of knowledge from their past lives, you may see in some of their words and actions how they may relate to a past life. Watch how they speak and react to other people—family, friends, and strangers—and you may see past life portraits begin to emerge. If the child talks about people or places or things that seem to be imaginary or that you cannot identify, you may have a good place to start to help them gather information about their heritage.

Many times the past life memories will surface spontaneously. They might be triggered by a place they are in, something they see or experience, music, a taste, a smell, or a feeling that opens up their memory album stored in their unconscious mind. It's always advisable to have a notepad and pencil handy so that you can jot down pieces of information when they surface. If you have time to plan, a tape recorder or a video recorder are great tools for capturing these precious moments. The more variety of ways you have to collect the information, the greater opportunity you will have to piece together the child's past lives.

It's a good idea to keep a journal along with any recorded material. Remember, if you're using a computer, back up your information on an external disk as well as on your hard drive. If you're keeping only written records, make sure that you make copies and never keep them together.

For follow-up sessions, review your material before jumping into new areas. One great advantage in doing this is that you will be "priming the pump" for more information. You can use past knowledge as a cross-reference to see what correlates from session to session. Make sure this is a pleasant experience for the child. If any unpleasantness crops up from the past, steer away from it until the child is ready. If the child is mentally stressed, it's a good idea to seek the guidance and the wisdom of a professional counselor or therapist trained in past life recall and therapy techniques.

Remember that a child's attention span will be short. Gathering the clues should be a positive experience for him. He shouldn't feel bored or deprived of other activities. Try not to interpret what the child is telling you. Just encourage him to provide as much information as he is interested in at the time.

It's also possible that a child may have nothing to say about memories from a past life. The child may not remember them at all. Never press a child into an experience that may be uncomfortable.

KARMIC CAUTIONS

If your child is old enough to realize what you are doing, set aside a quiet time to have a chat. You might call it story time. Rather than you telling her a story, let the child tell you a story. Or you could take turns, but be careful not to lead the child into false memories that might be influenced by your storytelling.

It's possible that the length of time might be only a few moments, or it might be several minutes, all depending on your and the child's attention span. It could take a little time to develop a routine that provides consistent information, and as the child grows, the routine and the information may vary. When you have established an initial time period or an order to what you are doing, you can start to collect and organize the child's information.

As you progress, you may find that you are getting clues on more than one past life theme. It is also possible for other elements to be mixed in with past lives. For instance, the child may be seeing an angel, a ghost, or a spirit guide. A spirit guide is a highly evolved being that may come to the child as a voice in her mind. Sometimes the child is also able to see the guide. The purpose of the guide is to assist the child through her life journey. A deceased relative may visit the child from the other side. At this time in life, the child has not yet learned to become prejudiced about the information that is received, either internally or externally. Everything to a child is natural and real.

She might like or dislike a certain kind of music. These responses can start almost at birth. When Carter was an infant, music was very familiar to him. And yet, every time that he heard Mozart's "Kinder Music" he would get upset and cry. He even woke out of a deep sleep crying in response to that particular song. Perhaps he had an issue with Mozart in a past life.

The Least You Need to Know

- Children bring past life memories with them when they are born.
- Children may continue to act out past life situations in their present lifetime.
- A child may treat you as if you were the child.
- Some children may have a hard time adjusting to their present life.
- You can help a child become adjusted to this life and keep memories alive by helping the child understand his or her past lives.

How to Create a Trance

In This Chapter

- Understanding what trances are all about
- Trance and your imagination
- A relaxation exercise that focuses on your breathing
- Finding your own mental zone
- How you can use trances every day

Many people think that to experience hypnosis you need to go to a hypnotist who will put you into a deep sleep. Many believe that while you're in this sleep trance the hypnotist has a secret power to change you somehow. When you leave the session you will magically be changed. That's really not the case. The hypnotist doesn't have the magic power; you do. The hypnotist's job is to help you change a habit or even take you into a past life.

In this book, you can become your own guide. A relaxing imagery trance can become a very effective tool for you, not only in examining your past lives, but for many other things as well. As you become experienced in the use of imagery trances, you will be able to use this state of relaxation to give yourself suggestions that will help you regress to your past lives.

The Different Kinds of Trances

You already learned in Chapter 1 that trances are altered states in which your unconscious mind accepts a suggestion without question by your conscious mind. What actually happens in a trance is a gradual shifting of your focus from the reality around you to another reality that's created by suggestion. That reality is real to you but may not be noticed by others. On the extreme end of altered states of reality are *phobias*.

> **DEFINITION**
>
> A **phobia** is a fear that becomes so powerful the one who experiences it temporarily loses touch with his or her surroundings and enters a second reality that is connected to a traumatic moment in the past. (That past may not be in this lifetime!) When the phobia starts, the memory is experienced again without the person realizing what is happening.

You can experience that dual reality on a lesser scale when you step into your imagination. That imagination may be based on real moments in your life. There may be no known basis for the images you experience—at least not yet.

In this book, any suggestions will be phrased with "you may." There is no need for you to enter a deep trance to discover your past lives. You will always be aware if the phone rings, of traffic going by, or of people talking. Yet at the same time, you may not need to be as aware of these interruptions as you might be at other times. Remember, if at any time you feel confused or uncomfortable when you're experiencing a trance, you can always return to your conscious mind by taking a deep breath and opening your eyes, feeling positive and relaxed.

> **AGELESS INSIGHTS**
>
> Your goal in a trance will be to keep your analytical mind out of the way so that you'll accept the suggestions you give yourself. The more you get used to the process, the easier it will be to enter your own trance. It's useful for much more than past life discovery. It can help you relieve stress and make positive decisions.

The type of imagery you'll be experiencing is derived from Neuro-Linguistic Programming (NLP), which was developed in the 1970s and is widely used today. This concept will help you build image models for collecting past life information. It can help you change your focus from your conscious reality to the reality of your past lives. It will enable you to do so without the fear of reliving a negative memory from the past.

So to sum it up, a trance is really a combination of imagination and communication. Communication creates the imagination. Almost every word produces an image in your mind. At the same time, an image projects a thought or a communication. The two are linked together. In the following chapters, you will learn that no one on Earth creates images the same way that you do. Therefore, no one else will experience a trance exactly like you.

Use Your Imagination

Even though the explanation of what actually happens when you enter a relaxed trance can sound very complicated, it's really a lot easier than you might think. It is very natural, and you already do it all the time! If you can imagine, you can experience a trance.

Let's see how you imagine. Do you have a special place where you like to go and relax? This place could be real, or you may have a place that you think about in your mind. If you don't have one or can't remember such a place, it's all right to make one up. See how many questions you answer with a yes in the following imagination exercise:

1. Make yourself comfortable and think about a place where you like to relax. Close your eyes, if you'd like. Can you put yourself there in your imagination? Can you experience what it feels like to be there? If you can't, that's okay because your imagination experience is the way you naturally do it, not necessarily the way these questions suggest you do it.

2. Can you imagine a picture of your place? Can you see yourself in the picture as if you were watching a video of yourself? How clearly can you picture your relaxing place?

3. Can you hear your favorite relaxing music or another sound such as water flowing? If you can imagine hearing these sounds, does the experience help you to relax?

4. Can you imagine a relaxing smell? If you can remember one, can you experience the feeling of being relaxed when you smell it? Can you picture what you imagined smelling?

5. Can you imagine the taste of a relaxing food? Can you imagine how this food feels in your mouth? Can you smell it? Can you picture it?

All of these questions are designed to show you that you do imagine, and show the way you imagine. You may have been able to answer all of the questions with a yes, or you may have only answered some that way. Whatever your total was is the right one for you. You will learn more about how differently each person imagines in the chapters to come.

SOUL STORIES

I can tell you that most of my answers to those questions would be no. I discovered when I was studying hypnosis that I cannot imagine pictures, sounds, external feelings, smells, or tastes. I knew I was different, but I didn't know how much. That still didn't discourage me from learning my own way of doing imagery trances. I have lost more than 50 pounds using relaxing trances, and the amazing thing is that it has stayed off for more than 20 years.

The goal of this little exercise is to prove to you that you experience trances naturally. It's really as easy as imagining. There is no way to do it wrong. Each time you imagine, you will do it differently, even if it's the same subject. Each time you will focus a little differently. Sometimes the focus will be deeper, and sometimes when your conscious mind is cluttered with other thoughts it may not be easy to let your imagination go.

You have just completed your first exercise in imagery. It wasn't very hard to do, was it? Next, you will have the opportunity to experience an imagery trance exercise to help you focus even more on relaxing.

You may already practice meditation or other forms of relaxation. If you do, you may use any technique that will help you focus and relax.

KARMIC CAUTIONS

Imagination can have a positive influence on you. Unfortunately, it can also have a negative influence. If you focus on worries and fears, it's easy to slip into negative trances. This can be especially true if you worry about future outcomes or continually go over a negative memory from the past. If you experience a negative image, try to refocus on a positive one.

Take a Breath and Relax

There are a couple of ways you can try the following relaxation exercise. You can read it first and memorize the wording, or you can record the words and play them back to yourself as you experience the induction. You can also have someone else read them to you as you experience the exercise. You may notice that many words are repeated over and over. There is a purpose to that. It's to help remind you to experience the words.

If you're ready, find a comfortable place to sit or lie down that is away from interruptions. You'll want to wear something comfortable and not too tight. You may start by taking a deep breath, if that's comfortable for you, and slowly exhale. Do this several times. Next, focus your mind on the center of your forehead—your third eye—and continue to breathe slowly and deeply. As you do this, let your eyes go out of focus and feel yourself begin to relax. You may be aware of sounds and other things happening around you, and that's okay. You will always be aware, but you need not focus on them.

Sometimes it's really hard to let your body relax. You may have all kinds of thoughts bouncing around in your head. There may be negative thoughts interfering with your relaxation. Slow, deep breathing can help you bring yourself to a calmer state.

You may be aware that you have many muscles in your body, and at all times there are some that are relaxed and some that are stiff. If you feel a muscle stiffen up, relax it and let yourself feel even more relaxed as you continue to breathe in and out comfortably and slowly. With each breath you may feel yourself relaxing more and more. You may let your eyes close and feel yourself relaxing even more. If at any time you want or need to, you may always open your eyes, take a deep breath, exhale, and come back to the surface of your conscious mind, relaxed, refreshed, and ready to continue on with your day or night.

In a moment you are going to count backward from five to zero, and with each number you will feel yourself going 10 times deeper, into a very comfortable relaxed state. It's a good feeling and as you go deeper and deeper you will feel yourself relaxing more and more. As you go deeper and deeper, you may feel yourself becoming more and more in tune with your focus on your forehead. If you are ready, you may start with the first number.

- *Five.* You may feel all the muscles from the top of your head down over your forehead to your nose, cheeks, mouth, chin, and neck relaxing. You may suggest to yourself to relax and go deeper and deeper as you slowly count yourself down to zero. In between each number you may allow yourself to breathe deep and focus your mind on your forehead. With each number you tell yourself that you will go 10 times deeper.

- *Four.* You may now allow yourself to become more and more comfortable as you relax all your shoulder muscles down to your upper arms, to your elbows, your forearms, your wrists, hands, and all the way to your fingertips. As you relax, you may feel yourself going 10 times deeper than before. You may feel yourself relaxing more and more as you go deeper and deeper.

- *Three.* You may now feel the muscles in your body relaxing down over your chest and your back, all the way to your waist. You may feel yourself going deeper and deeper. You may feel yourself relaxing and going 10 times deeper with each count downward. You may feel very comfortable as you breathe slowly in and out.

- *Two.* You may let your muscles relax all the way to your knees as you go 10 times deeper into a comfortable relaxed state. You are getting closer and closer to being very relaxed and in a comfortable trance as you count yourself down to zero. With each breath you are relaxing more and more.

- *One.* You are almost there. You may feel yourself relax all the way down to your ankles as you breathe slowly in and out, 10 times deeper than the last number. You are feeling yourself becoming more and more relaxed. Now, as you slowly count yourself all the way down from five to zero, you may enter a deep relaxing trance.

- *Five. Four. Three. Two. One. Zero.* You are now in a very comfortable trance state as you feel the muscles in your total body relax. You may feel a positive, soothing energy flow through your entire body. Take a few moments to enjoy where you are as you feel positive, relaxed, and very comfortable.

AGELESS INSIGHTS

Some people are more comfortable counting themselves up rather than down. If this is the case for you, just reverse the image suggestions you give yourself and count upward from your feet to begin the exercise and down from your head to end it.

When you are ready, you may begin slowly counting back to the surface of your conscious mind when you reach five. You may go back to this place at the same or different trance level every time you experience a very relaxed state. You will continue to have a positive and relaxed feeling after you end your trance. If you're ready, you may start counting yourself back up.

- *One.* You are slowly counting yourself back to the surface of your conscious mind. You may continue to breathe slowly in and out.

- *Two.* You are slowly coming back to the surface of your mind feeling relaxed and comfortable.

- *Three.* You feel so relaxed as you continue to come back upward. You are getting closer and closer to the surface.

- *Four.* You are almost there.

- *Five.* You may now take a deep breath, exhale, and open your eyes feeling calm, relaxed, and positive after your imagery trance. Isn't it great to feel calm, comfortable, and relaxed?

Creating a Daily Practice Schedule

This relaxation exercise can be beneficial to you in many ways. If you develop a habit of experiencing it at least once a day, it can help you stay focused and relaxed. It will also be very helpful to you as you progress through this book.

Some of the potential benefits of using self-imagery include the following:

- Reduce stress

- Lose weight

- Stop smoking

- Lower blood pressure

- Perform better athletically

- Communicate more effectively with yourself and others

- Be a better student

- Overcome a fear

- Increase creativity

Remember that no one else will experience trances exactly like you. You may not have been able to relax as much as was suggested. That's okay. If you felt any benefit, you experienced something positive. The relaxation exercise you completed earlier in this chapter is a great way to begin preparing for your journey into discovering your past lives. You will be adding to this script and learning how to enter into a trance faster and deeper.

A script is the words that help you enter your trance. When you are entering a relaxed state, it's the words you say to yourself, either by recording them and playing them back during the exercise, or thinking them to yourself, that help you enter your trance state. The script should lead you step by step into a more heightened state of focus or into your comfort zone.

DEFINITION

An **anchor** is a special word, physical touch, or movement that can help you recreate a state of heightened focus.

The following exercise shows you how to create an *anchor* to help you focus:

1. Start by experiencing the relaxation exercise that appears earlier in this chapter. Count yourself all the way down to zero to your relaxed state. When you have gotten there, imagine your special place, and for a few moments let yourself experience how good it feels to be there.

2. When you're ready, give yourself a special word, or place your thumb and finger together, or both. Suggest to yourself that any time you want to experience this heightened state of relaxation you will trigger your special anchor(s), and you will be able to experience this state instantly. Suggest that you will be able to have this relaxed feeling, but you will always be aware of where you are at the time you experience it.

3. While you're in your heightened state of relaxation, practice triggering your anchors several times. Suggest to yourself that you will be able to have this experience any time you use your triggers at a focus level that is right for where you are. In other words, if you are in a place where you can experience your anchor more strongly, you may do so. However,

if you're in a place where it's impossible to go into a deeper state of focus, you may feel less of an effect.

4. When you are done, suggest that you will remember your anchor after you count yourself back up out of your trance. Now count yourself back from one to five, take a deep breath, exhale, and open your eyes.

AGELESS INSIGHTS

It's important for you to practice the longer relaxation exercise at least once a day. At the same time, practice triggering your anchors so that you can return to your relaxed state several times a day. Plan on specific times so that it becomes part of your daily routine.

Now try triggering your anchor and go back into your relaxed state of heightened focus. Take a moment to experience the benefits and take a breath, exhale, and return to your normal conscious state.

Once you get into your routine, you will be amazed at how it will help you relax. The more easily you can relax, the more it will help you as you prepare to discover your past lives.

The Least You Need to Know

- Relaxing trances are not the complicated process you may have been led to believe they are.
- Deep breathing is a good way to help you relax.
- No one else experiences an image trance exactly like you do.
- You can create positive anchors for yourself that help you find your zone.
- The more you use relaxing trances on a daily basis, the better at entering them you will become.

Peeking Through the Veil

Now you are ready to start honing your investigative skills. You will learn to understand your own mental DNA and develop a profile of your own thinking. You can look for the clues within yourself that will help put together your own case for your past lives.

Practice helps fine-tune your imagery trance skills. As you learn to focus your mind, you will find it easier and easier to create images that feed you back information that has been stored in your unconscious mind.

You will have the opportunity to see how a past life specialist helps facilitate a session, and you can use these same techniques to help you discover your past lives.

You Live in a Trance

In This Chapter

- Learning to create a relaxing image trance
- Identifying an interest in things from another era
- Living in a different time period
- Have you ever experienced dèjá vu?
- The link between dreams and your past lives

In this chapter, you will discover that you may have been spending a good part of your life in a trance all along. It could have been a pleasant trance or at times a negative trance.

How so, you ask? Can you remember when you were in school, and you had a very boring teacher? No matter how hard you tried to stay focused on the lesson, your mind would keep wandering off to something else. You might even have left the classroom in your mind. All of a sudden the teacher decided to call on you. You didn't have a clue as to what he was talking about, and you got into trouble for not paying attention. That boring teacher had helped put you in a trance.

Have you experienced driving on the highway and losing track of time? All of a sudden you realize that you've gone right by your destination. You were experiencing something called highway hypnosis. A trance can occur when your conscious mind just spaces out and your unconscious mind takes over. The trance continues until something brings your focus back to your conscious mind.

Do You Like Old Things?

Now it's time to begin to zero in on some of the ways that you have been imagining already that may be keys to unlocking the memory of a past life. Perhaps you like old things, whether the study of history or collecting antiques from a certain time period.

As a child, Beth felt a need to go to a church near her home. Her parents were not particularly religious and did not attend Sunday services. Beth was persistent and convinced her mother to take her there. She continued to attend through her teen years and became a member of the youth group. As an adult she still felt close to God. She wondered why, given the views of her parents. She discovered that in a past life she had been a nun who had died feeling her work was incomplete. As a child she was influenced by her soul's memories.

You probably know an old-car buff who isn't old enough to remember the age that consumes their passion. You may be drawn to music, art, and literature, or other subjects that come from a different era. You may be drawn to something old without even realizing it. Perhaps you have thought about your interest in old things and perhaps you haven't. As you get ready to discover your past lives, now is a good time to become aware of what you already know.

Keep in mind as you consider the following questions regarding your interests in old things that you may not have much interest in them at all. Maybe you had enough of them or didn't have a good experience when you actually lived with them in a past life. There are no wrong ways to answer the questions.

What old things do you like? Can you identify the time period that they came from? Is there more than one time period that holds your attention? Does your interest go back hundreds of years ago or from a time not long before you were born?

Do the things you like have a theme to them, such as old bottles, tools, clothes, books, or other things? Do you collect or research as much as you can find about things that relate to a certain time period?

> **AGELESS INSIGHTS**
>
> Keep notes of the things you are interested in that may relate to one or more of your past lives. You can keep a small notebook with you or close by at all times so that when you have a thought, you can just write it down. Once you have captured it, you can always add it to a more permanent past life diary later.

Do you like old things that relate to certain countries or geographic locations? Can you imagine what it would be like to live during the time period that you're interested in? Do you feel a sense of comfort when old things surround you?

Feeling Comfortable in a Different Time

Perhaps you feel so strongly about a different period of time that you actually wished you lived there rather than the time you live in now. Besides collecting old things, you may live in a period house, complete with interior decorations and exterior landscaping. You may have chosen your neighborhood because it looked like what you had in mind. You may feel out of place and awkward trying to exist in a world where you're uncomfortable. If you feel this way, you're not alone. It's easy to spot someone who consciously or unconsciously longs to live in a different time period. Just look at the way the person dresses. Someone with a passion for the old West may look and act like a cowboy. Someone interested in the Civil War may grow a beard like an enlisted man in the army of the North or South.

The goal in past life discovery is to update the strengths that you brought with you from an earlier time into the world where you live now.

Do you wish you lived during a different time period? Even if you like where you are now, what other age would you have liked to live in? Do you try to recreate that age where you live now? Would you if you could?

Do you wear clothes, cut your hair, read books, collect art, or watch movies from a different time period? Can you imagine what it would be like to actually live then?

Is there a time period that sends shivers up your spine just by imagining it? There may be a time period that you positively do not want to visit. Just the thought of living back then brings negative images to your mind. You may be so repelled that you don't even want to watch programs or read books about it. These negative images are just as important in researching your past lives as positive images of different time periods. What is it about that period that you can't stand? Is it the food, the social environment, turmoil such as war, the art, the music, or something else? Are there certain locations or countries that you absolutely would not want to live in?

Do you enjoy certain foods and ways of preparing them that were popular way back when? Do you need to make sure you are as self-sufficient as possible? Do you wonder or imagine what it would have been like to walk the land as a pioneer or early settler, near where you now live?

Is there a specific culture you are absolutely attracted to? Do you try to learn as much about that culture as possible? You may have an interest in Native American culture. Mark always had a fantasy about a life as a Native American. He went to a powwow and became hooked. He even went so far as to adopt a Native American name and take part in the ceremonies. He was so obsessed that he existed in a dual reality, one fueled by his imagination.

Perhaps more than one member of your family has the same strong interest in a particular period of history. Do you go to or take part in functions where all of the attendees wished they lived in the same time? Do you take on specific roles of someone who actually lived during a different time period, such as a Civil War enactment group? What other thoughts about living in the past do you have?

You may want to make notes of the responses you had to the preceding questions. You may not have had a response for all of them. That's okay. Every clue you uncover can help identify a past life you might have lived.

I Think I've Done This Before

Have you ever had *dèjá vu?* Basically this means being aware that an experience you are having may have occurred before. It's like you already know what's going to be said or happen next as if you were reliving a memory. Sometimes the image itself is so powerful that it puts you in the reality of the previous experience. It can be very confusing as you try to balance what is happening with already knowing that it happened.

DEFINITION

Dèjá vu is a French phrase that means "seen before."

Dèjá vu can be a wonderful feeling, like connecting with an old friend again. It also can be a warning signal to avoid something unpleasant that may have happened in the past. Perhaps you have had either or both of these experiences.

Dèjá vu can happen any time, anywhere. It could be a conversation with a friend, a chance meeting with a stranger, or a visit to a certain location. Something is triggered in your unconscious memory, and you are suddenly pulled into a memory of the past, only you're acting it out again.

Have you ever gone someplace for the first time and found that you knew where you were going without reading the directions? Perhaps you got lost, and someone else in the car who had never been there before was able to give you accurate directions as if she already knew the way.

Allison, a teenager, was invited by a friend to join her family on a trip to France. Everything went well until she visited the Palace of Versailles. Standing in the square, she suddenly became distraught that the beautiful white cobblestones were dark and dirty. She could not understand what had happened to this beautiful place she knew so well in a past life. Without realizing it, she had been transported back in time in her soul's memory.

Have you ever had a dèjá vu experience? Have you had more than one? Is there a pattern to any dèjá vu experiences that you may have had? Did you have the experiences with the same or different people? Did any of them have a similar dèjá vu at the same time as you?

Do you have the feeling that you and someone else have had the same conversation or experience together before? Do you feel that you and a group of people have been together before during different times and are reacquainting with each other? Do you feel that other people you are now with have known you in the past? In other words, do you feel that you might have taught them before and are teaching them now? Or maybe they taught you?

SOUL STORIES

Have you ever had an experience where you visited a place you had not been before and felt that you had experienced it in an earlier time period? This happened to author Taylor Caldwell. She and her husband arrived late at night in a hotel in Italy. She gazed out of the window and noted the splendor of the courtyard below. The next morning she was amazed that what she had seen the night before was not what she saw in daylight. She later learned that what she had experienced was the view from the window a few hundred years before. Many of her books reflected knowledge of periods of history that she knew in her mind without doing actual research.

Melanie decided to take Spanish her junior year in high school. There was something about South America that sparked her interest. She seemed to be a natural at learning the language until she was asked to read a passage in class. The teacher told her she was pronouncing the words all wrong. From that time on she had a hard time with the class. A few years later, in college, she had a chance to study in South America. On the visit she found out that she had been speaking the language correctly. After all, she had lived there in a past life. Perhaps you have had similar experiences of dèjá vu. Many times it happens when you create a light trance by relaxing your conscious mind and shifting your focus into your imagination. Or is it really just imagination?

Dreaming About the Past

We all have dreams, but we may not remember them. Can you remember your dreams? Have you ever had a dream that repeats itself either in theme or actual scenes? Dreams are a treasure trove of past life memories. It's very possible that you will actually get more information about your past lives when you're asleep than when you are awake. The reason for this is quite simply the fact that while we are awake our active minds don't give us as many opportunities to let the messages come up from the unconscious mind.

While you are asleep, your thinking mind takes a break. While it is taking a break, there are a lot of other things going on. All your experiences of that day and the days before are floating around in your unconscious mind. Just the littlest experience, such as dèjá vu or a contact with something old, a conversation, or something else, might connect with a memory you have stored. That might trigger an anchor in your unconscious mind that focuses on a memory from the past.

This memory will then work its way up into your sleeping mind as a dream. You can have a dream that goes on for a certain length of time before you even become aware that you're having it. When you wake up, the last moments of your dream may still be very vivid in your mind. A great example of this is a nightmare. You may wake up in a cold sweat caused by the memory of a traumatic past life experience.

Dreams can come through in many different ways. They might be realistic, in which you relive a scene that is very similar to your life now. The cast of characters in the dream play is recognizable to those in your life. However, it's possible that they may be playing different roles. It's possible that someone whom you know remotely, or with whom you've had only a chance meeting, turns out to be one of the stars in your dream.

Dreams can also be symbolic. This can be particularly true in dreams that have a certain theme to them. You may see symbols such as animals, bridges, houses, food, or metaphors that play out their story while you sleep. You may see strange, fanciful characters. Or you may experience certain feelings or emotions over and over again in different scenarios.

Another type of dream is a precognitive dream, usually related to a psychic insight that can also relate to a past life. It's possible to dream of going to a location and experiencing a situation that happened in a past life. If you visit the place later, you might notice the similarities. You might even be able to locate certain landmarks you had seen in the dream.

You may also experience a lucid dream. Unlike other types of dreams, it can continue after you have awakened. It's possible to put yourself back in the dream and control its outcome.

AGELESS INSIGHTS

Trance state is a great tool for revisiting a dream. When you're in a state of heightened focus, it's possible to relive the experience of your dream state and gather many more details. When you wake up from a dream, you could, in fact, put yourself in a trance and examine the dream right away.

Keeping a dream journal will help you remember dreams that you might otherwise forget. Any notebook will do; keep it and a pen handy so that you can jot down your dream right after you have it. A dream journal will give you an idea of any pattern developing in your dreams and could provide clues to your past lives. Include as many details about the dream as you can, including these:

- Where did you have the dream (at home, while traveling, etc.)?
- What was the location in the dream?
- Who was in the dream that you recognized?
- What strangers were in your dream?
- What were you doing before you went to sleep?
- What did you eat before you went to sleep?

Dreams can definitely be a very important window to your past. If you'd like to find out more about dreams, you might start with the books listed in Appendix B.

The Least You Need to Know

- Your imagination may include past life memories coming to the surface of your mind.
- Your interest in things from a different era may be a continuance of a past life experience.
- Wishing you lived in a past time period may indicate that you actually lived there before.
- Dèjá vu experiences may indicate that you are remembering a past life experience.
- Some of your dreams may be your memory reliving a past life experience.

Making Use of Your Senses

In This Chapter

- Understanding the past, future, and present experiences of your mind
- Roles of your conscious, unconscious, and universal minds
- The mental DNA composition of your mind
- Determining the strengths and weaknesses of your image recall in each of your five different senses

Perhaps this illustration can help you understand how your mind works. Imagine that your mind lives in a house that has three rooms. They are the same size and are constructed side by side with doorways connecting them. You are free to pass back and forth between the rooms, and you can spend as much time in any of them as you want.

The room on the left is filled with memories from your past, and the room on the right is filled with plans for the future. The one in the middle focuses on your present. You can visit these rooms in any of your five different senses: seeing, hearing, feeling, tasting, and smelling.

Each one of you will live in the house in your mind differently than anyone else, whether you want to or not. That is because you're unique, and no one thinks or remembers like you. It's just the way you naturally go about living in the house in your mind.

The Past, Future, and Present

Did you know that your mind focuses in three different tenses— the past, the future, and the present? The past is the total of all your memory experiences up to this moment in your present life- time. These memories are contained in your unconscious mind and they will continue to be stored there until they come back up to the surface and are noticed by your conscious mind. Have you ever had a memory that you hadn't thought of in years appear in your mind from out of nowhere? If you have, you have experienced *spontaneous memory recall*.

 DEFINITION

Spontaneous memory recall is a memory that is stored in your un- conscious mind and suddenly becomes part of your conscious thinking without any effort to remember it. This is different than a memory that you may have been trying to remember.

Spontaneous memory recall can be triggered by an experience that taps into your unconscious mind's memory storage area. It might be a similar experience relating to an earlier one that causes a flashback. Sometimes a memory can be so powerful that it actually seems real to you. When this happens, it can be very confusing and even a little scary. This type of experience often takes place when you are already in a light trance such as a daydream and are unwittingly open to spontaneous memory recall.

Fears and phobias are usually triggered by a spontaneous memory that brings a disturbing image back to the surface of your conscious mind. You relive it in the same way you experienced it the first time. You are actually in a self-hypnotic trance while you're having an experience like this, and you are unaware of anything but that mem- ory until it has run its course.

Not all spontaneous memories are bad. You can also suddenly remember a very pleasant experience that's almost as enjoyable when you relive it. Your mind is constantly reaching into your past whether you are awake or asleep.

Besides past memories from your present life, you can recall memories from your past lives. These usually are spontaneously triggered through your unconscious mind. You actually have many more memories than you may realize from past life experiences. Many times these images are overlooked unless you know what to look for. By the end of this book you will.

Besides remembering the past, your mind can focus into the future. You may plan ahead and perhaps even live an event in your imagination before it actually takes place. Perfectionists usually have the ability to experience the future so strongly before it happens that when it does happen, it quite often doesn't meet the expectations they had in their imagination. They have pictured every little detail and put the outcome together with perfection. This ability to imagine so vividly can be a real problem for a perfectionist.

You can project a past memory into the future. In this situation you may be so focused on reliving a past memory that you miss what is actually happening in the moment. Again, for the perfectionist, the result is usually a disappointment.

Your mind can also focus on the present. Athletes call it the "zone." When you're in a state of hyper-focus, you are able to mentally change time, distance, and energy. When you are focused in the moment, you may not even be aware of what you're experiencing. It's in this altered state that an artist can paint a picture and not be aware of doing it until after he or she has finished.

You are constantly moving back and forth between the three tenses of your mind. Every thought or word creates an image that relates to a past memory or a future expectation. You will eventually bring these images back to your present where you have the opportunity to assess them. Under normal circumstances it's very difficult to stay focused for any length of time in any one of the three mind tenses.

Your Conscious, Unconscious, and Universal Minds

You have access to three different minds: your conscious, *unconscious*, and universal minds. Your conscious mind is your thinking mind. It is constantly processing information it receives from external stimuli as well as the images that surface from the unconscious and universal minds. Sometimes your conscious mind handles so much information that it will overload itself and induce you into a trance or sleep state.

DEFINITION

Your **unconscious mind** is the storage area for all your memories up to this point in time. You are constantly adding new information to your database. Your conscious mind is analytical, but your unconscious mind is passive and accepts what is stored there without question.

Your conscious mind makes up only about 10 percent of your total mind. It can easily get out of balance with your other minds. This happens when your unconscious mind takes over and creates an outcome that your conscious mind isn't happy with. When your conscious mind stays on alert too long, it can cause you to experience stress, which, over time, can result in health changes. It's good for you to be able to relax your conscious mind as often as possible so that you stay in balance with your whole self.

Your unconscious mind has been compared to a computer that has programs installed in it to do specific tasks. If it doesn't have the right program, the only way you can change the computer's function is to install a new one. Like your unconscious mind, the computer doesn't question the data it stores.

The unconscious mind may send the conscious mind stored information at any moment, sometimes when the conscious mind is not prepared or expecting to receive it. These images may be so powerful that they can cause you to enter a light trance that shifts your focus from conscious thinking into an unconscious memory experience.

Your universal mind is the part of you that connects to all the knowledge of the universe. You go through your unconscious mind to communicate with your universal mind. Every person is a part of and has the opportunity to access this mind. Many people choose not to, and they miss many opportunities to use their past life strengths and talents in their current lifetime.

Your universal mind is your connection to your soul's memories. These have been collected and stored since the beginning of its journey. Psychic Edgar Cayce referred to the soul's storage area as the Akashic Records, and he would enter a trance and go there to look up the record of the soul of the person for whom he was doing a reading.

How Do You Rate Your Mental DNA?

As you learned in Chapter 1, your mind is different than anyone else's on Earth. You'll now learn how you process in each of your five senses. It may be that you are strong in all five, or you may be strong in just one of them. For many of us, our visual sense is strongest. We recall our past memory in picture images and visualize what we expect to experience in the future. Everything we observe is recorded in our unconscious mind. Learning how you image can be very beneficial to you in many aspects of your life as well as in a past life experience. (The word "image" when used as a verb means experiencing a mental impression through your five different senses.)

Consider the following questions to help you determine the type and strength of your visual images.

Seeing with the Mind's Eye

Can you think of a pleasant memory and imagine it in pictures in your mind's eye? If so, can you see these images in color, or are they in black and white? Are your visual images clear or dull? Can you watch your memory as a moving picture? Can you stop the images, rewind them, and play them again?

There are two different ways that you can experience visual images. One way is to be able to watch yourself in the image. It will be like looking at a snapshot or video of yourself as you remember your image from your unconscious mind. This type of visual image doesn't have emotional feelings attached to it.

The second way is to see the image as if you were experiencing your memory all over again. When you experience a visual memory in your mind, you are also usually connecting one or more of your other senses to your visual image. Emotional images are often a part of the pictures in your mind.

Some of you may be able to experience both types of visual images. Some of you may only be able to visualize just one or the other, and a few of you will have no visual images in your mind at all. It's not necessary to be able to have visual images in your mind to experience a past life discovery.

Can You Hear It?

The second of the five senses is hearing. Technically, it's known as your auditory sense. Can you imagine sounds in your mind? If you can, what do you hear? Can you imagine a song in your head? Can you imagine turning up or down the volume? Can you slow down or speed up the music? Can you listen to music in your mind to calm you down or energize you?

KARMIC CAUTIONS

One of the keys to having a successful past life discovery experience is to be able to understand your own mental DNA. Make sure you understand how your mind works so that you can get the most out of your experience. If you're not visual and you try to have a visual experience, it can be very frustrating to you. Be very aware of this if you are working with someone who only processes in his sense strengths and doesn't take yours into account.

Can you imagine other sounds, such as nature? Can you remember a conversation with someone and hear it all over again? Do you replay conversations with others in your mind? Can you both picture and hear sounds of the same image in your memory? Can you move around in your visual memory and hear different sounds, or the same sounds from different locations?

Are you sensitive to sound? Do loud noises bother you? Can you listen to something that is mechanical and tell how well it's running by the way it sounds? Do you hear the voices of your guides or your angels? Do you have a positive voice that acts as your guide and comes to you when you need to hear it?

SOUL STORIES

George, an older man, had always had an interest in the unknown, but had an experience one day that he could not explain. He was driving down a rural road in upper New England and heard brass band music. The selection sounded right out of the late nineteenth century. He checked the radio, and it was off. As he continued to drive on, the music faded away. Had it been real, or had he imagined it in his mind? Had he stepped into a time in the past or experienced a memory in his soul?

Some of you may not have any sound recall at all. You may not imagine any sound in your mind. You don't need to recall sound to experience a past life memory. The hearing sense is only one of five, so if you have no sound recall at all, you can make up for it with your other senses.

How Do You Feel?

How do you feel about this so far? Actually feeling is one of your five image senses. It is known as your kinesthetic sense and covers two different areas. You can have a tactile experience, which simply means touch. If you have a strong tactile memory, then you will be able to recall what something feels like and experience it all over again when you are remembering it.

You will have both comfortable and uncomfortable touch memories. You might imagine how good something felt in the past and then expect that it will feel exactly the same in the future. The same can be true of a memory about something you touched or ate that was very unpleasant. Fears and phobias can be the result of a touch experience that your unconscious mind recalls from the past. That may be why you want no part of touching a spider, a snake, or some other animal or reptile.

Your tactile memories are created from actual physical experiences. These experiences could have happened any time in your life up to this moment and are recorded in your unconscious mind. When you are born, you also bring with you the memories of past life physical tactile experiences. This is why you may be repulsed by the thought of touching something that you have never come in contact with before in this lifetime.

Can you recall the touch of something that is pleasant? If so, how well can you experience this feeling right now? Is it as strong as when you first experienced it, or is it stronger or weaker? Can you change the intensity of your touch image in your mind? Do you also imagine pictures and/or sounds when you recall a touch memory?

Besides tactile images, the kinesthetic sense also includes emotional images. Emotional memories are internal feeling experiences that have been stored in your unconscious mind. You may remember a happy experience that will bring a smile to your face. You may recall a sad experience that brings tears to your eyes when you think of it again.

Can you imagine emotional feelings in your mind? If so, can you increase or decrease the intensity of these feelings? Could you imagine a memory and watch it with little or no emotion, and then place yourself in the memory and experience again the feelings that come from your unconscious mind? Can you increase or decrease these feelings?

AGELESS INSIGHTS

Do you have emotional experiences that come all of a sudden and you have no idea what caused you to have them? These experiences may have their roots in past life recall. An emotional image comes from your unconscious mind and can be triggered by many different things, including a picture, a physical location, a sound, a touch, a taste, or a smell.

Do certain sounds or music evoke emotions? If so, are these intense or slight? Can you control them, or do they control you? Some of you may have a very strong emotional image recall, while others of you may have few or no emotional memories. You will experience emotional images in the way that your mind naturally takes in and recalls them. If your emotional sense is not strong, that's okay, as you will make up for it in one or more of your other senses.

Let's Add Taste and Smell

There are two more senses to consider, and they are also very important in your mental DNA makeup. They are your taste and smell senses. The sense of taste is known as the gustatory sense. Everything you have tasted in your life is remembered in your unconscious mind. Some of these are good memories, and some of them are not so good.

Can you remember a taste that's very pleasant to you? Can you imagine a picture of a certain food and experience the taste of it as well as how it feels as you eat it? Can you imagine a food that tastes bad? If so, think of something pleasant instead.

Do you get a bad taste in your mouth when you think of an experience that was unpleasant and not related to food? Do you relate tastes to images in the other senses such as sound, pictures, or feelings? Can you change the intensity of a taste that you're remembering from a past experience?

Your smell sense is known as your olfactory sense. Do you have a favorite smell memory? Can you take a deep breath and experience the feeling right now? If so, how strong is your smell imagery? Can you experience it again the same way as you did before? Do you relate smell images to any one or more of your five different senses— seeing, hearing, feeling, tasting, and smelling? You may or may not have a keen sense of smell. If you don't, that's okay, as your other four senses will pick up the slack.

Jean has very poor hearing as a result of severe ear infections as a child. However, she does have an extremely sharp sense of smell. She can pick up an old jar that has been empty for more than 50 years and imagine what it had been filled with. She can also pick up old leftover smells from specific locations and then develop an image in her mind of what might have been there a hundred years ago. This is both a good and a bad thing for her. Some of the lingering smells are not pleasant and are a distraction to her.

Making Sense of It All

Have you been able to make any sense of your sense imagery so far? To review a little bit, you have five different senses—seeing, hearing, feeling, tasting, and smelling. Every one of you will process in those five senses differently. No one else on Earth does it exactly like you do. Your mind works backward into your memories from the past, and you recall them through one or more of your five senses. Your mind also projects forward into the future, experiencing events before they happen in those same five senses. In the present, you constantly are processing information through, guess what, those same five senses.

If you are hard of hearing, you will not recall sounds around you very well. If you are visually impaired, it will affect how you remember or project into the future your visual sense. The same thing is also true of feeling, smelling, and tasting.

Let's see how well you remember in each of your five senses. First of all, let yourself relax, using the trance exercise you experienced in Chapter 4. Suggest to yourself that you will remember and experience in all your five different senses a very pleasant memory from your past. You can memorize the questions, tape them and play them back to yourself, have someone read them to you, or consider each one by itself, using this book.

Rate each question in terms of a very strong image, a good image, a fair image, or no image. It's possible to be strong in all of them or strong in only one of them. You will score differently than anyone else. There is no pass or fail, just the opportunity to learn your image strengths. When you are ready, answer the following questions:

- Once you have focused on your pleasant memory, can you imagine in color? Can you see the image as a moving picture? Can you stop the picture and look at one image? Can you move in and out to get close-up details or see the image from a distance? Can you replay a scene over and over? Can you place yourself in the memory image and move yourself around? Can you go back and forth between experiencing and watching?

- Can you hear any sounds or voices related to your memory image? Can you turn up and down the volume of the sounds or voices? Can you slow down or speed up your sound images? Can you move around in the image and hear the sounds and voices from different locations?

- Can you experience what the temperature feels like in your memory image? Can you move around and feel different temperatures from different locations? Can you feel textures of different objects in your image? Can you feel what it's like to be someone other than yourself in your image? Can you feel emotions that are in your image? Can you feel someone else's emotions? Can you increase or decrease the intensity of the emotions you feel? Can you step out of the image and not feel any emotions?

- Can you experience any taste images in your memory recall? Can you experience different tastes in your image? Can you move around in your image and sample foods if there are any? Can you increase or decrease the intensity of your tastes?

- Can you experience smells in your memory recall? Can you move around in the scene and experience different smells? Can you increase or decrease the intensity of your smell imagery? Can you step out of the scene and not have a smell experience related to your memory recall?

What if you have no image recall? Some of you may ask this question after completing the assessment exercise. Mark, for example, found that he did not recall images in pictures, sounds, tastes, smells, and external feelings. He only experienced emotions. He found out that by focusing on the present he was able to receive spontaneous past life memories in feeling images. He learned to trust what his unconscious and universal minds let him know.

Once you have completed this assessment of your mental DNA, you will be able to develop a profile of your image strengths. These will be very valuable for you as you prepare for a past life discovery experience.

The Least You Need to Know

- Your mind is constantly going back and forth between your past, future, and the present.
- Your conscious mind is your analytical mind.
- Your unconscious mind contains all your memories from your past.
- Your universal mind is the link to your past lives.
- Your mental DNA is different than anyone else's in the world.
- You may be strong or weak in any one of the five different senses—seeing, hearing, feeling, tasting, and smelling.

Now Get Comfortable

In This Chapter

- Finding a comfortable, relaxing place in your mind
- Your destination when you experience an image trance
- A trance-deepening exercise
- Enjoying your deep trance experience
- Continuing the trance experience after you come back to consciousness

John has always had an active imagination. He was able to tell amazing stories when he was a child. He could also draw pictures that flowed from his unconscious mind. When he experienced a past life discovery session, he easily slipped into a deep trance.

Eric, on the other hand, had never been able to relax. He felt that he could not let himself enter a trance. After he identified the memory of a special place, he started to revisit it using his image senses that were the strongest for him. After a couple weeks of daily practice, he was ready and open to his first experience of discovering his past lives.

Your mind may be similar to John's or Eric's, or different from either one. In this chapter you will be able to determine the best way for you to experience past life imagery. Once you have decided what you like the best, practice every day, and you will soon be doing it like a pro.

Where's Your Favorite Relaxing Place?

You are now going to learn how to deepen your natural trance. Deepening means to bring yourself into a more focused state of imagery. When this happens, you are able to step into a holographic image, or, in other words, move from the reality around you into the reality of your trance. You may already be naturally escaping in your mind if you daydream a lot or immerse yourself in a good book, for example. If you do, this will really be easy for you. If you don't, the goal is to let you understand how easy it is to go to your comfort zone.

You will be able to apply your new knowledge of your mental DNA to help you focus even more. As you now know, every one of your minds is different, and the exercise in this chapter is designed to help you use your natural abilities to enter and deepen your relaxing imagery trance. This technique will be helpful to you as you prepare to experience a discovery journey to a past life.

Take a few moments and let yourself relax. Now think of a place that is very relaxing and comfortable to you. Don't be surprised if it takes you a little time to come up with one. Some of you are very busy and don't have much time to relax. Still others of you may meditate daily and are easily able to think of a comfortable place.

This place may be one from a pleasant memory where you used to go. It may no longer exist, or it may be hard or impossible for you to go there physically at this time. That's okay. A positive memory that you can revisit in your mind can be a good mental comfort zone. You may have a place in your imagination that you have visited many times and go there when you need to get mentally away. That may also be a good place for you to focus on. If you can't think of an actual place, you can make one up if you want to.

Your relaxing and comfortable place in your mind may be an outside or inside image. It could be an experience like floating in water, feeling the warm sun at an ocean beach, or bathing in a warm tub. You could be high on a mountain, relaxing in your bed, cruising on your motorcycle, or reading a book. There are so many places you can find to relax in your mind that you can choose the same one every time or a different one each time you experience your trance state.

KARMIC CAUTIONS

A relaxing, light trance can be good for your health. When you fail to allow yourself a chance to escape in a positive way, you can build up stress. This buildup can result in future health problems.

Once you've identified a comfortable place, begin to focus on it through your five different senses: seeing, hearing, feeling, tasting, and smelling. Remember that you may not be strong in all of them even though they are addressed here. You can use the ones that help you focus most deeply and most easily.

Picture your favorite relaxing place in your mind. If you can, view it both from a distance as if you were looking at it on a television screen, and place yourself in the image where you can move around and see it from several different positions. Let yourself hear the relaxing sounds that are in your relaxing place. Turn the volume up or down and hear different sounds as you move around in the image. Now let yourself feel how good it is to be there. If there are positive and relaxing things to touch, you may allow yourself to do so.

If there are any positive and relaxing tastes in your image, you may experience them. Let yourself experience any relaxing smells that are in your image. You may move around in your mind and enjoy the smells from different locations. Let yourself become aware of what it's like to experience your relaxing and comfortable place in all your senses.

You may also have a favorite relaxing smell that is not a part of your comfortable place. If you do, it's okay to include it in any way that will help you relax. You are also free to add to the imagery with any of your other senses. If you want to try a nonphysical place, you'll be able to after the completion of this exercise.

Take a Deep Breath, and Let Your Eyes Go Out of Focus

Now if you're ready, you may experience how to deepen your trance by going to your relaxing place in your mind. Find a comfortable place where you won't be disturbed, and sit or lie down. Make sure your clothes feel comfortable and are nonbinding. You may burn a candle with a relaxing smell and use music or other calming sounds if you wish. You may record this and play it back, memorize it, or have someone read it to you. You may rewrite the words any way you want to help yourself deepen your trance state.

AGELESS INSIGHTS

It may help you to focus if you record the following exercise and play it back to yourself. Read slowly and emphasize words like "relax" and "breathe in" and "breathe out" to help you step into your unconscious mind. You can also ask someone else to read it to you.

To begin, take a deep breath of your favorite relaxing smell. If this is a candle or something else that's actually in the room with you, focus on the scent as you exhale and continue to breathe in and out in slow, deep, relaxing breaths. If you are imagining your smell, do the same thing. Suggest to yourself that with each breath you will let yourself feel more and more relaxed.

As you continue to breathe in and out, let yourself focus your mind onto the spot in the center of your forehead known as your third eye. Let your eyes go out of focus as you continue to breathe in and out, relaxing more and more with each breath.

You have many muscles throughout your body, and some of them are stiff and tight, while others are relaxed and loose. All the way through this exercise you may be aware of different muscles that may stiffen up. If they do, allow them to relax, and suggest to yourself that you will go deeper and deeper into your relaxing trance as you focus on your special comfortable and relaxing place in your mind.

In a few moments, when you're ready, you may begin to slowly count yourself downward from five to zero. You may suggest to yourself that when you reach zero, you will be able to experience your relaxing place in your mind in all your five senses. You may totally let yourself experience your image and let yourself have a very relaxing and positive experience.

Count from Five to Zero

As you prepare to count yourself downward, suggest to yourself that with every count you will feel yourself going deeper and deeper. If it's comfortable to you, you may physically feel yourself sinking deeper and deeper as if you were descending down a spiral staircase into the recesses of your unconscious mind. Once you reach the bottom level, suggest that you will step into your special place and experience it in all your senses.

If for any reason you want or need to, you may always take a deep breath, exhale, open your eyes, and come back to the surface of your mind, feeling wide awake, and very positive and relaxed. If you feel uncomfortable during any exercise in this book, you may end it at once.

Are you ready? Take a deep breath of your favorite smell and slowly exhale. At your first number let a positive, relaxing feeling start to flow downward over and through your body from the top of your head, down over your forehead, eyes, nose, mouth, chin, and down to your neck.

- *Five.* Feel yourself sinking deeper and deeper as you breathe in and out. The relaxing feeling begins to spread through and around your body. You may relax any muscle that is stiff as you continue with each breath to feel yourself sinking deeper and deeper.

- *Four.* You may let yourself sink deeper and deeper into your positive image as the relaxing feeling flows down over your shoulders and down your arms, all the way to your fingertips. With each breath you may feel yourself going deeper and deeper as you relax more and more. You are getting closer and closer to your special place in your mind.

- *Three.* You may experience your favorite smell getting stronger and stronger as you feel yourself relaxing more and more. You may feel a relaxing energy spreading down over the rest of your upper body, all the way down to your waist. With each breath, you may feel yourself relaxing more and more and focusing your mind on the images.

- *Two.* The relaxing energy is now spreading downward to your knees. You can feel it flowing over and through you. You feel yourself sinking even deeper and deeper. With each breath you are relaxing more and more and feeling so comfortable.

- *One.* As you continue to relax more and more and sink deeper and deeper, you may feel the relaxing energy move down to your ankles. With each breath you continue to relax more and more as you go deeper and deeper. In a moment, you may count slowly from five all the way down to zero when you will be totally filled with a relaxing energy and focused on the special comfortable and relaxing place deep in your unconscious mind.

- *Five. Four. Three. Two. One. Zero.* You are now deep into a very relaxing trance. With each breath you may relax more and more. You may now prepare to experience the comfortable, relaxing place in your mind.

Enjoy Your Comfort Zone

Now allow yourself to focus on your special relaxing place. You may see it in a very clear picture image. Let yourself step into your image and experience it with all its relaxing beauty. You may move as slowly as you want, and you can stop and rewind your image and replay it again so that you may see it clearer each time.

SOUL STORIES

Athletes use mental imagery to train for their sport. They will find a comfortable place and practice in their minds. They can practice variable conditions, feel their muscles, and experience their moves over and over again until their muscles automatically remember. When involved in the actual sport, they go into what is often called the "zone."

Totally immerse yourself in your special image and experience it through all of your senses at once. Take your time and experience as many different details as you like. Suggest that you will be able to visit this special place in your mind and experience it even more any time you want or need to. You may give yourself a special word or touch anchor to help you come back to your special comfortable place in your mind. Also suggest that you will continue to have your relaxed, comfortable feelings long after you have counted yourself back up to your conscious mind. When you're ready, you may begin to slowly count yourself back up to your conscious mind.

Count Back to Reality

You may now begin to leave your special place in your mind and begin your return to consciousness.

- *One.* Continue to slowly breathe in and out and experience your favorite relaxing smell. You will feel comfortable and relaxed as you continue your way back to the surface of your mind.

- *Two.* You are continuing upward. With each breath you will feel comfortable and relaxed, enjoying your visit to your special place in your mind.

- *Three.* You are now halfway back. You are beginning to move from your special place back into the world of your conscious mind. You are feeling very comfortable and relaxed as you breathe slowly in and out.

- *Four.* You are almost all the way back. Let yourself prepare to come back into your conscious mind on the next count, feeling very calm and relaxed from your positive experience in your conscious mind. Continue to breathe in and out slowly as your favorite smell lingers in your mind. Now take a deep breath and hold it for a moment.

- *Five.* Slowly exhale and let yourself come back to conscious awareness. You may open your eyes and adjust them to the light. You feel very comfortable and relaxed from your visit to your special, comfortable place in your unconscious mind.

AGELESS INSIGHTS

Consider this an exercise of your imagination. That is really what it is. It's a great way to prepare for a past life discovery experience. If you establish a daily routine of practicing this technique, you will form the habit of shifting your focus from your conscious to your unconscious. Your goal is to work with your imagination to help the images become sharper and more in focus. This ability to let your mind wander and experience all your five senses will be very helpful in the chapters to follow.

Take a few moments and allow yourself to reflect on your experience. You may want to make some notes on what you would like to add or change the next time you go to your special place in your mind. You are also free to go to other places and have other experiences any time you want.

What If I Don't Have a Special Place?

It's possible that you can't imagine a special place or any place in your unconscious mind. You may be like Jim, who is nonvisual. He could not think of a specific place that he could imagine visiting, so he focused on connecting to his faith. Jim was used to communicating in the form of prayer. As he relaxed, he asked that a peaceful, healing energy flow into his body. He asked his faith to help him with his worries and to guide his words and actions. The more he practiced his praying trance, the easier it was for him to bring himself back into the state when he wanted or needed to relax.

You don't have to fit into a specific mind mold to be successful in discovering your past lives. You are learning how to create your own natural image strengths. All you need to do is recognize, develop, and allow yourself to trust what you already are able to do. This exercise will help you focus on your abilities.

The more you practice, the more your mind will be prepared to experience discovering your past lives. The more you learn to accept and trust the information your mind gives you, the easier it will be to explore your past lives. Remember, all you have to do is take a deep breath and open your eyes to come back to the surface of your mind whenever you are experiencing a trance.

The Least You Need to Know

- The more you learn to relax your mind, the easier it will be to experience image trances.
- When you experience a positive, relaxing memory through your five senses, you will relax even more.
- If you establish a specific routine to experience imagery, you will automatically begin to enter your relaxing trance.
- It's not necessary to be visual to develop a technique to enter a trance.
- The more you develop and practice your own technique, the better prepared you will be to experience discovering your past lives.

A Visit to a Past Life Discovery Specialist

In This Chapter

- What to expect when you visit a past life discovery specialist
- Portions of three past life discovery transcripts
- Brad's discovery of why he is so sensitive
- Stephanie's journey to Atlantis
- Dora's discovery of why she feels panic

In this chapter, you will read the transcripts of three past life discovery experiences that were done by a professional specializing in past life recall. Even though the *facilitator* is trained to guide his subjects into a state of trance that will help them enter a past life, as you progress through this book, you will be able to accomplish the same thing yourself.

All image trances are self-trances. The specialist does not have the power to create a trance; only you have that power. You will read how three people like yourself were able to discover information in their past lives that helped them understand and change their current lives for the better.

> **DEFINITIONS**
>
> A **facilitator** is someone who can help you journey through a past life experience. The facilitator can read the script that helps you create an imagery trance and then ask questions that focus on the right information to bring back. The facilitator can also be there to help guide you back out of your trance.

What Should You Expect?

Many people who want to discover a past life have read or heard about others who have already done it. The subject may have a set idea in their mind of what the experience will be like, and they come into a specialist's office with expectations that they hope to accomplish. Some may want to just have the experience of visiting a past life, while others are looking for specific answers that they hope will provide enlightenment on a certain situation in their life.

Try to keep an open mind. If your expectations are too focused, you may miss the real purpose of discovering your past lives. You could be expecting an insight to occur in a certain way and when it doesn't, you focus on what you didn't want when you could have been open to what you needed.

It is good to have an idea of what you would like to learn when you visit a *past life specialist*. However, you also want to be prepared to go with whatever takes place during the session. There will be plenty of time later to analyze the experience.

Always check on the credentials of a professional past life specialist. That includes inquiring about the person's training, certifications, and even talking to his or her previous clients.

Ask if you can bring a friend to videotape your experience, or ask the past life specialist to tape the induction for you when you are being induced into your relaxing image trance. Sometimes the specialist does this, and sometimes she turns the tape on after the induction has been completed. This is done to save tape space for the past life information. If you supply a video camera, the tape usually lasts a minimum of two hours, which should be plenty of time to get the induction also.

DEFINITION

A **past life specialist** is someone who has been trained to guide you into a past life discovery experience and interpret what you experience. The training may be certified by an organization such as the International Board for Regression Therapy (IBRT).

The better prepared you are, the better the chance for a positive past life discovery experience. You may want to give the specialist a written list of some of your past life interests.

One of the biggest disappointments to a client when experiencing a past life experience is the failure in his or her own mind to enter a deep image trance. Many good and successful past life trances are not as deep as you might think. The specialist is trained to observe every expression and every movement, and hear every word or phrase the client uses during the session. That is the benefit of videotape as you get to see yourself offer clues about your past life that you didn't realize you were giving.

It's okay to imagine the answers to the questions you are asked, even if you consider yourself completely awake. The specialist can actually help your imagination become a mind reality experience if you will let him or her. The answers you give lead to more questions, which are designed to help you enter into a light trance, and perhaps eventually a deeper trance. The specialist will focus on your image strengths to help you shift your view into the hologram that is contained in your unconscious mind.

SOUL STORIES

Rachel had a fear of needles. Now that she was expecting a baby, she was faced with constantly getting her blood checked. She discovered in a past life session that she was a prisoner in a Nazi concentration camp and had died from a lethal injection. With this information she found she could focus on her unborn child and have her blood tested without distress.

The more you let yourself go with the flow, the better the possibility of your having a successful past life discovery experience. Remember that there is no scientific proof up to this point indicating that you are, in fact, recalling a past life. You are ultimately responsible for interpreting what took place.

After you finish your session, you may want to make some notes about your experience. The past life specialist may give you the suggestion that every time you listen to the tape of your experience, you will remember more details. You can use the tape as a work tape to help you actually go into a trance and allow you to focus on the images you experienced during your session. Each time you go over it, you may be able to fill in details that you missed previously.

A past life session usually lasts no more than an hour. The entire office visit with pre- and post-talks can last from an hour and a half to two hours. Follow-up visits usually take a little less time as the specialist is already acquainted with how your mind produces images.

Let's look now at how the experience went for one past life discovery session.

Brad's Past Life Discovery Session

Brad had been very sensitive his entire life. Even though he felt great joy for other people, he also experienced a touch of emotional pain. It was easy for him to get down on himself when he wasn't holding up his part of the "bargain" for other people. He wanted to find out the roots of his sensitivity.

PLS: Brad, I want you to just allow the first impression that comes to you without feeling pressure to come up with an answer one way or another. I'm going to do an *affect-bridge* technique and I want you to imagine a time within the last year when you have felt that oversensitivity.

PLS: You don't have to state what it is. Can you remember a time in the last five years when you may have felt it?

Brad: Yup.

> **DEFINITION**
>
> An **affect-bridge** technique takes the subject back through his life to events that relate to a specific emotion. As he goes back, he may transfer the emotion to a similar emotion he experienced earlier. In a past life experience he bridges back to another lifetime that has images with the same or similar emotions.

PLS: Fifteen years? Twenty-five years?

Brad: Uhum.

PLS: What is the earliest incidence you can remember?

Brad: Nursery school perhaps?

PLS: Is it okay to talk about this scene?

Brad: Sure.

PLS: Tell me what you see.

Brad: I see fire trucks, toy fire trucks, and tricycles riding around the basement.

PLS: What are you doing?

Brad: I'm part of the fun.

PLS: Can you see yourself?

Brad: Yes.

PLS: So what happens to create the feelings of sensitivity?

Brad: Just watching the joy and pleasure in other people's eyes.

PLS: What did it feel like to you when you felt the joy?

Brad: It was like I was feeling everybody's thoughts, feelings, and positive interactions.

PLS: Can you remember any times earlier than that?

Brad: Yup, being with grandparents at their house.

PLS: And these were good memories?

Brad: Yes.

PLS: Can you remember anything earlier than that?

Brad: Not really. Ah ... (Brad hesitated) probably doesn't relate to it.

PLS: Go on.

Brad: I had a dream at one point of being an infant and something bad happening somewhere in a hospital.

PLS: Can you picture that dream in your mind?

Brad: Uhuh. I was in a crib in the hospital.

PLS: Why were you there?

Brad: I'm not sure.

PLS: Can you see any doctors or nurses?

Brad: Not really.

PLS: So you're by yourself?

Brad: No. They're milling about and I'm just there.

PLS: What's your mood?

Brad: Scared.

PLS: Tell me what happened to this child in the hospital?

Brad: The child just wants to get out of the crib badly because he's very scared of the atmosphere around it and feels like he's trapped.

PLS: Now I want you in your mind to go to a different scene, perhaps in a different lifetime, where someone was trapped.

Brad: In an airplane.

PLS: Watching this for a moment, can you see it through the eyes of a person?

Brad: Yes.

PLS: Go back to the time before the airplane took off. What do you see?

Brad: A couple in line, waiting to get aboard.

PLS: Why are they getting on the plane?

Brad: For pleasure. For vacation.

PLS: Have they flown before?

Brad: No.

PLS: So follow this along and tell me what happens.

Brad: The plane crashes.

PLS: Go back to just before the plane crashes and tell me how he finds out the plane is going to crash?

Brad: He can feel it.

PLS: How did he feel it?

Brad: He felt the turbulence, a sharp downward decent.

PLS: What were his last thoughts?

Brad: Family.

PLS: Did he pass in the accident?

Brad: Uhuh.

PLS: What were his thoughts after he passed over?

Brad: A sense of relief that it was over.

PLS: Why was he relieved?

Brad: Because there was so much fear as he was going down.

PLS: What is the relationship to this and the dream you had as a child?

Brad: Entrapment.

PLS: Now go to another life where your feelings of sensitivity came from.

Brad: Perhaps a priest. He's got a robe of some type on. It's not modern day, but he's a good healer.

PLS: Go to the point in life when he learned how to heal.

Brad: He was hurting emotionally. He saw a scene that depressed him somehow. A wife and kids being hurt by an abusive husband.

PLS: What was his connection?

Brad: He wanted to step in and heal them.

PLS: Did he do that?

Brad: Yup. He was able to read how they were feeling and take them to the next step to help them heal.

PLS: Go back to when the priest first knew.

Brad: When he was an infant, he just knew. It was something he just had inside of him. He had sadness as a child because of his family situation, but he just knew how to heal.

PLS: Where did he learn to feel joy about his healing ability?

Brad: Toward the end, he finally accepted it.

PLS: Connect with his thoughts toward the end and tell me what he was feeling.

Brad: That he brought some joy to other people's lives.

PLS: Connect to that body for a moment and know how he used the healing.

Brad: With great compassion.

PLS: For a moment take a deep breath and feel what that priest knew, the connection of love and healing energy, and in your mind allow that energy to flow over these and other lifetimes to heal and to heal oneself within, knowing that sensitivity is a gift. It's an awareness to use in a positive way without carrying the great weight of it.

PLS: Imagine where you are now and look at how you have been feeling in your life and see how it is all coming together in a positive way to help you. Can you see that?

Brad: Uhuh.

PLS: Feel the healing of the past as it comes through and allow it to connect to each part of your soul so that you're free to walk the life together again now with joy, light, and love. Know in a moment that when you come back to the conscious surface of your mind, you will be able to use this positive element in your life. You will be free to use this energy now to help many people as they move along their life maps with a feeling of joy and gratitude as you see this coming all together again. The details will fill in more and more as you come to the surface of your conscious mind.

Brad was able to use this past life discovery experience to come to terms with his over-sensitivity. He knew now the reason for feeling joy at other's happiness. He became aware how his compassion helped others who crossed his life path. He was not the victim on the plane anymore. A part of him was still Father Brad.

AGELESS INSIGHTS

It can take time and patience to find the right information. In Brad's case, the past life specialist went with whatever his response was to the previous question until a bigger picture began to emerge. Then he began to focus on the roots of the sensitivity, both good and bad.

Journey to Atlantis with Stephanie

Stephanie loved the Bahamas and swimming in the warm ocean. She had even gone so far as to swim with dolphins. She wanted to discover her past life connection with the lost continent of Atlantis.

PLS: I want you to look in your mind's eye and see an image of Atlantis.

Steph: I see two columns and a book. It feels like I'm under water and it's very blue and I'm breathing.

PLS: Is it easy to breathe under water?

Steph: Very, and I'm actually able to stay on the sand.

PLS: Look down and tell me whatever is touching the sand.

Steph: I have human feet and, huh? (Stephanie was surprised at what she saw.) There's actually web between the toes. It's like a foot but there's web between the toes.

PLS: How do these feet work with the water?

Steph: They're really not long webs, so you can walk if you need to, then if you want to swim, they are like flippers. You can actually swim like a fish.

PLS: Can you feel the top of your head?

Steph: It seems like its something flowing. It seems like it begins with hair and ends like plants or seaweed. It's very fine and soft and when it turns to plants it's like rubbery and thicker.

PLS: Can you look at something that resembles hands?

Steph: The hands are the same as the feet. They have a bit of web between the fingers but there's more appendage. They have more fingers than toes but there is a joining of a web between the fingers.

PLS: Step back into this body and describe what it feels like.

Steph: Feels all-knowing.

PLS: What is your mood?

Steph: Happy. It seems like there's something that I need to get done. It's happy but a sense of urgency. Coming for an appointment. Something has to get accomplished.

PLS: Know what it is you have to do.

Steph: Just to remember that the universe is part of the co-creation of this and to always be checking my every step with the universe, not where my mind leads me.

PLS: How do you check in with the universe?

Steph: In my heart. That's the way they do it.

PLS: What happens when they think of their heart?

Steph: It feels warm and it glows and it expands, more than it was before they were thinking of their heart.

PLS: Can you go through the columns now?

Steph: Yah.

PLS: Tell me what happens next.

Steph: I'm a little hesitant. I'm afraid to continue now that I am on this task and feel how important this is now. I feel like I've got butterflies in my stomach right now.

PLS: You don't need to feel the butterflies. You can watch if you want. Have you been there before?

Steph: I think so, and I didn't accomplish something I was supposed to do before, and, wow, I can feel this, it feels funky.

PLS: Go back and know now what you didn't accomplish before, without feeling the effects of it. Remember, you can always open your eyes and come back to the surface of your mind any time you want.

Steph: Wow! This is bizarre to what is happening in this lifetime. I went in feeling as if I had this headstrong taskmaster with an attitude, and I just wanted to get done. I got this feeling I was not going to be able to accomplish this mission because the last time I tried it, I was overwhelmed and I failed.

PLS: Why are you on this mission?

Steph: 'Cause there's information in books I'm supposed to share with people, but I got so impatient that it actually came out all mixed up because I was worried that I wouldn't be successful, and instead of relaxing, I worried that I wouldn't be able to absorb all the information.

PLS: Where is this information?

Steph: There are shelves with books but you don't have to open them to get the information, you just have to stand around them.

PLS: Take a deep breath and let yourself now know what you need to learn from these books.

Steph: There's never a moment too soon or too late and when it doesn't feel right, don't push it, and just allow and be patient. When it feels right, all the information we need to know is in that moment, and when it doesn't feel right, to not pass that moment. It's only how our heart feels that we know how to go at the right tempo and to always know that we are not alone.

PLS: Were you able to accomplish that in that life?

Steph: It seems like in that life the first time "no," but as I am speaking about it now, it seems that as I am walking through the columns, it's getting okay, and at this point it does feel successful.

SOUL STORIES

Stephanie was actually able to go back into her Atlantis life and correct what she failed to accomplish earlier. She was also able to apply this information as a way of guiding her in this life. Further on in the session she started to channel information from the knowledge in the books in what appears to be the Atlantis version of the Akashic Records.

Dora's Panic Attacks

When Dora was three years old, she and her mother, who was carrying her younger brother, were climbing the stairs to their apartment when she saw a fly. Dora instantly panicked, and her mother did all she could do to get her to keep going. The past life specialist asked her to imagine a scene from another life where there was panic.

Dora: It goes back to Europe. I'm little again and I'm looking at my parents at the time of a plague. They have maggots and flies all over them.

PLS: Can you go back to a happier time?

Dora: Yes, I'm in a wheat field and I'm playing in the middle of all the grass. It's the end of summer, and I'm very, very happy.

PLS: Where do you live?

Dora: In an old stone house.

PLS: Who lives there?

Dora: My grandmother and my parents, but my parents are sick.

PLS: How long have they been sick?

Dora: Weeks. My grandmother is taking care of them.

PLS: Now step out and watch the scene and tell me when the little girl begins to panic.

Dora: I seem to be coming back to the stone house. It's as if Gram and I went away for a while, and my parents had died there alone, and now I walked into the house and saw them covered with flies and maggots.

PLS: What could you see from that life that is connecting to you now in your current life?

Dora: My parents and brother both died of cancer, and I had that feeling of panic again.

The past life specialist had Dora go back and hold the hand of the little girl in the field when she was happy, and tell her she did not need to experience the same panic anymore in this life. She was now free to explore this life as a child feeling love and good health.

The Least You Need to Know

- Every past life discovery experience is different.
- It's not necessary to enter a deep trance to be successful.
- Go with your first image without analyzing it until after the session is over.
- Keep an open mind, because what you experience may not be what you expected.
- Be aware of the many small image details in a past life experience.

Preparing for the Adventure

It's time to begin to prepare for the journey into your past. Now that you have been to detective school, you know how to start looking for clues about your soul's memory. In fact, you may already have a lot of the pieces of your past life puzzle laid out.

You have read about other experiences and may wonder if you, too, will be able to journey into your past. You will consider what a past life discovery session will be like as you prepare for your own. You will also learn how your faith is an important part of your travel.

In this part you will begin to spread out your puzzle so that you can decide what pieces you want to look for in your past to help complete the picture. There may be an unresolved karma, an old fear, or a soul mate connection. It's time to create a travel plan and pack the tools you'll need to take on your journey back to your past lives.

What Is It Like to Discover Your Past Lives?

In This Chapter

- Going with the flow of your images
- Can you get stuck in the past?
- What will you be like after discovering a past life?
- How imagination can help you discover your past lives

The process of discovering your past lives can be like attending a powerful performance. Although the experience is different for everyone, this chapter explains more about what you can expect.

What Will You Experience?

Now that you've had the opportunity to read about others' experiences of discovering their past lives, you may wonder what it was like while they were in their trance. The answer is simple. Your experience will be different than anyone else's.

Many factors enter into the experience of discovering your past lives. Your state of focus can change each time you enter your relaxing trance state. It is possible that your mind could be cluttered with day-to-day business at one time, while another time you may be totally relaxed and focused on the experience. You could feel differently each time emotionally, physically, or spiritually. There may be interruptions that were not anticipated that could interrupt your focus.

You may start with an expectation of what you're going to or should experience, only to end the session disappointed with the outcome. You may have a specific time period or place that you want to visit, only to go someplace completely different. You may have read about, heard of, or observed a past life discovery experience that was particularly dramatic. It could have touched on famous characters in history or had an unbelievable outcome.

SOUL STORIES

Fred came to a past life discovery session with specific expectations. He had been told that he would go off into a sleeplike trance and would not be aware. Fred, however, did not go into a deep trance. His conscious mind was active throughout the whole experience. He refused to accept the images that came to him because he thought they were only his imagination and not real. Sadly, he missed the information that was actually coming to him through his unconscious mind.

It is possible that your first past life images may be of a traumatic situation, and it's important for you to be able to move yourself out of the experience just as a past life discovery specialist would. You will learn to ground and protect yourself before you take your first past life discovery journey. This sounds much more serious than it is. Grounding means that you will be able to have an experience without getting totally caught up in an image that might be negative for you. Protected means that you are in balance between what you experience and your faith so that you will not have an unsettling past life image.

The way that you process with your five senses (see Chapter 6) will have a big impact on your past life discovery experience. Because your mental DNA is different than anyone else's, you will have an image experience that no one except yourself will have. You can expect that you will recall past life information in the same manner as you do a comfortable memory in your mind. If you image visually, you should be able to see your past life experience. You may be able to step back and watch it, or you may be able to step into and see what you are experiencing. You may be able to do both or neither.

As discussed in Chapter 6, a past life specialist can help identify one's image strengths before a past life journey starts. He would then be able to ask questions related to the subject's mental DNA that he knows the person could respond to. It would probably do no good to ask a visual question of a nonvisual subject. Both the specialist and the subject could become frustrated and disappointed by the experience.

AGELESS INSIGHTS

The more you practice your relaxing image trance, the more you can sharpen your focus on your strong senses. At first you may have to remind yourself to see, hear, feel, taste, and smell in your mind. You may need to practice a bit to sharpen your sense imagery. Every time you work on your technique, you will become more confident and comfortable with it.

All your other senses work in the same manner as your visual sense. If you have a strong smell sense, it can help you to gather valuable information about the lifetime you're visiting. The more you understand how you can use your senses, the more confidence you will have in your ability to experience and collect information during a past life discovery experience.

A strong sense experience can also help deepen your trance state. You can practice entering your comfort zone and imaging through each of your five senses to help you focus with a higher intensity on the experience. The more your image experience intensifies, the easier it is for you to step into the reality of the experience. A relaxing imagery trance is an altered state of reality. It's possible to change your reality so that your image experience becomes your reality. When that happens, you are entering a deeper state of focus.

And remember: the less you expect to experience when you visit a past life, the more open you will be to what you will actually experience. If you are looking for something specific, you may pass by something that is very important. In fact, the littlest clue could be an integral element as you put the pieces of a past life together. Something you may have dismissed might eventually turn out to be the missing link. Of course, you may collect some information that doesn't fit into your past life discovery goals. At the same time, even that information may be very important to something else that you're looking for or need to know.

The more you can allow yourself to accept that every past life discovery experience is important, the more open you will be to understanding the lessons that may be there for you to learn. There are no failures. There are no ways to do it wrong as long as the experience is one that has a productive outcome.

It's not necessary to gather all the information in one session. Many times unconscious images will continue to surface in your conscious mind long after the trance has ended. More information may come up to the surface through your dreams or thoughts at any time. The best thing that you can do is to think of it as an adventure, and the process of discovering past lives has the potential to be just that, a great adventure.

Is It Possible to Get Stuck in the Past?

As you'll recall from Chapter 1, the television show *Soap* had a storyline one season about a character that became trapped in a past life. It was very funny to watch him try to adjust to a culture that was much further advanced than he was accustomed to. This character stayed stuck for several episodes of the show.

So could this happen to you? The answer is no, you won't get stuck in a past life. You may have an experience that's so strong that when you come back to conscious reality it can take you a few moments to adjust. This is no different than being absorbed in a good movie, a play, or a good book. Have you ever had the experience of becoming so focused on what you were reading or watching that you shifted your reality to the experience? If you have, you know that sometimes when you are jerked back to conscious reality, you still continue to focus on the other image for a moment as well as your actual surroundings.

This same feeling can happen after you have experienced a deep trance state during a past life discovery session. This is why it's important for you to come back to your conscious mind slowly so that you can easily make the adjustment back to your conscious reality. It's a good idea for you to plan to give yourself some time to reflect on your experience and get accustomed to your surroundings again.

> **AGELESS INSIGHTS**
>
> You should always suggest to yourself that you will come back to the surface of your conscious mind refreshed and relaxed and in a positive mood. This way you will be more open to letting your past life journey slowly make its way into your conscious mind at a pace that's good for you.

It is also very important that if you're receiving treatment or counseling from a professional, you discuss your goals of past life discovery before you try the process. Some people have such an extreme ability to be influenced by suggestions that it's easy for them to lose track of reality. That is not the goal of this book. It's good for you to always know where you are on some level. Once you are comfortable with that, you are free to experience your reality imagery trance for a past life discovery journey without the fear that you will be trapped somewhere in the past.

The experience of discovering your past lives is sort of like wandering around in woods that you are slightly familiar with. It's very easy to get turned around if you aren't paying attention, and yet the woods are not so large that you won't be able to find your way out in a reasonable time. Then again, if you had a compass with you, you could wander around and be confident that you could always find your way out quickly. If you have a tendency to get lost in your mind, then you will want to be sure of your ability to come back to the surface of your conscious mind and know where you are. The more you practice your relaxing self-imagery trance, the more you will know and trust your ability to return to your conscious mind.

It's always advisable to know where you are physically, mentally, and spiritually. People who get lost in their minds can lose track of reality. You might compare it to a war veteran who was so traumatized in battle that when he hears a car backfire, he instantly shifts his reality to a memory still playing in his unconscious mind. Once the veteran has focused on that reality, he will continue to do so until the battle trance has run its course.

Fear and phobia trances can work the same way. Some of them can last for days, weeks, and even years. All this time the conscious mind is powerless to change the course of the trance.

AGELESS INSIGHTS

Some people actually live in a past life trance. They may realize where they are, but they have compelling images they cannot explain that flow from their soul's memory. If they are able to understand these images when they first start, they can stop a trance by pulling back and focusing on something that keeps their mind in the present, such as feeling the temperature of their surroundings and being aware of sounds, smells, and their body sitting on a solid chair.

There is no more danger of getting stuck in a past life then there is getting stuck in this life. By understanding and grounding yourself in normal reality, you will have the opportunity to experience the reality of a past life without the fear of being stuck there. It's just like going to the movies, only they are in your mind.

After Your Past Life Discovery Experience

So what will you be like when you return from your past life discovery adventure? What are you like after you have read a book, or gone to a play or a movie? A great many different elements can influence your response to that question.

The quality of the work in a book or play and your interest in the subject may affect your response to the material that you have experienced. If it's done well, you may be drawn into the material even if you didn't have an initial strong interest in it. You can actually become mesmerized by a good presentation. You will shift your focus and become totally absorbed in the subject, remaining in your trance state until the presentation is over or until something interrupts you. When that happens, you sometimes need a few moments to regain your balance and come back to your normal reality.

A past life discovery expert knows how to help you change for the better after your journey. They help you sift through the image material you've just experienced so that you may gain a different perspective on a situation that needs to be clarified in this lifetime. The goal of the therapeutic session is to resolve a past life memory that keeps resurfacing through your unconscious mind. Once you can understand the surfacing images, you can resolve them and move forward in your mind to other more positive and productive images. When you have done this, there is a good possibility that you will have a different outlook about your life. Yes, you may change from your past life discovery experience.

Keep in mind that when someone who is unqualified tries to do therapy, the results may not be helpful to the person experiencing the session. An old trauma may be brought up to the surface of the conscious mind, and an untrained person might not know how to deal with it. Leading the subject to imagine a reality that never really existed can create what are called "false memories." An untrained person could also jump to the wrong conclusion about the meaning of the experience.

SOUL STORIES

Ann had always been fearful of trying to help others. She had studied therapeutic arts such as hypnosis and Reiki but could never allow herself to open a practice. She was even doubtful that she had lived in other lifetimes. When she went to a specialist for help, she found herself imagining the story of a young woman gathering plants in the woods to make poultices. The woman was a healer. It was determined that she had eventually been burned at the stake for her abilities. No wonder she was reluctant to use her old skills in this life. After she went back and connected with the young woman in her past, before she had experienced the trauma at the end of that life, she was then able to allow herself to use her abilities to help others with pain.

Then again, you may have read a book that changed your life. There may have been just one piece of information that became your motivation for change. Was it what you read that changed you, or did the book unlock the knowledge that was already inside you? What if you had not read the book or paid attention to its message? Would you have eventually found another source to provide you with the insights to bring about your change? Only you know the answer to that.

The experiences of reading a book, of going to the movies or a play, can be similar to experiencing your past lives. You may be profoundly changed after your journey back, or you may come away from it disappointed. The more you are prepared, the better the opportunity for a positive experience that will encourage you to have more.

You can prepare by reviewing and practicing the exercises in this book up to this point and those that are still to follow before you experience your first past life discovery journey. Not only will the exercises help you with your expression, but they will also help you become more relaxed in general. The more you are able to relax your conscious mind and escape your daily stress, the better prepared you'll be for the adventures that lie ahead for you.

KARMIC CAUTIONS

It might take more than one past life journey to bring about your desired change or give you all the information you want. Don't be discouraged if this happens to you. The more patience you have, the better your chances for finding the answers to perhaps help you change.

Experiencing or Just Imagining?

It's not uncommon for someone who is going to experience a past life discovery journey for the first time to wonder if she will really be having a past life recall or if she is making the whole thing up. That is a good question, and many times the individual will supply his or her own answer.

Mental images come from *imagination*. They may be made up of a single memory or a composite of different memories. Remember in Chapter 7 how you found your relaxed comfortable image in your mind? You experienced a positive memory through seeing, hearing, feeling, tasting, and smelling. To do this, you entered a trance that helped you to enhance and strengthen your images. When you did this, you were using your imagination, or memory recall, to put you back in your mind to your special place. You were also able to physically experience what your mind was imaging.

DEFINITION

Part of the *Webster's Dictionary* definition for **imagination** is, "the power of the mind to reproduce images or concepts stored in the memory." Consider that definition with the exercises you have been doing to help you identify and use your five different sense images to recall positive memories from your unconscious mind.

When you had this experience, you were able to shift your focus from the reality of the moment to the reality of your memory. You might say that imagination includes the use of the images you recall from your unconscious mind. So were you experiencing or imagining? It just might be all the same thing.

During a past life discovery journey, the real question may not be whether or not you were imagining, but "What is the source of your imagination?" Where did the images in your imagination come from? Were they from something that you read, saw, heard, or otherwise experienced in your current lifetime?

Sometimes these questions are difficult to answer. You may not have a conscious recall of something that you heard, saw, or experienced during your life, but it's possible that your unconscious mind does. That is the nature of something that doesn't have readily provable facts. Just because it seems real doesn't necessarily make it real. At the same time, if there is no way of proving it to be true, there is also no way of proving it to be untrue. It's a reality that only the person who experiences a past life discovery journey can answer, and it is possible that even he may not know for sure.

One past life discovery session may not provide enough information to make a determination, even if you wanted it to. Sometimes a lot of information surfaces all at once, and the images themselves can be unclear. Think of the experience as similar to an event you may have just witnessed that you will be asked to report on. If you give this report right after you've witnessed it, you may be a little fuzzy about what took place. It often takes some time for the unconscious mind to process the information for it to be recalled accurately.

A witness to a crime can offer more vivid details several months after the event rather than right afterward. The term used for hypnotic memory recall is "memory revivification." However, hypnotic enhanced memory recall has come under great debate by the legal system. Why? Lawyers and experts question whether witness recall is real or imagined. No one really knows what the unconscious mind really knows.

You may want to make several past life discovery journeys to the same lifetime so that you can bring out details that can be historically researched. You will be given ideas in a future chapter about what to look for during the session. It may be possible to establish a link from the memories you recall to actual events before you were born.

Each of you will experience your past life discovery differently and at different depth levels of your relaxing imagery trance. Some of you will be able to visit your special place in such a deep trance that you'll lose all awareness of your present surroundings. Others of you will have just a mild experience, perhaps recall a pleasant memory, but never lose track of your conscious reality.

The real benefit of experiencing a past life discovery with someone else watching you is that he will see and hear you express things that you may not be aware of. Better yet, have someone else video the session so that you can watch yourself afterward. When you watch the replay, you may be able to decide if you were experiencing more than you thought during your past life discovery session.

KARMIC CAUTIONS

There are many depths of imagery trances, from a light daydream to somnambulism. You don't have to be in a deep trance to have a productive past life discovery experience. All you need to do is just let the images flow, whether you are aware of them or not. If you spend your time analyzing whether or not you're imagining it, you may miss much of the information that is coming up from your unconscious mind.

One of the best ways to prepare for your past life discovery experience is to practice your imagination. The more you become comfortable with the way you recall your images in your five senses, the easier it will be to have a positive experience, no matter how deeply you enter a relaxing imagery trance. This is why it's important for you to establish a regular relaxation routine so that you'll be prepared to let your imagination take over. The better you can imagine, the clearer your experience will be.

The Least You Need to Know

- Every past life discovery session will be a different experience.
- You will not get stuck in a past life.
- Returning from a past life experience can be the same as going to a movie, watching a video, or finishing a good book.
- You may find that you will improve your life through the insights gained from a past life.
- It isn't necessary to determine if the experience was real or imagined to receive positive benefits from it.

The Karma Club

In This Chapter

- How past karma can catch up with you
- Identifying karmic cycles
- The connection to people, places, and things
- The roots of your fears and phobias
- Do you know where your aches and pains come from?

Have you ever found yourself stuck on a highway rotary? Perhaps you drove around and around, not knowing where to exit. You may have tried to get off and taken the wrong road. Your only recourse was to turn around and start over again.

You were caught in a cycle that went around and around because you didn't know how to exit correctly. It may have taken you some time to learn the right route to get to your destination.

Likewise, until you learn the correct route to resolving your left-over karma, you will continue to cruise the highway rotary of your mind. Identifying and plotting the right route through the karma of your past lives will help you chart your course for your soul's journey through your current lifetime.

Your Past Lives Can Catch Up with You

You learned in Chapter 1 that you may be constantly dealing with karma or leftover issues from your past lives. You also know that it's your choice or free will as to how you will resolve these issues. Of course, you may not even be consciously aware of some of your karma. You may not have looked at your life situations from this perspective. This is a good chapter for you to start looking at some of the clutter in your life that may have come from unresolved situations in a past life.

Once you become aware of the possibility that you have karma, you will begin to examine some of your life situations differently. Remember the idea of two different views. If you are stuck in just one view, that's all you will see until you have the opportunity to get a different perspective. The second view is the other perspective. As you know, this is what happens when you enter an image trance. You shift from one focus to another. In this case, the second focus is the chance for you to gain a different view on a situation in your life by examining it from a past life experience.

Now we're back to your willingness to imagine again. It's not necessary to have a vivid past life discovery experience to benefit from examining a situation from the viewpoint of unresolved karma. All you have to do is take a moment and imagine. It may help you to imagine how you would respond to a situation if it had happened during a different lifetime.

The first step is to consider the multitude of past situations in your life that may have resulted from karma from a past life. There are several different types of karma that you can identify. Remember, karma is unfinished business from a past life that resulted from a missed opportunity to follow your soul's purpose and the lessons in that lifetime. Karma is the result of your or someone else's (or even a group of people's) choice to exercise the right of free will and not follow soul lessons.

The first questions you may wish to ask yourself are, "When did I first become aware of my situation? When did I first see it, hear it, feel it, taste it, and smell it?" You may find many different things that bring out an emotion in you that can't easily be explained—a picture or a certain selection of music, a feeling, or the touch of a specific material. It could be a certain food or smell that creates an emotion in you that isn't easily resolved.

If you think about it, every thought you have is related to an image. Some of these images can be explained in terms of your memory recall and others can't. The key to identifying karma is a reaction to a situation or image that isn't normal. It could be a heightened attraction or repulsion to someone or something.

Ask yourself when and where you first learned to react that way, and it will automatically open the door for the possibility of a past life connection. This is especially true if there is no plausible explanation in your current life as to why you or someone else would react that way. The reaction had to be learned somewhere. It gives you an excuse to consider the possibility beyond one view.

SOUL STORIES

Some people who have a hard time stopping smoking find, when discovering their past lives, that they once lived as Native Americans where tobacco was used in sacred rituals. It is the pull from the past that keeps the use of tobacco still sacred in their current lives. To become smoke-free, they need to realize that this isn't the same tobacco and that it's full of nonsacred chemicals.

For a moment, think of a relationship or emotional feeling in your life that has no plausible explanation. Perhaps it's one that you have been trying to understand. It may be a good topic for you to consider when you pick a destination for a past life discovery experience. When you seriously start to think about it, ask yourself the following questions and make notes that may eventually help you when you explore your past lives:

1. When was I first aware of this situation?

2. Does this situation relate or connect to others?

3. What are my strongest images relating to this situation?

4. Is this situation currently positive or negative for me?

5. In my five different senses, how do I react positively?

6. In my five different senses, how do I react negatively?

7. What else about this situation can I relate to a past life karma?

How did you make out? Could you identify a possible karma? Maybe some of your karmic images are so powerful that it's hard for you to examine them rationally. If that's the case, a good way to do this is to view them from your comfort zone, which you can enter with your self-imagery trance to bring you to your special place (see Chapter 7). From there, you can get a different perspective of the situation in a less emotional and more detached manner. You may be able to step back and run the images you want to examine like a movie in your mind. Then you may be able to determine a possible karmic connection to them.

Does Your Life Run in Cycles?

One of the most common past life karmas is the continuing of a situation that started during one of your other *life cycles*. It is a lesson that you get a chance to work on again if you choose to. If you don't, it will keep coming up again and again during your soul's journey.

 DEFINITION

A **life cycle** is a theme or situation that keeps coming up or happening over and over again. Many times these conditions or situations start out full of hope and end up with your swearing never to do it or get involved again. Unfortunately, the bad memory doesn't last for long, and before you know it, you are immersed back in the same old karmic conditions.

Once you start the old pattern again, you actually enter a type of trance that impedes your conscious mind from making rational decisions. Like any other trance, it will continue until something or someone breaks your focus so that you're able to get a second view of the situation. Does this sound familiar to you? You're back to considering the concept of two different views or focuses again. That sounds like a cycle itself, doesn't it?

A life cycle trance is one that starts at the beginning of the cycle. It can begin innocently and simply, and before you know it, you're hooked again. A cycle is often connected to a bad habit such as smoking, overeating, or stress. It's possible to stop the habit for a period of time, but unless the reason for the habit is addressed, it may be only a matter of time until the habit trance starts its cycle all over again.

Can you identify a possible karma in your life that runs through cycles? It may surface in one of many different ways. Some of them may be very powerful and disrupt your life, while others could only result in a slight aggravation. It's an aggravation that after a while you begin to anticipate before the cycle actually begins again. Simple and less severe karma can relate to different seasons and how they affect you. Most everyone knows someone who goes through a mood change during a specific season of the year. A normally happy individual may go through a period of depression before she suddenly emerges from her mood as if nothing had happened. Some people require counseling to help them deal with their problems, while others just weather their mood change, knowing that it will eventually improve.

Of course, many mood changes are related to situations that have occurred earlier in the person's life. Holidays and other dates or events that have sad memories can plunge someone back into the emotions that are connected to the actual time the event happened. What has happened is that the person has shifted his focus from the present onto an event in the past. When this happens, he enters a memory trance that puts him back to that time again rather than being able to move forward in his current reality. At this point, the trance runs its course until it ends or is interrupted, and the person is able to refocus on his current life.

David was having a lot of trouble getting over a failed relationship. It was not his choice to end it, but she felt a need to be free of him. He was loving and kind and could not understand why the breakup had happened. Looking into the history of his past lives, David discovered they had been together before. In a previous life he had killed her in a jealous rage. In this life he had always felt the need to keep close watch over her, while she, on the other hand, began to fear that he might harm her.

As I mentioned in Chapter 8, a past life specialist may use an affect-bridge technique to take you back into a past life to help identify a cyclic pattern that has happened not only in this lifetime but in others as well. You will learn more about this technique in Chapter 14. It can take you through the cycle of the karma in your current life and then work it backward into other lifetimes. By doing this, you have the opportunity to return to the karma's source so you can break the cycle and create a new positive direction in the future using your new past knowledge to resolve the old situations.

A cycle that involves relationships usually begins with the prospect of one that will last forever. Often, one of the parties will see something in the other that she hopes to change. She knows that she can help her partner reach his potential, one that perhaps others do not see. Once a relationship like this has started, the optimistic member fails to see potential problems until it's too late. By then, the other member has taken control and has succeeded in bringing the other one down to his level. They are now trapped and will continue to be until something finally causes them to break free.

As you give it some thought and read on in the chapter, you may identify one or more karmas in your life that are cyclical in nature. If you can, make some notes that you may want to refer to when you prepare for your past life experience. You might want to try your relaxation exercise to help you consider the possibility of karma from a place in your mind that is comfortable for you.

The Connection to People, Places, and Things

It's very possible that you have traveled through your different lifetimes with a group of souls that keep coming back together to work out old karma. That unfinished business could be either something that needs to be resolved or something that was good but still could be developed in this life. What makes this all the more interesting is that we are most likely playing different roles than we did before. That doesn't mean that it's impossible to have had the same relationship over several lifetimes.

Psychic Edgar Cayce had a very strong attachment to his secretary, Gladys Davis. Through his readings on her past lives it was determined that the two of them had been together before in many different lifetimes. In this lifetime, however, despite their bond, Edgar remained faithful to his wife, Gertrude Cayce. He was able to overcome his karmic attraction and focus on the continuation of the work that he and his secretary had begun many lifetimes before.

AGELESS INSIGHTS

You have traveled with many soul mates before. You may have had a close relationship or a casual one in the past. You may have been family or friends, lovers or adversaries, rich or poor. You may recognize a connection, either positive or negative, the first time you see someone, or it may be after you've known him for a while that something brings a past life memory to the surface.

Unexplained Fears and Phobias

Past life karma can also be connected to a fear, phobia, or even an unexplainable health problem. Some of these may only be minor, and some others may be serious. A condition from the past can manifest itself again from an unconscious soul memory that is triggered by a situation or event that occurs. It could be a single experience that is triggered by participating in or observing something that relates to a past memory.

SOUL STORIES

Jack was very uncomfortable around heights. He especially hated getting close to drop-offs that didn't have well-defined protective barriers. To him it felt like he was trying to be propelled over the edge by an unseen force. One day a friend told him of a dream she had had where he was a ruler of a country in ancient times. There was an uprising, and she had been unable to save him from being thrown over the edge into a seemingly bottomless pit. It made sense to Jack and helped him come to terms with his fear of exposed heights.

A birthmark on your body might indicate a continuation of a condition that started in a past life. It could be a mark with a special symbol that could actually be researched to determine its origins. Some cultures would look for a child with similar markings after their leader died, believing they would find him again. Other birthmarks can continue the scar from a wound suffered in a past life.

The seeds of your fear or phobia could have been planted in your subconscious mind earlier in your life, or you could have been born with a memory that developed into a phobia as you encountered similar situations. Phobias often have their first onset during the teen years. Interestingly enough, the teen years are also the time when people often become aware of their psychic abilities. Children are much more open to natural trance and can be caught off-guard when the unconscious mind sends up a response to an earlier experience long since forgotten by the conscious mind.

Most people have fears or phobias to some extent. Can you identify one or more in yourself? If you can, this might be something that you'll want to examine through a past life journey. As you can see, there are enough past life discovery ideas in this chapter to keep you busy working on resolving your past life karmas.

Mysterious Aches and Pains

Alice didn't have any allergies until her mid-twenties. One day while picking strawberries in a grassy field, she felt her airways begin to close up, and she could hardly breathe. After that experience, she continued to have allergic reactions to many grasses and pollens.

Years later she discovered that at the same age in a past life she had died face down in a hayfield.

> **KARMIC CAUTIONS**
>
> Do you have any mysterious aches and pains or other medical conditions, such as asthma, that the doctors can find no reason for? You may have been told that it's all in your mind and maybe it is—deep in your unconscious mind. The condition could very well be an incident from a past life that has manifested itself for you to deal with again.

It's always important to remember that a past life discovery experience is not a substitute for medicine. It doesn't mean that you can go to a past life to cure an actual physical condition that requires medical treatment. This being said, it is also possible that an insight gained from researching a medical condition in a past life may help modern medicine bring about healing in a shorter time. If you have any thoughts about doing a past life discovery with the objective of gaining knowledge that can help provide a cure for a present medical condition, check with your doctor first.

You may gain an understanding of your present life situations by experiencing a past life discovery journey. You can try out any of your ideas when you're ready to begin. Adventure awaits as you learn to work with your leftover karma through past life experiences. In Chapter 20 you will have an opportunity to study the karma you have found in your past lives and learn how you can resolve it.

The Least You Need to Know

- You may have a lot of karma from your past lives.
- Karma may come and go in specific cycles.
- It's possible to recognize a soul mate from a past life.
- Some of your fears and phobias may have their roots in a past life.
- Unexplained medical conditions may begin in a past life.

Keeping Yourself Grounded

In This Chapter

- The importance of being grounded in your faith
- What it means to be in balance
- Do you have angels, guides, or other beings watching over you?
- A relaxing image trance grounding exercise

When discovering a past life, you often don't control where you begin your experience. You could be at the end of the life and involved in a traumatic event such as a battle or a sinking ship or a plane crash. An experienced past life specialist will ask you to follow an emotion or fear back to *before* the traumatic scene starts.

It's important to always have an escape route and believe that what you are going to experience will be positive information you can use in your current life. The belief that you are having a helpful experience is a way to stay grounded and not be overrun by the fear of uncertainty. Learning to go with the flow can help you gather more information that may prove useful to you later.

When you are totally prepared to travel into your past, you can experience the journey with the assurance that whatever insights come to surface in your conscious mind through your imagery, you will be able to relate them to your current life. When someone isn't prepared, he can get out of balance when he encounters something unplanned. The best strategy is to plan for everything and nothing so that you will not be thrown off-balance.

Travel Insurance: Understanding Your Faith

How do you protect your assets when you travel? Do you carry cash? If so, do you keep it all together or do you hide it in several places? Do you carry credit or debit cards? Do you take traveler's checks? If you are in a foreign country, do you convert all or some of your funds to their currency?

What kind of trip insurance do you carry, if any? Perhaps you are willing to take the gamble that nothing will go wrong and that you'll save money by taking the risk that everything will go just fine on your trip. Perhaps you are the type who worries about everything that can go wrong and overprepares by purchasing too much insurance.

There are several things that you can do to help ensure that your travel back into a past life discovery experience will go successfully. You have already taken the first steps by identifying your mental DNA, developing your imagery trance technique, and using it to help you find your special relaxing places in your mind. You also now know the importance of letting yourself imagine in your five different senses so that you can shift your focus into the reality of your unconscious mind. The next step is to develop an understanding of your faith and confidence in your conscious reality to ensure that your past life session will be a positive experience. I'll discuss this more in a moment.

You are a product of a combination of different influences. You inherit certain physical and mental traits such as size and color, and different sensory strengths such as a photographic memory and perfect pitch. The environment in which you were raised also influences you. Your parents and others can make a large contribution to your character development and to the values you were born with. These often don't relate to the other influences you have experienced. The feeling may be as simple as knowing that there is something more to life and a deep passion to go in a direction that is different from what would seem normal for other members of your family. The values from a past life could make you feel out of place in your present lifetime.

If you have ever had nightmares related to a past life or a disturbing dream, you know that they can be very unsettling. At the same time, if you can detach yourself from the nightmare or dream, you may be able to figure out the reason you had it. The same thing could happen when and after you experience a past life discovery session.

A past life specialist will have given you an "escape route" in case something traumatic surfaces while you are in your trance. That could be permission for you to come out of trance in case you feel uncomfortable. If you know that you can always come back to your conscious mind, you are more likely to allow yourself to enter a deeper trance state than if you were worried about facing a potentially unpleasant situation. The past life specialist will watch your physiology to determine signs of discomfort and distress. He or she will know how to move you away from something that's unpleasant and yet at the same time let you experience just enough of the negativity to help you produce an image of your past life discovery.

The past life specialist also usually gives the client permission to open his eyes and come out of his trance any time he wants or needs to. This helps diminish any fear that he will be stuck in a past life while having a traumatic experience. Knowing that you can change your past life travel plans is part of your insurance package that the experience will have a positive result no matter where you go.

SOUL STORIES

Sal's first past life image was suddenly feeling very cold. In fact, he was so cold he started to shiver almost uncontrollably. Fortunately he was with a friend who knew how to move him out of his trance. He was experiencing a past life where he had frozen to death.

Lorraine found herself tied to a stake, and she could feel the heat from the fire that was about to consume her. She woke herself up and had no desire to investigate that or any other past lives. Had she been prepared, she could have moved herself to another image in that lifetime and slowly refocused from a safe vantage point on her death scene to learn how that lifetime was affecting her now.

Also included in your insurance package is the ability to keep yourself balanced between the past and the present, a secure feeling that you are in tune with your faith and that your journey will be protected and guided by your team from the other side—your guides, angels, or other spirit beings. This type of travel insurance only requires the patience to practice your imagery trance technique, and you will be covered on your journey into the past.

SOUL STORIES

Sometimes the past life specialist encounters situations that were unexpected. During one session, the specialist found himself engaged in a conversation with a Confederate officer who wanted to know why the specialist was there asking him questions. The officer was in the process of riding his horse and leading a charge against the enemy. The specialist waited until the battle ended to continue the dialogue, when the soldier was in a calmer state.

When Belinda experiences a past life session, she first goes through the Native American who watches over her as one of her guides. As she enters her trance, Belinda begins a ritual of protection that she is not consciously aware of.

Part of the balance you are looking for in this lifetime could very well hinge on your understanding of the lessons of your past lives. As you learned in Chapter 10, each time you resolve a past life karma, you help to balance your present journey. If you're not prepared to experience and resolve the karma of your past, it will follow you into your future.

Another very important step to take before you embark on a past life discovery session is to make sure that your internal and external guidance systems are balanced and grounded. We will talk about that next. It's also important for you to help your physical body get and stay in tune and in balance. You are the amplifier for the messages that flow from your unconscious mind. If you are out of balance, you may not be able to interpret the lessons of your past.

Include Your Faith

Your faith—your core set of values—is one of the most important elements of keeping yourself grounded and balanced, not only during a past life experience, but also in most aspects of your life. One of the reasons you are probably reading this book is because a part of you believes that there is something beyond your daily existence. As you know, that view may be difficult to express to your friends and family. As you become comfortable with what you already know deep inside your soul's memory, the more you will begin to believe in your connections to the past.

It's easy to get off balance when trying to work with your faith and other people's beliefs. Many religions and their followers are not very tolerant of beliefs different than their own. In their eyes, if you don't follow the rules of their religion, you risk the possibility of damnation in hell. That form of intimidation can make it difficult to break away or try out other religious philosophies. The more you are pulled by conflicting beliefs about past life reincarnation, the more you are drawn away from your own faith. This conflict can keep you off-balance and ungrounded.

Your faith can communicate with you through your unconscious mind. It can send up messages to you in one or more of your five sense images. In other words, you may get a feeling, a taste, a smell, a voice, or a visual message. The message can come from the universal mind, an angel, spirit guide, or a deceased relative or friend. Your inner guidance can reach you when you're awake or through your dreams when you're sleeping. If you are open to your inner faith, you will be guided to make the right decisions in your life, including how you will use the knowledge you gain from your past life discovery sessions.

SOUL STORIES

Listening to your inner faith can be life saving. This faith is a part of intuition, or what your soul knows. Jerry waited patiently for a stoplight to change to green. When it did, a voice suddenly came in his head yelling, "Stop!" He slammed on his brakes just as a car sped through the intersection. It was running a red light, and Jerry would have been right in its path if he had not heeded the warning in his mind.

You can ask your faith for guidance on many things, including help to get you in balance with your soul's purpose. An answer may come right away, or it may take a little time. It may come in any of the five sense images, or it may come from an outside source. It may also come when you are sleeping, either from a dream or a feeling you have when you wake up. The more you're in tune with your inner faith, the more you are prepared to visit your past.

Being comfortable, balanced, and grounded in your faith doesn't mean that you are able to define what it is to anyone else. Most people actually cannot. Those who absolutely think they know what they believe in may not be flexible enough to make adjustments when something different surfaces. So if you are unsure, that is really okay. The main concept of staying balanced and grounded is that deep inside you know there is something to help guide you on your soul's journey. There is an exercise at the end of this chapter that will help you.

Once you learn to trust and are comfortable with your inner faith, regardless of how you define it, you will be able to keep yourself balanced and grounded. You will be prepared for any images that might come through while you're having a past life discovery experience with the knowledge that it's there to help you progress along your life map. That feeling can go with you all the time, anywhere you go, as long as you stay in tune and connected to your faith.

Include Your Guides or Angels

Besides your faith, you also have a guidance system that travels with you throughout your life journey. Many people choose not to use it even though it's always available. It can materialize in many different forms and ways. It's a part of your soul connection, and you have been developing it over many lifetimes. Your psychic or intuitive gifts are a part of this rich heritage. You may not realize all of them yet, but a past life discovery session is a good way to discover them and bring them up to date in this life.

Psychic Edgar Cayce said that there are two types of realities— manifest and unmanifest. Manifest reality is all that everyone has the ability to see, touch, hear, taste, and smell about him or her. Unmanifest reality is that which is also real but isn't acknowledged by most other people. You can experience a reality in the nature of your external guidance system, which is composed of angels, spirits, guides, and other unseen elements that are a part of your daily life. Your guidance system will appear to you in the way that you can accept, if you choose to.

> **AGELESS INSIGHTS**
>
> Your guides can take many forms. They may represent ancient connections to your soul. They may be old souls who have finished their earthly life cycles and are now there to watch over you as you continue yours. They may represent one or more cultures from your past lives. They may even be animals or other beings. Whatever form they take, their main job is to help you as you continue on your soul's journey.

Even though your external guidance is different from your faith, it can still communicate to you in your mind as well as in your dreams. It can also get the message to you through someone else, or even from electronic media such as the radio or television. You may have someone tell you exactly what you were thinking about. You will usually hear, feel, see, taste, or smell something more than once. When that happens, your guidance system is trying to tell you something. It's time to pay attention!

An angel may be thought of as someone who was with you on the earth plane before he or she passed over. It could be a deceased relative or a friend. They have come back to keep an eye on you if you will let them. Some people are so closed to that possibility that they miss all the clues their angels have given them. You may be aware that something is watching out for you, but you have no idea who it is. That's okay. Just believing in the possibility that something is there can be a great comfort to you in many aspects of your life, including exploring your past lives.

You could actually go back to find out when you first became associated with your guides. You can also go back in time to reconnect with some of your psychic abilities. You can also visit a psychic who specializes in talking with the other side to help you identify who your angels might be. Once you are confident that there is something with you that is unmanifest to most people, you can experience a past life experience with the knowledge that you are being looked after and protected.

KARMIC CAUTIONS

Some people may not be open to the view that angels, guides, or other beings exist. Don't expect others to believe you if you tell them about your imaginary friends. You may not want to tell everyone about your beliefs.

You may communicate directly with your universal mind or God for guidance and protection. You could say that you are just bypassing the middlemen, your guides and angels. You can also use all of the above, your internal and external and universal minds, all at the same time. The more you feel grounded, in balance, and protected, the freer you will be to explore the unconscious regions of your mind.

A Ground-Level Exercise

Now it's time to add something more to your relaxing imagery trance technique. This exercise will take you a step beyond your comfort zone and put you in touch with your guidance and faith. Once you are comfortable and confident in this process, you will be ready to start planning your first past life discovery session. Just as with the exercises before this one, the more you practice, the more you will become proficient at using it. You may want to memorize, record, or have someone read to you the following imagery trance induction. Find a place where others will not interrupt you while you are trying it.

If you are ready, you may get comfortable and loosen your clothing. Take a deep breath, slowly exhale, and continue to do so as you let your eyes focus on the center of your forehead. If you can imagine a relaxing smell, do it as you let yourself prepare to count downward from five to zero to the special place in your unconscious mind. With each breath you are relaxing more and more.

You may begin to feel the connection through the center of your forehead to a peaceful flow of energy that's connected to the guides, angels, and other beings who are there to watch over you. You may feel the peace and love of the universe entering and surrounding your body as you slowly count yourself from five to zero, downward into your imagery trance. You are feeling so comfortable and relaxed as you feel the energy begin to flow over and through you. Remember that you can always count up from your toes to the top of your head if that works better for you, and then reverse it.

- *Five.* You are beginning to start your countdown to your special place where you will feel the peaceful and loving energy of the universe surrounding and protecting you. You can feel it slowly spreading down over your head to your shoulders. With each breath, you relax more and more.

- *Four.* You are going deeper and deeper. You can feel the peaceful and loving energy spreading all the way down over your arms to your fingers. Your inner and outer guidance systems are there with you as they work with your faith to help you feel balanced, protected, and grounded. With each count you focus more and more.

- *Three.* You can now feel the peaceful and loving energy of the universe spreading all the way down to your waist. You have many muscles. Some of them are stiff, and some of them are relaxed. Every time you feel a muscle stiffen up, you may relax it, which will help you relax more and more. You can feel yourself sinking deeper and deeper with each breath you take. You are feeling so relaxed and comfortable.

- *Two.* You are getting closer and closer to your special place, deep in your unconscious mind where you will feel totally connected to your faith and guidance systems. You can feel the universal energy spreading all the way down to your knees. You are relaxing more and more and feel the peaceful energy of the universe and your guidance systems watching over and protecting you. With each breath you are going deeper and deeper.

- *One.* You are almost there. The peaceful and loving energy is flowing all the way down to your ankles. You are going deeper and deeper with each relaxing breath you take. In a moment you will be all the way down to zero. You will be in your special place, deep in your unconscious mind. When you get there, you may feel the peaceful energy flowing over, around, and through your entire body. You will be in balance, grounded and protected by the universal mind, and you will be open to the intuitive energies of the universe connected with you. You will feel your guides, angels, and other beings with you, watching over and protecting you. You will be open to their guidance.

- *Zero.* You may now feel yourself totally immersed in the peaceful and loving flow of universal energy. You are in your special place, deep in your unconscious mind. You feel in balance and grounded by your guides, angels, and other beings. You may ask them to help watch over you in every aspect of your life. If you have something you need help or guidance with, you may ask them for their assistance. Let yourself feel grounded in universal love as you prepare to experience a past life discovery session that will help you be in tune with your soul's journey. You feel comfortable and ready to have a positive experience when you journey into your past.

You will continue to feel safe and grounded after you count yourself back up to the surface of your conscious mind. You can easily come back to this grounded state every time you experience your imagery trance. When you're ready, you may count yourself back up to consciousness.

- *One.* Continue to breathe slowly.

- *Two.* You are coming slowly back to the surface, feeling grounded and in balance.

- *Three.* You are halfway back.

- *Four.* You are almost there. On the next number you may take a deep breath and exhale, open your eyes, and come back to your conscious mind.

- *Five.* You are all the way back, grounded and in balance with your faith and guidance systems. The more you practice this technique, the easier it will be to slip into a grounded and relaxing self-image trance.

The Least You Need to Know

- You were born with your faith already inside you.
- Unless you are properly grounded in your faith, it's easy to get out of balance while discovering your past lives.
- You are balanced when you are in tune with your faith and guidance systems.
- You have guides, angels, and other beings who watch out for you if you choose to acknowledge and accept them.
- Practicing your relaxing image trance grounding technique will help prepare you for any kind of past life discovery experience.

Creating a Travel Plan

In This Chapter

- Choosing a destination for your past life discovery experience
- What to look for in your past lives
- Traveling alone or with the help of a partner
- Tools that can help you gather information during your past life session
- How long do you want to spend at your destination?

How do you plan when you prepare to go on a trip? Perhaps you are used to going places often and keep a bag of essentials packed and ready. Maybe you seldom travel, and when you do, you find that there are items you wish you had remembered. How much detail do you put into planning?

Do you spend days developing a checklist, or do you put together a rough idea of your plans and hope that you've included everything? Do you make your own trip plans, or do you depend on a travel agency to handle the details? Do you go on package tours, or do you customize your plans to meet your own interests?

Now it's time to start planning your first past life discovery journey. Of course, you may already have naturally been traveling back. You have had the opportunity in previous chapters to examine what can influence you from your past lives through your interests, relationships, and even your dreams. Past lives can spill over into virtually every aspect of your current life.

Where Do You Want to Go?

Just as you would prepare for any trip, doing the same for a past life discovery session can help give you the best opportunity for a positive and fulfilling experience. Usually you travel to a destination for a specific purpose. It may be because of an interest, work, or for relaxation. Many of you combine business and pleasure. The same can be true for a past life journey. You may have a destination that you currently enjoy or would like to go to. Perhaps you'd like to go there during a different time period. You can examine the culture, try the foods, and experience the music and art or any other thing that you want to. You can immerse yourself in that time in all of your senses, stepping into the imagery of your mind.

> **SOUL STORIES**
>
> Dean Bennett has a passion for the wilderness. In his book *The Forgotten Nature of New England* (see Appendix B) he identified and visited every place in that region that still remained untouched from the time before the white man first explored it. He literally put himself in a trance and regressed hundreds of years. The reader has a chance to do the same through his descriptive writing.

You may want to visit a specific location or a certain time period, or investigate a culture. You may want to understand a feeling about someone in history whom you've been interested in. You may have done a lot of research already and wonder if you'll get any new insights or just make up a past life experience using the information you already have.

Start with a pad of paper (or the computer) and make a list of the places that you would like to visit during a past life journey. You may have several or only one. You may not have any place at the moment that you feel you want to visit. You may have a destination that you don't want to go back to. If you do, make a note of it, but find a place for your first experience that seems like it would be really neat to visit. Just like the special place in your mind, if you are comfortable in your first past life trip, you may be encouraged to continue your past life discovery sessions.

To get an idea of where you'd like to visit during a past life discovery session, ask yourself the following questions:

- **What place or places in the world would you really like to visit?** Maybe you have visited there several times and feel a special connection to it beyond this current lifetime. You may feel at home again when you are there. It could be somewhere you've never been but have always had a special place in your heart for. You may have read or studied about it. You may have already imagined being there in your mind.

- **Is the location you want to visit real or imaginary?** Ellie has a special magical place she travels to in her mind when she sits at her altar. It is lush green, warm, and has a large waterfall. Sometimes when she goes there, she swims. Other times she goes behind the waterfall and listens to the power of the water as it rushes over her head. It's a place that is filled with love for Ellie, and when she comes back from her journey, she always feels mentally, spiritually, physically, and emotionally refreshed. Could it be that this is a place buried deep in her unconscious memory that connects her to a sacred time in her past?

- **Is your choice of destination one that you visit in your dreams?** Perhaps you have had a dream of a specific location throughout your life. If you have, you may want to investigate it in a past life discovery session. So your destinations may come from a real place, an imaginary place, or a dream. These possible destinations may come from your childhood or be somewhere that you haven't consciously thought of before. It doesn't make any difference as long as it's a place that seems like an interesting travel destination.

What to Look For

Maybe your reason for visiting a place is to determine where you first learned an emotion, ability, or interest. It may be to understand a relationship with one or more other people who may be family, friends, or casual acquaintances. Ask yourself a few simple questions to help define what you want to look for in a past life discovery experience:

- **What feelings have you had in your life that you would like to know where you first learned them?** These feelings could be something you long for. It may be the sense that a part of your life is incomplete without understanding why you have those emotions deep inside of you. You may have a feeling of belonging or not belonging, or of being in sync or out of sync with your current place in the world.

- **What emotions that are normally out of character for you do you experience from time to time?** These feelings may be triggered by music or other sounds, smells, food, or pictures. You may find yourself suddenly reacting in a way you didn't anticipate. If this is the case, make a note of it as a part of your checklist of something to look for in your travels.

- **Do you want to investigate the history of some of your relationships through a past life discovery session?** You may have one or more friends or family members that you know you've been with before in different roles. It may be an attraction to someone that goes beyond normal. If this is so, add relationships to your list of things you are looking for.

You may want to go back and connect with the roots of an artistic or athletic ability. You might want to use a past life discovery session to enhance your natural-born ability. You could look for a connection with your psychic talent from another lifetime.

Working by yourself or even with a past life discovery specialist doesn't always produce the desired results. Your soul seems to have its own agenda as to how it reveals the memories from your past. Even though it may be frustrating at the time, that may be a good thing, as it may not have been the right time for you to discover that particular part of your past.

It's also possible that you don't have an idea yet of anything that you might want to research in a past life discovery session. In that case, perhaps you could go to a time when you can apply what you learn to your current life situation. Remember that your soul will already have an agenda for you to investigate, which your conscious mind may not yet be aware of. Just the fact that you're reading this book indicates there is something in one of your past lives that will be helpful for you to learn now. You will have an opportunity in Chapter 15 to review your final preparations.

AGELESS INSIGHTS

You may feel that you and someone else are soul mates. You know that you've been together before. If so, you can plan to investigate your relationships in one or more past lives. The result may be insights into your current feelings about this person. Be sure to make note of the relationships you want to investigate in one or more other lifetimes.

Traveling Alone or with a Partner?

Do you like to go places by yourself or with other people? Perhaps you enjoy taking a tour with a whole group of people. If so, you'll want to use the help of a *facilitator*. Right now, though, let's consider whether you would go alone or with someone else.

DEFINITION

A **facilitator** is someone who can help you journey through a past life experience. The facilitator can read the script that helps create an imagery trance and then ask questions that focus on the right information to bring back. The facilitator can also be there to help guide you back out of your trance.

The first few times you try a past life discovery journey, you may want to consider working with a partner by taking turns being the subject and the operator. There are several positive reasons for doing this. If you have someone who might be interested, you can read this book together and compare how your minds are the same and different. You can help each other practice relaxation and trance imagery techniques before you have your first session.

Besides having the support of someone else when you do a past life discovery session, a partner can sometimes give you more insights into your experience. He or she can watch your facial expressions and body language and run a recorder or video camera to capture your experience for you to hear or watch later.

If you're working with someone, you both may come up with some good ideas for questions to ask during your session. Together you can develop a script that will help guide you. Chapter 14 will talk more about scripts. In the meantime you can make notes about what you would like your partner to help you look for in your travels. You can decide if you want to record and play back questions you want to ask yourself, or have someone else read them. If you have a partner, he or she may also be able to ask questions about your responses during the session that will clarify your answers.

Psychic Edgar Cayce used someone to guide his trance sessions. He would first put himself into a trance state and then open up to questions about the subject he was doing a reading for. In the beginning, sometimes the people who conducted the sessions would experiment with him to test his abilities or gain information for themselves. Finally his wife, Gertrude, became the one who conducted the readings while his secretary, Gladys, transcribed the information.

Another benefit of having a partner is to help you move out of any past life images that might be unsettling. It's good to have them available to remind you that you can open your eyes and come back to your conscious mind if you want to. Sometimes, if your partner is psychic, he or she may be able to actually see into your past life images and remember things you forgot to note during and after your trance.

It may not be an option for you to work with someone else, or even if you do, after a few sessions, you may want to continue the work by yourself. That's okay. You will probably approach the session differently by yourself than with someone else. You may choose to record your induction and the script for your past life journey or memorize it and talk to yourself internally or out loud during your session. You can experience it in silence, or you can verbally describe and record the details of your travel.

You may choose to use a form of automatic writing as a way to discover your lives. This means that you would place yourself in front of your computer or sit comfortably with a pen or pencil in your hand poised and ready to write on a piece of paper. Once you have induced yourself into your relaxed imagery trance, you can suggest that you will begin to let your fingers write down the images that come from your unconscious mind.

KARMIC CAUTIONS

Past life discovery specialists have a lot of training and are experts in guiding their clients into their past lives for both discovery and therapeutic reasons. This book is not designed to provide the education to become a professional, and your past life discovery sessions are not meant to take the place of getting help for any serious issues you may have in solving the karma of your past. At the same time, this can be an exciting adventure for you and your partner.

Have you decided whether or not you want to travel alone? If you want a partner, have you approached the person yet? If not, now is the time to do it. If you are traveling alone, then you are one step closer to beginning your journey.

Tools to Bring with You

Now that you have made some notes about where you want to travel and what you would like to experience, you may want to consider what other tools are workable for you. A couple of these devices you have already heard about. They are the tape or video recorders to capture any reaction you have, either verbal or physical, to the images you encounter during your session. You also can use automatic writing, which I discussed in the previous section.

Another potential tool to help you get unconscious soul memories is the pendulum, which is a weight such as a crystal, a pendant, or anything that can dangle from a chain or string. It could be as simple as a washer on the end of a string or as intricate as a gold watch on a chain.

The use of the pendulum is also a technique for gathering psychic information and is known as dowsing. Dowsing is the ancient art of divination, or determining information through one of several different devices controlled by the unconscious and universal minds of the individual holding them. Dowsing tools include "Y" rods or sticks, "L" rods, bobbers, and the pendulum.

If you want to try using a pendulum, find something you already have or make something simple that's light enough to hold comfortably between your thumb and first finger and yet heavy enough to swing freely in different directions. Once you have selected your pendulum, try holding the string, chain, or cord with the thumb and first finger of either one of your hands. Let the weight dangle about 6 to 8 inches and hold it out in front of you, about 12 to 18 inches in front of your face with your hand at eye level.

Now ask the pendulum to show you the direction of "yes" and watch what happens. It could start moving in one of several directions, swinging back and forth from side to side, moving toward and away from you, or rotating clockwise or counterclockwise. It may start very slowly, or it may become very active right away. If it doesn't respond, don't worry. Practice concentrating on it moving in a direction of your choice. Then ask it to go in a different direction. When you have accomplished this, ask the pendulum to come to a stop. Did it work for you?

Once you get comfortable with the movement of your pendulum and have found the direction of yes, ask it to show you "no." Each time you try dowsing with a pendulum, yes and no may be different movements. Therefore, you will want to go through this procedure whenever you begin to dowse. When you have established this, ask the pendulum if you can receive answers from your soul memories regarding the past life information you are looking for. Obviously you will need to ask questions that can be answered with yes and no answers.

If you have a partner, you can prepare a list of questions for him or her to ask you. If that's the case, or even if you're alone and using a video camera, you can answer with your eyes closed, letting the pendulum go its own way. You can ask your questions out loud or silently. Dowsing may be a useful tool for you to take with you in your past life travels.

You may want to use music or other sounds to help you go back in time. For instance, you may have the feeling that you lived during a time where music from that period was important to you. Playing some period background selections may help you deepen your imagery trance. Certain sounds such as the ocean may help bring you back to a lifetime connected with the nearness of water. Smells, tastes, visual images, and even something you might have worn may also prove to be useful tools in helping you regress into one or more of your past lives.

How Long Should You Spend There?

What is the right length of time to spend experiencing a past life discovery session? The answer is that there is no exact amount of time, but at first, generally no more than a half hour to an hour. Each time will vary according to the level of trance you achieve and the amount and clarity of the images that you experience.

The most important thing is that you are comfortable in the time you spend there during and after the experience. You might want to come back and revisit an uncomfortable situation after you get used to the images you're experiencing. When you do this, you are actually desensitizing the impact of the images so that each time you are able to work with them a little more easily. You can even choose different views of the same images to make the experience easier.

Remember that your discovery session may be similar to going to the movies or reading a good book. There may be times when you feel all the emotions that are going on in the story. Have you ever been so involved in a book that your heart rate speeds up, your hands become sweaty, or you feel the sadness or happiness of the characters? If you have a health condition where you're not supposed to become excited, you should check with your doctor first to make sure that a past life experience will be all right for you.

SOUL STORIES

Prolonged periods of intense emotional feelings can be unhealthy for you. Your physical, mental, and spiritual bodies can all be impacted. Edgar Cayce was told by a reading of his own health that he needed to cut back on the number of daily readings he gave near the end of his life. By then he had become much in demand, and it was impossible to keep up with the requests. He ended up with health problems that are often attributed to his failure to listen to his own warnings. This doesn't mean that you will experience the same exertion as Cayce did, but it's always wise to be aware of your own health condition.

Some people who enter into a deep level of trance may experience some physical discomfort during and after the session. Feeling cool or cold is fairly common. This can result from being very relaxed and staying in one position for a period of time. If it occurs during the past life discovery session and is because of an image that's being experienced at that time, you or your partner can make a suggestion to feel warm. You can also move away from that image to a warmer one.

If you consistently have a problem with being cold during or after a past life session, you may want to have a blanket over you or ready to cover you if you need it. You can also address the temperature problem in the suggestions you use in your script. Tell yourself that you will be warm and comfortable as you relax in your deep trance and that you will wake up calm, comfortable, warm, and relaxed.

Once you get used to your routine, then you will be prepared for temperature changes while and after you travel.

Another sensation that may be experienced during but especially after your past life session is that of heaviness in all or part of your body. You may feel as if you gained 50 pounds while you were away. This result may stem from the level of your focus when you are experiencing the trance. If you use words such as "sinking" and "deeper," you may wake up with these feelings if you don't remove them when you come back to the surface of your conscious mind. Other feelings such as lightheadedness, dizziness, or even nausea can result from past life images while you are in deep trance.

It's important to be able to move away from these images without taking the feelings with you. A death scene can also bring a past life session to a close if you're uncomfortable with the images you encounter. Again, it's always important to feel confident that you will be able to come back to the surface of your conscious mind any time you want. All of these factors will influence the length of time that you travel back in time.

If you are using automatic writing, you may be able to spend a little longer in trance. In fact, you may even be able to break up your session by moving about or sipping some tea, etc., and going right back into your trance when you start again. The more you let yourself experiment with past life discovery, the better you will understand the right length of time for you to travel in your mind. Just remember to focus on your current life when you're not in a trance. It's sometimes easy to forget the reality of the moment.

The Least You Need to Know

- You can choose your destination, but be prepared for changes in travel plans.
- You can define what you want to look for by considering the feelings and abilities you currently experience.

- Working with a partner can help you gather and record your information.
- Many different tools are available to help you delve into your soul's memory.
- You can expect your past life discovery sessions to vary in time length.

What to Do When You Get There

In This Chapter

- Using your mental DNA in your past life discovery session
- Getting used to the experience
- Brushing up on your detective skills
- The characters you meet in your past life journey
- The themes of your past lives

At one time or another almost everyone has imagined what it would be like to be a detective and solve a mystery. Public interest has even led to the development of mystery dinner theaters where the audience participates in determining who did it. Some of the most popular television shows are about detectives or invite the audience to be a part of the hunt for the criminals. *America's Most Wanted* is an example of one of these types of shows.

Well, now you have a chance to take a crash course in gathering evidence. It's time to get yourself ready to start piecing together the clues of your past lives. You are becoming the expert detective of your own soul as you prod its memory and search for evidence of your past.

Put Your Mental DNA to Use

The more you understand your mental DNA, the better you will become at recognizing the clues from your own images of the past.

This simple review of your five senses, discussed in detail in Chapter 6, will remind you of the way your mind works and how to use that knowledge to gather information your unconscious mind reveals about your soul memories that you might otherwise miss. It's often impossible to gather all the clues at first. Your unconscious mind records images in its memory that your conscious mind is not aware of. This will be the same for you when you go back into a past life. The way you experience the event will be different from anyone else's.

Your visual sense is usually one of your strongest senses. The way you see the events of your past will determine how many details you can recall. If you are very visual and can retain the images in your unconscious mind, they will always be there to revisit once your conscious mind is aware of them. A visual person has the ability to supply a great many details.

If you are not a strong visual person, you can anticipate that you won't see the vivid details from your past life discovery sessions. You may, however, be just as vivid in one or more of the other sense images. Remember that there are two different ways of being visual. The first is by detaching yourself from the image as if you were watching it from a distance or on a screen. Your other senses don't come into play as much from this vantage point. The other type of visual image is experiential, where you find yourself fully involved in your past life experience. A partner can be a big help here as he or she can ask you what you're doing and how you feel. By yourself, you may have to rely on how you remember the experience afterward.

AGELESS INSIGHTS

It's easy to tell if a visual author has written a book. Sometimes she sets the scene so vividly that you begin to wish she would just get to the point rather than focus on the background details. For the visual reader, however, these graphic descriptions help transport him into the story. You may have this same ability to report on the scenes in your past lives.

How well you can hear sounds when you're experiencing a past life discovery session can help a great deal in gathering your information.

If you can hear sounds, you will have the ability to listen to conversations that may take place and be able to repeat them so that they can be recorded for you to examine later. You may be able to gather information from different sounds such as running water or wind. You may be able to hear a battle as it is fought or music as it plays out in your past life. There are so many clues that can be gathered if you have the gift of hearing what your unconscious mind is remembering from your soul's memories.

Feelings and emotional images are also a great source of clues. Experiencing a temperature and the touch of something during your past life session can help focus your trance. A past life discovery specialist often uses the kinesthetic sense for just that purpose. They may spend a lot of time on small details at first to help sharpen your focus to help you as you experience the images. Once this is done, the subject can easily be moved around throughout that lifetime.

Perhaps you can put yourself in the mind of a character from a soul memory of your past and rediscover how you thought in another lifetime. Sometimes the smallest clue that isn't understood at the moment will mean a great deal later on as you solve your past life mystery.

Imagine that you could sit down to a 2,000-year-old meal. If you have a good sense of taste or smell, you can. All you have to do is step back into the image scene and experience it. You can take in the aromas and textures as you describe, in as many sense images as you have, what is taking place around you. The more you use your natural mental DNA in your past life experience, the better the opportunity to collect a vast amount of clues about the mysteries of your soul.

KARMIC CAUTIONS

Chances are you will not be able to produce clues in all five of your senses. If you focus on the senses that are weakest for you, you may get frustrated with the discovery process. If you go with your strengths and trust them, you should have much more satisfying results. There is no one who knows your mental DNA better than you.

Just Allow Yourself to Experience

Remember, you might not be able to experience images in some of your senses. You may become discouraged when you try to follow the method of someone who uses images in senses that aren't strong for you. It's usually developed around the way that person's mental DNA works and not the way yours does. That doesn't mean you won't be able to experience exactly like someone else, but the message is to be true to your own way of imaging.

A good detective will just collect the data and then mull it over, constantly comparing and working at fitting the pieces of his case together. Perhaps you have seen an investigation scene in a movie where the detectives have a large board and are constantly arranging and rearranging the information they collect. As you compile your own notes, you will be doing the same thing.

Remember, if you don't get all the information you want the first time, you can go back. There is no need to try and force clues to the surface of your mind before they are ready. At first you may gather a great many details within a very small range of imagery. If that's all you have to work with at the time, then work with it. Each time you go back, you may bring out a little more. Always be on the lookout for a new piece of information you might discover.

A past life discovery session is like going to a movie, only it's in your mind. To a certain extent you're at the mercy of your soul. The images that play in front of you may be pleasant or unpleasant, happy or sad, funny or serious, and even provoke you into examining a part of your life and your faith. You can stay or leave your theater any time you want.

You do have another option that a movie doesn't. You can change your scenes, zero in for a close-up, or pull back for a broad view. You can use all of your senses. You cannot rewrite the play that's your soul, but you can look at it from many angles and perspectives.

If you have ever acted in a play, you know what getting into character means. Many of the great movie stars spend months preparing for a role. They study the history of the character that they're going to play and even begin to imagine what it would be like to be that person. They change the way they speak, their hair, and may even gain or lose weight. When they finally act out their role onscreen they are totally experiencing what it's like to be the person they are portraying. You are the actor in your own play. The more you get into the characters of your past, the more you will go with the experiences of your soul.

As you probably know, some movies start slow and, just as in a good book, it takes time to set the scenes for the plot. You may have wanted to get up and leave, but for some reason you stayed. After all, it costs a lot of money to go to the movies today. You may have gritted your teeth and decided to tough it out. As you continued to watch, suddenly you found yourself engrossed in the story. By the end you forgot how you felt about it in the beginning. Again, realize it may take a little time and patience for you to begin to receive clear images as you start your past life discovery session. The more you're willing to just go with the experience, the better the chance of you getting your money's worth out of your performance.

You Can Be a Detective in Your Own Mind

Are you ready to be a detective? If you are, how do you begin to collect the clues to your case? Of course, you already have gotten started. You have been going to detective school as you have been reading this book. You've begun making notes and deciding on possible areas to investigate. You are almost ready to visit your first scene. Now is the time to make a checklist that will help you gather the information you seek.

When you experience a past life discovery session, what are you going to look for first? You already have an idea from your notes. Are you comfortable with the way you image in all your five senses? You may want to start collecting your information through the sense that you're the most sure of. For instance, if you are visual, start with what you can see. Make as many mental notes as possible, or have your partner ask you for visual descriptions. If you rely on your hearing or feeling senses, start with them. If you are strong in more than one sense, then after you have focused your first images, move to your other senses and report or make notes on what you're experiencing.

Start with a small area or view. Collect as many details from that place as possible before moving on. This technique actually will help you focus your imagery trance as you sharpen your collecting skills for your past life discovery adventure. Be patient and go with what you're experiencing. You may not even go beyond this spot in your first session.

Do you remember a television show called *Columbo?* The main character was a detective dressed in a rumpled trench coat who came across as unsophisticated and bumbling. The criminal often dismissed Columbo's ability to solve the case, and yet the detective would keep coming back and repeat question upon question until the culprit was tricked into admitting guilt. You may think you miss a great many details at first. Be patient, and, like Columbo, keep coming back and asking more questions until you have solved the case.

Detectives often take photos of the crime scene. They can study the photos to help them look for visual clues they may have missed when they were first investigating. They spend hours poring over the evidence, trying out different scenarios in their minds. When they have a new idea, they look for more clues in that direction. They are using a thought process called *divergent thinking* as compared to *convergent thinking*.

> **DEFINITION**
>
> **Convergent thinking** means that you focus on only one objective and continually work toward reaching it. The problem with this is that if you reach a dead end, then you're stuck and have no place to go. **Divergent thinking** means that when you get stuck, you begin to look for other directions to take. It may seem to you that you're going sideways or backward, but eventually you will find a way to go beyond where you were. In the meantime, the convergent thinker has given up.

Some detectives will stay on a case for years, long after others have given up and even forgotten about it. They may have files filled with clues, or perhaps there was little evidence to gather at first. As they continue to let their unconscious mind work, even if they are busy on another case, there is always action taking place. They may wake up with an idea that surfaced to their conscious mind. Now they plug it into their investigation. It may help them move forward, or it may not, but sooner or later they will be back on their case with a renewed vigor.

Your unconscious mind will do the same thing after a past life discovery session. It will take the pieces of information collected and play with them while your conscious mind is occupied with something else. Something that may not make sense at first will begin to make sense as you keep the files on your past lives open. Keep your note pad or recorder with you, ready to make a note of the ideas your unconscious mind sends up to you.

If you have even a little artistic skill, make sketches of what you encounter during your experience. Just as with your other observations, focus on the scene that's the easiest at first. Put in as many details as possible. You are, in effect, making a composite sketch of what you're witnessing. Once you have the basics down, you can always go back and sketch in more information. Think of the flow of your unconscious information like priming a water pump. In order to get the water going, you have to put a little bit back in the line first. Always have a little bit of information to work with for your next session that can help get the information flowing again. The more it's used, the easier it becomes to start it again the next time you look for clues.

> **SOUL STORIES**
>
> In her first past life discovery session, Angel visited four different lifetimes. Each one provided sketchy details of the experiences. Within a couple days she remembered many more details than she had experienced during the session. She had opened up her unconscious mind.

Study the Cast of Characters

A good detective not only takes note of the scene but of the different characters who are encountered during the investigation. Profiles are developed on each one. What is each character's personality type? How do they think? What are their habits? What are their interests and likes and dislikes? There are many questions you can ask about each of the characters you encounter in your past life discovery session. You might begin with who, what, when, where, and why:

- *Who* are the characters you want to profile? Are they people you recognize from dreams or other images from your unconscious mind? You will want to gain as much information as possible on their relationship to other characters in your session, if there are others. Who is the most important character you encounter?

- *What* are their physical descriptions and their approximate ages? What are their personalities? What do you see them doing? What do you hear them saying? What are their emotions? What do they smell and taste? What is their role in your experience? What is their relationship to you, or are any of them related to you in a past life?

- *When* do the characters live in your past lives? Can you determine the time period? If you are able to follow the main character through that lifetime, when does something significant happen that relates to that life or to your life today?

- *Where* are your characters located during your past life? Get the best description that you can. Remember to consider all these questions with all five of your senses, using the strongest one first. You may want to ask yourself where the personality of the main character in your discovery session fits into your life.

- *Why* are the characters that you are profiling important to the case you're working on? How do they relate to your life? It's possible that at first you will find a character popping up who seems to be unrelated to what you are working on. If this happens, just collect all the information and have it ready to review when and where you think it will fit.

It may be possible for you to put yourself in the mind of more than one character in a lifetime. How can that be? It means that you may be able to draw upon the past life memories of other souls besides your own. This is sometimes referred to as collective unconscious—the place in the universe where it is believed all thoughts and experiences from the past are recorded. Edgar Cayce called this the Akashic Records. You'll learn more about this in Chapter 18 after you have experienced your first past life discovery session. If you encounter this situation before then, just go with the experience and collect the information.

AGELESS INSIGHTS

Look for similarities in different characters in more than one lifetime. Remember the principles of karma: unresolved business will keep coming back until the lessons are learned. You may be able to trace the karma from one lifetime to another, following the similarities in the different characters that you come in contact with during your past life discovery sessions.

Everything you observe about the characters in your past can be important clues, as well as anything you experience through their eyes. Every piece of the puzzle you can collect and have ready and waiting to put in place when its position is recognized will help you gain a better understanding of your soul's purpose. Remember that all the pieces might not fit right away, and all of the characters may not seem to relate, but chances are that they will sooner or later.

Follow the Story's Theme Wherever It Goes

Every one of you will have different reasons for wanting to investigate your past lives. You may have a pressing need to discover something in your past that relates to you now and the route your life will take in the future, or you may have only a casual interest in finding out about your past. You may be considering studying the techniques used in past life discovery for the purpose of becoming a past life discovery specialist as a part of your vocational work.

You might not want to invest a lot of time and energy into investigating your past lives. You really can go at your own speed. There may be periods in your life when you can devote more time to studying your past, or you may be pulled in many different directions. You can start and stop any time you want. Just remember that the better you make notes or record your discovery sessions, the easier it will be to get back on the track of your soul's history when you begin again.

Good detective work takes time, energy, and patience. It takes the willingness to follow leads wherever they go. There might be many dead ends before something is discovered that advances the case forward. Even then the path may seem to dry up, and the detective is back to square one. Sometimes it seems as if the case will never be solved. Just as in a busy life, a detective may be working on more than one case at a time. Priorities need to be established.

Have you ever seen the plate-balancing vaudeville act? The goal is for the performer to twirl a plate fast enough on a stick so that it will stay balanced and not slow down, fall off, and crash to the floor. He is supposed to balance up to 10 or more plates on sticks. The trick starts easily enough, but by the time they are all spinning, the performer is racing back and forth trying to keep them all going at once. You may feel the same way about your life. You are the plate-balancer, and it's hard to see everything at once, including your past lives.

KARMIC CAUTIONS

The themes of your past lives can relate to the karma or unfinished business that you have the opportunity to resolve during this lifetime. The karma itself may interfere with giving you the time and energy to solve it. In other words, you may be so caught up in your life play that you don't realize the same theme is playing itself over again.

Consider for a moment the benefit of taking a little time each day to experience a relaxation exercise as you have practiced in this book. It could be an instant one, or one that takes a few minutes. It could be just before going to bed or the first thing in the morning. Go to your favorite place in your mind.

This is the time to think about your past lives and how they may relate to your present life. It only takes a moment, and you may ask your faith to supply you with more clues after your conscious mind has gone on to the other happenings in your life. If you consider doing this, you are actually staying with the theme of your soul's path. Your unconscious mind will then help bring you the insights when it's time for you to make note of them.

The Least You Need to Know

- Use your mental DNA image strengths to help gather past life information.
- Let yourself experience whatever takes place during a past life discovery session.
- Imagine that you are the detective on your own past life case.
- Every character you encounter may be important.
- Stick with the past life themes during and after the experience.

Going Through the Window

Okay, mind detectives, it's time to open the window and enter into the experience. You've finished your training and you are ready for your first encounter with the past. Before you go, you'll be given some important dialogue to help you enter the scene.

You will go back in time and meet the characters in your past life adventures. You will use your skills and ability to image in order to collect important clues. When you return from your research in the field, you will organize and analyze the material you have just retrieved. You may decide to revisit the same location to look for more past life clues.

You will learn about one of the most important past life stories of the twentieth century and how to decide what is truth or fiction in your own case. Get ready. It's time to lift the veil and step through the window into your past.

Past Life Discovery Scripts

In This Chapter

- Read about your past lives in a library
- Go to a movie theater in your mind
- Watch a mental television program
- Learn to count yourself back in time
- Trace a feeling to where you first experienced it
- Which past life discovery technique works best for you?

In this chapter you'll find several different ways to experience your past life discovery session. As you read each section, you can decide which technique you want to try first. You probably already have a tendency toward one or another.

Do you often go to the library, the movies, or watch television? If you do, with the use of your relaxing image trance you should feel right at home traveling back in time. If you start by imagining something you enjoy doing, it will make it easier for you to experience the images you encounter during your past life session. In other words, any way that you are already comfortable imagining a story is okay for you.

You can adapt any of the following scripts to fit your own way of regressing. Each time you try one out, you can continue to make adjustments to it. Eventually you will probably be able to reduce your induction time as you learn to relax and enter your imagery trance.

Each technique is a vehicle for helping you enter and achieve a successful past life discovery session.

Going to the Library

Do you go to the library for research or for pleasure? Do you have a home library? Perhaps you like to read in bed or a favorite chair. If you do, and if it's possible, that may be a good place to experience your past life discovery session. If being there is impossible, you may be able to remember a positive reading experience and imagine going there in your mind. If you're ready, you may give the library past life discovery technique a try.

AGELESS INSIGHTS

Your definition of a library may be totally different than anyone else's. It could be a real place or one that you imagine in your unconscious mind. You may find that you have one book of your soul's memories or a series of books, each featuring one of your past lives.

Find a comfortable place where you won't be interrupted. If you are working alone, you may want to record and play back the induction, or if you have a partner, you may have him or her read it to you. You can rewrite it to fit the way you relax and imagine. Start in with your relaxation exercise and use your faith and guides to help you stay grounded while you travel. Just read the following induction without fully experiencing it to see how it might work for you in the next chapter.

Take a deep breath and slowly exhale. Do this a couple more times. Let your eyes go out of focus as you slowly breathe in and out. You may be aware that there are many muscles throughout your entire body. Some of them are stiff, and some of them are relaxed already. Every time you relax a muscle, you may feel yourself relaxing more and more. For a moment, imagine what it's like to be in your special, comfortable place deep inside your unconscious mind. Slowly breathe in, and as you do, feel the experience of being there with all your five different senses.

In a few moments you may begin counting slowly backward from five to zero. When you get to zero, you will be in a very special library deep in your unconscious mind. This library is filled with many different volumes of books. Each one is about a special past life that your soul has experienced. When you get there, you may select one that's appropriate for your past life discovery session. If you want, you may ask your guides or angels for help in choosing the right one. You feel very relaxed and comfortable as you prepare to start counting backward into a positive imagery trance to take you to the library of your mind. You may feel and hold the book if you want to and let it open to the right page.

You may end your past life discovery session at any time by taking a deep breath, exhaling, opening your eyes, and coming back to the surface of your conscious mind. Tell yourself that you will always have a positive experience even though you might witness things that seem negative. You will come back to the surface of your conscious mind relaxed, refreshed, and comfortable, whether you choose to stop early or finish your past life experience. All the information you find in the books of your past lives can be used positively as you learn more about the journey of your soul. If you're ready to go to the library of your mind, you may now close your eyes, take a deep relaxing breath, exhale, and begin to count yourself backward.

- *Five.* You can feel yourself focusing more and more on the images that help guide you into your trance. You are beginning your journey to the library of your unconscious mind. You will focus on your imagery trance state as you relax more and more.

- *Four.* You are now getting closer and closer to the library of your unconscious mind. You are relaxing more and more as you slowly breathe in and out. You feel very comfortable and look forward to choosing a volume of your past life stories.

- *Three.* You are now halfway there. You are allowing yourself to focus more and more on the images that are coming to you. You feel the library getting closer and closer. You are very comfortable and relaxed.

- *Two.* As you slowly breathe in and out, you are relaxing more and more. You look forward to entering the library of your unconscious mind. In a few moments you will be there. You are only two steps away.

- *One.* You are almost there. You feel relaxed and comfortable and surrounded by your faith, your guides, and your angels. You feel warm and positive and ready to select a volume on one of your past lives. Now count slowly from five to zero and let yourself relax more and more as you focus on your imagery trance. *Five, four, three, two, and one.*

- *Zero.* You are now in the library of your unconscious mind. Using your five senses, let yourself become comfortable with your surroundings. You may see the books, feel them, and even smell the material they are made of. Take a moment to select a volume and hold it in your hands.

You are now ready to open a book on one of your past lives. You know that any time you need or want you can always close the book, take a deep breath, exhale, open your eyes, and come back to the surface of your conscious mind, calm, relaxed, and feeling positive about your imagery experience.

AGELESS INSIGHTS

When you open your book and start to read, you may see the images of the story. You can step into the minds of one or more of the characters. You may experience your story in all of your five senses. You can re-read any part of the story you want.

This is a sample script that you can use for your library past life discovery session. The next portion, your actual past life experience, will be in the next chapter. The more prepared you are, the better the chances are that it will be positive and productive.

Movies of Your Mind

If you like to go to the movies, you may want to consider using a movie theater of the mind induction for your past life discovery experience. The beginning relaxation exercise and counting procedure will be about the same as the library induction. Here is a sample of how you would create and use this type of relaxing imagery trance.

Once you are ready and comfortable, you may begin counting backward from five to zero. When you get to zero, you will be in the movie theater of your unconscious mind. You will be able to experience the film that you select about one of your past lives in all of your five different senses.

You will notice that this is a very special movie theater. You can watch the action or you can step into the play and experience what it's like to be one or more of the characters. You can change the view by zooming in or out, turn the sound up and down, and even experience the smells and tastes of the movie during your past life discovery session.

KARMIC CAUTIONS

Any time you need to or want to, you can stop the movie, take a deep breath, exhale, and come back to your conscious mind feeling relaxed and positive. You can always turn down disturbing sounds and move forward beyond a scene that might disturb you.

Every time you go to the movie theater of your unconscious mind you can select a different film or one that you have seen before. You can replay them as many times as you want. Each time you will notice something that you may have overlooked before.

I Saw It on TV

Another effective technique to help you in discovering a past life is to watch television in your unconscious mind. This is the same concept as going to the movies, but you will imagine a television instead.

If you frequently watch television, this might be a more natural way for you to visit a past life.

Again, just as with the other techniques, you would experience a basic relaxation exercise to begin focusing on your imagery trance. You will count yourself back from five to zero and when you get to your unconscious trance level, you will imagine that you're watching a television set. It could be your own TV, or it could be the big-screen TV you wished you had, for watching your past life program.

You may choose a comfortable chair or a bed for your past life discovery experience. You can actually be there when you have your session or you can imagine the feeling of being there. Imagining something familiar to you like a television is a good way to help you relax and focus.

If for any reason you need or want to turn off your past life television program, you can push the off button in your mind, take a deep breath, exhale, open your eyes, and come back to the surface of your conscious mind, relaxed and positive. You can always change a scene or turn down the volume and other senses if you should become uncomfortable for some reason during your past life discovery experience.

When you count yourself backward to zero, you may feel the remote control in your hand. This control is special. You can turn your volume up and down, as well as alter the images in your other senses. You can zoom in and out for the best view. You can turn the emotions up and down and feel the temperature and textures in your past life program. You can also enhance the smells and tastes during your experience, stop the action, and replay it any time you want.

AGELESS INSIGHTS

Many people use the sound of television as a way to screen out other noises. Some even leave it on all night while they sleep. Others watch programs to relax. If you can imagine watching television, it is a great way to help you enter into an image trance.

When you are ready, you may select the proper channel to watch the program that includes the right past life for you to discover. Just imagine that you can feel the controls in your hand. Relax and enjoy a program featuring one of your past lives.

You may like to watch videotapes or DVDs on your television set. If you do, you can combine the library and television techniques. You may go to the video library of your unconscious mind and select the past life album to watch. Just put it in, take the controls in your hand, and start the program. You will be able to work the controls of your past life discovery session the same way as in the television method.

You may have a home theater—a special place where you can get the experience that you would when you go to the movies. You may have a great sound system, a big screen, and comfortable chairs. You may even have the smell of fresh-popped popcorn. You can imagine such a place deep in your unconscious mind if you want to. You can combine any of these techniques to create the one that works the best for you.

Going Backward in Time

Another technique to help you in discovering your past lives is to count yourself back into a different lifetime. In this induction you would journey through your unconscious mind to a place where the memory of your soul is kept. You could research your past in the Akashic Book of Records, you can update the old book to a contemporary computer system, or you can just step into a past life experience. As in the other methods, you can mix and match to find the best technique for you. The key is to be patient and go with the experience.

In this method you would use different wording than in the earlier inductions in this chapter. Always start by getting comfortable and connecting to your faith, your guides, or angels, to ask for the right assistance in your past life discovery session. Concentrate on your breathing as you focus on your third eye to begin focusing on your relaxing image trance.

At zero, you will be at the place where the records of your soul are kept. You always know that any time you want or need to, you can take a deep breath, exhale, open your eyes, and come back to the surface of your conscious mind, relaxed, comfortable, and positive about your past life discovery experience. We'll pick the count up at five.

- *Five.* You are beginning to slowly count yourself backward from five to zero. With each count you will go further and further back before your current lifetime to another life that will help you where you are at the moment. With each count, you will feel yourself going further and further back, feeling relaxed, comfortable, and positive about your past life discovery experience.

- *Four.* You may feel yourself going back before you were born, journeying out into the universal mind and to the place where the records of your soul are kept. When you reach zero, you will step into a past life that is the right one for you to experience at this moment. You feel yourself going back and back through time.

- *Three.* You are going back further and further. You are halfway there as you continue to slowly breathe in and out. You are relaxed and comfortable and looking forward to your past life discovery experience.

- *Two.* You may have the sensation of floating out of your body as you go back in time. It is a positive feeling, and you feel safe and secure. When you reach zero, you will be able to experience your past life in all of your five senses. You can review and move around in your past life to collect the right information to assist you in this lifetime.

- *One.* You are almost there. You will be able to step into a past life image at zero. You will be able to experience it in all your senses. You can move out of any image that is uncomfortable. The records of your soul are now ready to show you your past.

- *Zero.* You are now at a place deep within your mind that is comfortable and relaxing. Your unconscious mind is open to the memories of your soul. Your angels and guides who are always watching out for you are surrounding you.

Once you have reached your destination, take some time to adjust to your surroundings. Use your five senses to help deepen your focus. The next chapter will provide the actual past life portion of your script. You can rewrite these samples to fit your own goals.

> **SOUL STORIES**
>
> Each person experiences a past life discovery differently than anyone else. Brett went to a past life specialist and was counted back into his image trance. He kept his eyes wide open during the whole past life session and to all appearances was just having a conversation with the specialist about the scenes he was imagining in his head. Afterward he couldn't remember anything that had taken place during the session. When you are doing the exercises, you may have excellent past life recall while in what seems to be a fully conscious state.

If your destination is the Akashic Records, after you have arrived, you can use the same concept as the library induction by opening the book to the right lifetime. You might find yourself in a hall with one or more doors. If you do, ask that the right door be opened for you. You may find yourself in a place with modern or futuristic electronics. These can work just as well for you by letting the past life information and experiences take place in a way that is positive and right for you. Sometimes your original concepts may transfer to another way of past life discovery. If that is the case, just go with the experience.

Where Did That Feeling Come From?

An affect-bridge past life technique is a method that takes an emotion, a relationship, a phobia or fear, or even an ache or pain back through your life into past lifetimes that are connected to your current situation. You can go directly into a past life after the induction or you can follow the feelings of what you want to investigate back in your current life first, and then back into a past life. It's possible that an affect-bridge technique could take you back through more than one lifetime. You may find that you have had an unresolved karma for quite a while.

To discover a past life, you can use any of the earlier techniques I mentioned in this chapter, such as the library, the movie theater, or the television. The affect-bridge technique takes you back through a series of images that all relate to a specific physical feeling or emotion. To start, you would experience your relaxation exercise and count backward to zero. You will suggest to yourself while you are counting backward that when you get to zero, you will select a lifetime with the information that you are looking for relating to the situation in your current life.

Getting focused on emotional images may be a little more complicated if you are following the feelings back through this lifetime to a past one. As you follow the feelings back, you may focus on other emotions and scenes that seem to be unrelated at first glance. Just go with the images as one situation may have transferred to another one as you progress through your lifetimes.

KARMIC CAUTIONS

While experiencing the affect-bridge technique, some of the feelings you're investigating may be intense or unpleasant, such as a fear or phobia. If so, suggest to yourself that you only experience enough of the unpleasantness to help you find its roots in one of your past lives. You can tune up or down any of your five sense images to help you get the best focus in your past life discovery session.

You will do your basic relaxation induction and count backward from five to zero. You may suggest to yourself that when you get to zero, you will be able to bridge your feelings back over your life to your earliest unconscious memory. From there you will bridge it back into a past life that relates to your feelings, and you can use your most comfortable past life discovery method. Don't forget to suggest to yourself that you are always grounded and watched over during the session, and you can always end your past life experience any time you want by taking a breath, exhaling, opening your eyes, and coming back to your conscious mind, relaxed and positive.

Here is an idea for a script that you might use after you have counted yourself back to zero. Think of a time within the past few months when you've had an experience related to the subject you are researching. Then think of another one within the past year. Now go back a couple years. After you have found one, go back five years. You may think of something else besides your original subject that may be related. If you do, you may want to continue with this new one.

Go back to a memory from about 10 years ago. When you have recalled one, you may go back even further. Work your way back to the earliest unconscious memory connected to the subject or a related memory. Once you have done this, go back beyond to another lifetime that's related to the reason you are going back. You can experience it in the way that is the most comfortable for you.

The Least You Need to Know

- If you're an avid reader, the library technique might be right for you.
- Going to the movies is a natural way to watch a film of one of your past lives.
- A television program in your unconscious mind is a good way to discover your past lives.
- You can count yourself back in time.
- An affect-bridge technique follows a feeling backward to its beginning.
- Experiment with all the techniques to choose the route that's the best for you.

Back to the Past: Time for Travel

In This Chapter

- Prepare for your past life discovery
- Deciding how and where you want to go
- Trying out the television technique
- Experience a past life discovery session
- Coming back to consciousness

You've done all the preparation; it's finally time to try a past life discovery session. Have you ever waited a long time for something to happen? All along you may have been anticipating and imagining what the experience will be like. Finally the time has arrived.

The more you give yourself permission to let the experience take a natural course into your soul's memory, the better the chance of not being disappointed. Each of you will have a different adventure and experience in your own way. Have a good journey!

KARMIC CAUTIONS

Usually when you're waiting, you develop a certain expectation of what the experience will be like when it happens. That can set you up for a major disappointment when things don't go as you had anticipated. This could easily happen in your first past life discovery attempt.

Check Your Final Preparations for Your Past Life Journey

Have you decided where you want to go first? It's very important to establish goals for your past life discovery session. In previous chapters, you considered how to determine what your travel priorities are. If you're facilitating your own image trance, you will want to have them clearly in your mind, or have made a recording to follow as an induction to help you focus.

Hopefully you have been making notes as suggested while you've been reading throughout this book. If you are working with a partner, you can write your script together. The more details you have for planning your trip, the easier it will go when you are ready for your session.

It's best to start with one specific destination rather than several. Keep it simple at first. As you get used to experiencing past life imagery, it will be much easier to get to where you want in a much shorter time. At the same time, be prepared to take a detour. You may go someplace you hadn't planned on visiting. If you don't arrive at the destination you're looking for, don't be disappointed. Some people are expecting to have a perfect past life discovery experience and get instant satisfaction when they go back in time. Wherever you go, you are usually there for a specific purpose. However, your destination may be someplace unknown. You may just want to have the experience without picking a specific place simply to find out what it's like to regress into a past life. That is a great reason in itself.

Have you composed your past life discovery script yet? You've been doing it all along. It is the language that will help get you to your destination. Once you are there, you are free to examine and experience your past lives in the way that your imagery works best for you. In other words, you are in charge of what takes place whether you have a partner or not. You may not consciously be as much aware of your experiences when you work by yourself as you would if you do it with a partner. That doesn't mean the information will be any better either way. You can still have the same insights by yourself.

SOUL STORIES

It would be to your benefit to create a video recording of your experience. Steve was not aware of his facial reactions when he discovered his first life. When he watched himself later, he was amazed at all the emotion that showed on his face when he was in his image trance.

To get to where you want to go, follow these steps:

1. Relax, count yourself backward from five to zero, and suggest that you are focusing more and more on your image trance with each count.

2. When you reach zero, use the technique that is best for you to start your past life discovery experience.

3. Take time to focus on your first image in all your five senses, using your strongest first.

4. Step into your imagery experience if you can and remember that you can move in and out, forward or back.

5. Begin to look for important pieces of information in that lifetime that relate to your present lifetime.

6. Follow that life through to its end and examine the last thoughts and feelings that your character had that he might have taken with him into other lifetimes, including your current life.

7. Finally, review the theme of that lifetime, look for the people there who might be in your life now in the same or different relationships, and understand how the new knowledge of this past life can help you in a positive way after the session.

Most stories have a general theme to them. So does a past life. The theme may be the opportunity to resolve karma, or to advance the soul's purpose. As I mentioned in Chapter 13, one of your goals in a past life discovery experience is to understand how the theme of that lifetime may relate to your current lifetime.

These steps will be illustrated in the sample script coming up. It's time to begin counting back in time. Are you ready to begin?

Begin Your Trance

This script will use the television method (see Chapter 14) to help you experience a past life. Remember that you can integrate any technique into your own script that works best for you. You can record it or have your partner read it to you, if you wish. If you think you might want to sketch or draw, you should have paper and pencil ready. If you are ready, find a comfortable place to begin.

Take a deep breath and slowly exhale. Continue doing this as you feel your body beginning to relax. With each breath, you may relax more and more. There are many muscles throughout your body, and some are tight and some are loose. Every time you loosen a stiff muscle, you may relax more and more. You may from time to time hear different sounds such as traffic or talking as you experience your past life images. If you do, that is all right. You may hear them, but you do not need to focus on them. You may focus on your third eye and the peaceful and loving energy of the universe.

As you continue to slowly breathe in and out, you may feel yourself relaxing more and more. You may feel the peaceful and loving energy of the universe beginning to flow through your body and surround you. You feel connected with your faith and your inner and outer guidance systems. Your guides and angels are with you, watching over and protecting you. You feel positive, safe, and secure. You know that any time you want, you may always take a deep breath, exhale, open your eyes, and come back to the surface of your conscious mind, feeling positive and relaxed.

AGELESS INSIGHTS

Notice that many words such as *relax* are repeated over and over. There is a purpose for that. Each time you say or hear them from someone else, let yourself relax a little more. Repeating the words helps your unconscious mind accept their meaning.

In a few moments, you may slowly start counting backward from five to zero. As you do, you will focus more and more on entering a relaxing and peaceful image trance with each count. If you are ready, it's time to let yourself begin to experience your relaxing imagery trance.

- *Five.* If your eyes have not closed yet, you may let them close now. Continue to breathe slowly in and out as you begin to feel yourself relaxing more and more. You may focus on your special place as you count backward and experience your positive images in all of your five senses. You will experience each image more and more strongly as you feel more relaxed and comfortable. In a moment, you will focus even more as you go to the next number.

- *Four.* You may imagine many positive images of your special place as you focus more and more on the images that are coming to you. You can see, hear, feel, taste, and smell the images as they float upward from your unconscious mind. With each breath, you relax more and more. You are look- ing forward to reaching zero and holding the controls to the television program about one of your past lives. You are pre- pared, and you'll remember the images shown to you about your soul's memories. If you're looking for specific infor- mation, you will let yourself be open to the experience, believing that the knowledge you'll gain will help you under- stand what you're looking for, especially as it relates to your life now. It is time to go to the next number.

- *Three.* You are focusing more and more on the images in your mind. You look forward to discovering your past lives. With each breath, your body is relaxing more and more. You can feel the positive love and energy of the universe surrounding you as you continue your journey into your unconscious mind and the memories of your soul. In a short while you will be able to view and experience a past life with all your different senses. You may ask that the right information come to you as you step into your past. You are prepared to go with the program that is selected for you, and you will collect the information that will give you the clues to the questions that you would like answered. You are now ready to go to the next number.

- *Two*. You are focusing more and more on the images in your mind as you continue to breathe slowly in and out. You are getting very close to the place in your unconscious mind where you will begin to view a past life on your mental screen. You are more and more focused on the images of your special place and will easily be able to focus on the program of your past life. You feel calm, comfortable, relaxed, and ready to experience the discovery of your past lives. You know that you are prepared and open to your past life experience. You are ready to go to the next number.

- *One*. You are almost totally connected with your unconscious mind and ready to experience a past life. You can feel yourself focusing more and more on the images that are coming from your unconscious mind. You will continue your focus as you experience your past lives. Your past life images will become stronger and stronger as the session progresses. You even have a control on your remote to help sharpen them. You feel relaxed and very positive about your experience. You may now count totally back to zero and experience a relaxing image trance.

- *Zero*. You are now connected and in tune with your unconscious mind. You may ask one of your thumbs or fingers to rise up in the air when your unconscious mind indicates that it's ready for you to discover your past lives. You may feel it floating upward. When it has shown that your unconscious mind is ready, you may begin.

Imagine that you have a television remote control in your hands. You can see and feel the different buttons that let you fast-forward through or review any image you want, turn up or down the intensity of any of your five senses, step in and out of the images, and stop your program any time you want.

Travel Time!

Focus on the television screen in your unconscious mind and select the correct channel for your past life program. Let an image come on your visual screen. It may be out of focus at first, but if you let yourself go with the experience, it will become clearer and clearer.

What is the first thing you experience? Which of your senses are you using? Take plenty of time and let your focus become clearer and clearer. If you are recording or working with a partner, you may speak out loud and describe what you're seeing.

If you are not getting a strong visual image, you may let yourself begin to experience in all your senses. You many answer any questions out loud and clearly. What does it feel like? What is the temperature? What is your mood? Can you reach out and touch anything? Are there any smells? Can you hear any sounds? If so, what are they? Where are they coming from? Do you have any tastes in your mouth? Are you comfortable there? What can you see? If there is no picture, can you see colors or energies? How clear is your visual image? What else can you collect for information about your past lives?

KARMIC CAUTIONS

Don't get discouraged if you're still having trouble getting images. Use your controls to move yourself forward in your soul's memory to where you will be able to experience the program that's right for you. You will continue to focus more and more as the images become clearer. You may focus on the information and images that are right for you.

Once you have found an image, look around and describe what you see. Slowly shift your focus to different views of this image. Ask your unconscious mind to show you what's important for you to note. Now place yourself in the image. What does it feel like to be there? What are your emotions? What is the temperature? What time of day or night is it? What do you hear? What can you smell? Are there any tastes in your mouth?

Can you feel yourself there? What position are you in? What does the nearest surface feel like? Now feel your hair. How long is it? What is its texture? Can you feel something under your feet? Are you wearing shoes? Are you wearing clothes? If so, what is the fabric like? What is the style?

If you can do it, change your view of the past life television program from experiencing to watching. You may describe the scene you are watching. Now is the time to draw or sketch if you want to. You may open your eyes to see the paper you are putting your image on. Remember that you can zoom in or out and stop the action or review it if you want.

When you're ready, move the program forward to an important event in that life that may have a connection to yours. Take your time and let the images flow until they stop at the right place. You may now step in and out of the images as you want to gather the information that can give you insights into your past life. Remember to use all your different senses for the strongest images.

If you are searching for something or someone specific, focus on that part of your past life program, and let the action stop at the right places. Look for a theme in this program that relates to your life. Take note of all the different characters that are in your past life program. The longer your past life discovery session lasts, the more focused on your past you will become. If at any time you want to focus more and clarify your images, suggest to yourself that as you count slowly from five to zero, you will focus more and more, and the image will become clearer and clearer on each number.

When you are ready, fast-forward your program to the end of the life that you've been viewing. How did the person die? What were her last thoughts? Did she leave anything unresolved in that lifetime that resulted in karma in your present life? How did she feel about her life as a whole?

> **SOUL STORIES**
>
> Patty took the death of a close friend extremely hard. They had been very close in life, bonding instantly the first time they met in college. After a long period of grieving, Patty looked for answers in her past lives. She found that the two of them had been family in several different lives and had actually begun their journey together at the creation of their souls. Patty realized that her friend was now still connected to her from the other side.

Now go back and review the whole lifetime and look for the theme that emerged. Look for the relationships your character had with others. Can you recognize any of them in your lifetime now? If so, how are the roles the same or different? What could you learn from a relationship in your past life that could give you insights into your current life? You will be able to remember more details from your past life after you have come back to the surface of your conscious mind and every time you refer to the notes or tapes you make about your experience.

Finally, is there anything else that could be helpful to you to watch or experience while you are still visiting this past life? When you are ready, it's time to come back to your conscious mind.

Coming Back to the Present

You may now turn off your television program in your unconscious mind. If you have had the sensation of leaving your body, you may now gently float back and become aware that you are totally connected with your mind, body, and soul. Take a few moments to enjoy the relaxed and peaceful feeling that you have created while you are still in your imagery trance. In a moment you will begin to count back up to consciousness.

- *One.* You are beginning your journey back to the surface of your conscious mind. You continue to breathe in and out, feeling very relaxed and comfortable. At five you will come back to the surface of your conscious mind, feeling relaxed and very positive. You will be able to remember more and more of your past life discoveries as you reflect on your experience.

- *Two.* You are continuing your journey back. You are breathing in and out at a very relaxed and comfortable pace. You feel positive about your experience. You are slowly coming back to the surface of your conscious mind.

- *Three.* You are halfway there. You are becoming aware of your body. Any heaviness you may have felt is returning back to normal. You can feel the warmth of the peace and love of the universe flowing through your body. You feel positive and very relaxed. With each breath you continue to come back to conscious awareness.

- *Four.* You are getting closer to the surface. You have almost returned to the surface of your conscious mind. At the next number you will be all the way back. Feel the warmth and positive energy of the universe flowing through your body. You are slowly and comfortably coming back to your conscious mind. Your body is back to normal. You feel very good as you slowly breathe in and out.

- *Five.* You have now returned to the surface of your conscious mind. You can feel the peaceful and loving energy of the universe flowing through your body, and it will stay with you after you are totally awake. You are warm and comfortable, feeling very positive about your past life discovery experience. If you are ready, take a deep breath, exhale, slowly open your eyes, and come back to the level of your conscious mind. You are aware of your surroundings, feeling positive, relaxed, and refreshed after your journey.

You are now back to the surface. You are fully awake feeling relaxed, comfortable, and very positive. You continue to feel the peaceful and loving energy of the universe flow through your body. You may take a few moments to let yourself adjust to being back to consciousness and reflect on your past life experiences. You will remember more of the details every time you review them.

The Least You Need to Know

- A relaxing image trance helps you regress into a past life.
- The more prepared you are for your past life discovery, the better opportunity you have for an informative experience.
- After you have reached zero, ask permission from your unconscious mind to begin your imagery.
- A good way to get permission is to let a thumb or finger rise into the air when you are ready to discover a past life.
- You will continue to fill in the blanks of your past life discovery session after you have returned to the surface of your conscious mind.

What Just Happened?

In This Chapter

- Collecting your impressions of your past life discovery session
- Sorting through any confusion
- Where you want to go versus need to go
- Taking notes on your past life experiences
- Keeping a past life journal

Now that you've had the opportunity to try a past life discovery session, your head may be spinning with everything that you encountered on your travels. In this chapter, you'll take a moment to catch your breath and collect your thoughts.

The post-experience wrap-up is a very important part of your discovery. It's your chance to capture the information while it is still fresh in your mind. Some facts will begin to fade from your conscious mind very quickly, while others will take some time to surface. Start with what is freshest in your memory.

Collecting Your Thoughts

Take a little time to let yourself adjust to the real world again. Continue to breathe slowly in and out, and enjoy being in a relaxed state. You were given the suggestion that you would continue to feel positive effects of the peaceful and loving energy of the universe flowing through your body after you counted back to consciousness.

Coming back from a past life experience is much like waking up from a nap in which you have been dreaming. That dream may still be buzzing around in your head. If that's the case, just come back to reality at a nice, slow pace that is comfortable for you. You may feel sleepy, or you may feel full of energy. You may even drift in and out of a partial sleep state. Everyone responds a little differently after they have experienced a past life discovery session.

Your eyes may not react well to full light when you first come back. If you find this to be true, you can always use softer lighting in the future. If the light is too harsh, just close your eyes again and slowly make the transition back to full vision. You can even use candlelight, which will not only help with your return to consciousness, but also provide a nice, relaxing focus when you are first entering your relaxing imagery trance.

AGELESS INSIGHTS

A person may come back to consciousness after experiencing a past life in a very relaxed state, especially if he's in a deep enough trance so that he's not yet consciously aware of what he has just experienced. An imagery trance can be very relaxing for anyone who has forgotten how to put himself at ease. You may not be quite so affected because you have been learning how to relax throughout this book.

How do you feel physically? Do you feel heaviness anywhere in your body? If you do, take a moment and count yourself back from three to zero and suggest that when you come back to three your body will come back to its normal weight again. This heaviness effect, as well as other sensations, can result from being in a deep hypnotic trance. Sometimes when you experience a vivid past life imagery trance, it will stay with you when you come back to the surface of your conscious mind. These effects usually disappear shortly after you have regained consciousness.

Do you have any other physical sensations? You may feel tightness in your third eye area from being connected to the universal flow. You may feel a slight buzz in your head. If you experienced something in your past life, you may have that sensation for a short period of time when you awaken. You might have been very cold or very hot and are still continuing to feel it a little. You might be thirsty. You may want to reflect over a soothing cup of tea or something else that refreshes you after your journey.

SOUL STORIES

It is a good idea to remember to suggest to yourself that when you come back to your conscious mind you will feel positive, very comfortable, and relaxed. Art experienced a past life where he had frozen to death. He was very cold when he came back to consciousness and could still feel the images he had experienced during his past life.

If you are cold when you come back to the surface, cover yourself with a blanket or warm clothing. Turn off air conditioning or fans if it's too cold, or turn up the heat if it's during the colder part of the year. If you feel a slight headache, suggest to yourself that it is drifting away, and you will be relaxed and refreshed. The important thing is for you to feel comfortable. How do you feel mentally? What were your first emotions when you came back from your past life experience? It's possible to carry over some of the emotions felt during that past life. You may feel empathy for the person you were in your past, especially if it was a trying life. The result could be a lingering feeling of sadness or loneliness. If this happens, take a few moments to feel the peaceful and loving energy of the universe and send some back to your soul's memory to help heal old scars.

How do you feel spiritually? Did any of your past life experiences challenge how you believe? Was what you encountered so powerful that it could affect you in a life-changing way? Perhaps you were given the opportunity to begin a new and much more positive and spiritual way of life after your past life session. Then again, you may have felt nothing physically, mentally, or spiritually from your journey into your past.

It Can Be Confusing at First

Now that you're back from your first past life adventure, what was it like? You may not be sure what just happened. That is the case when someone is in a high state of focus. You may feel a bit disoriented at first. The stronger the images you experience, the more powerful the experience. It's not uncommon to come out of a past life discovery trance remembering only bits and pieces of the experience that just took place. The more you focus on the images, the less you are apt to remember when you come back to your conscious mind. The pieces of information that you do recall can cause you to feel disoriented for a short period of time. As you continue to discover your past lives, you will find it much easier to come back to your conscious mind more in balance. It is also possible that you'll be able to focus even more as you become comfortable with the discovery process.

Think of coming out of your past life imagery trance as looking into a snow globe that has a scene inside. When you shake it, you can't see the scene because the globe fills with snowlike particles. When the snowstorm subsides, you are able to see the picture once more. When you come back to your consciousness, you may be staring into the blizzard of information inside your mind. It, too, will settle in time.

Confusion can result when your past life discovery goes differently than you had planned. You may have been so focused on where you wanted to go and what you expected to learn, that you missed what was actually taking place in the session. If you rehearsed in your mind what you expected, you might not have wanted to accept what you experienced. Did you go with the experience?

 KARMIC CAUTIONS

Certain physical, mental, or spiritual conditions in your life may prevent you from totally focusing on your past life discovery experience. Perhaps you have a cold, or got some bad news before your session. There are always issues—both known and unknown—that can interfere with your ability to focus. These conditions can lead to disappointment if the experience doesn't go as well as you had expected.

Were you worried or anxious about your past life discovery session? If you were, you may not have allowed yourself to relax and trust your imagination to take over. Your conscious mind may not have turned itself off the whole time. It's not uncommon to be a little anxious about the unknown, no matter how much you have prepared.

Remember that you are still learning the skills of regressing into the past. There is no such thing as a perfect past life discovery session because there will always be something else that you may wish you had looked for while you were there. That's the incentive to go back again.

You may have encountered something that you weren't expecting that was very unsettling to you. You may still have a disturbing image that was brought back with you into your conscious mind. The more you work with your faith to help you resolve your past, the better the possibilities to melt away any negative image. Remember to surround yourself with the peace and loving energy of the universe to keep yourself grounded.

Making Notes

Did you prepare to make notes right after your past life discovery experience? Just as soon as you have adjusted to being back to your conscious level and have collected your thoughts, you'll want to make a record of your first impressions of your journey. You can do this in several different ways. If you recorded the trip, you can capture your first impressions easily. Another way is to write down your thoughts. A laptop can be ready to go so that you hardly have to move after you have come back from your experience.

You may not be able to remember graphic details right after your experience. Just write down what you remember at the moment and fill in more impressions later. How do the different characters relate to each other and you, not only in your past life but in your current one? After you've described the actors in your story, review them to see if you missed any details.

Write down your answers to the following who, what, when, where, and why questions to help you collect your past life data:

- **Who did you meet in your past life?** Were there other characters present? How many different ones can you describe? Start with ones that you have the best images of. Remember to note sights, sounds, feelings, touches, smells, and tastes. Look around for as many details as possible.

- **What was the big picture?** Once you have figured this out, zero in on the little picture. Describe the clearest image that you can remember. In other words, get down as much information as possible. You may change some of your first impressions as you get further away from your discovery experience. If you don't make notes in the first place, you might forget some of the information after a few days.

- **When was your past life?** Can you figure out what time period in history you went back to? One of the values of describing the characters and their dress is that you may be able to research the fashions to help give you a concept. If you are unsure of the time period, you may want to dowse your unconscious mind for an answer. Just pick your tool and follow the directions in Chapter 12. Count the dates backward in larger numbers at first, such as 100 years if the date is back far enough, or 10-year increments if it's not as far back in time. Finally you can count back in single years when you get close.

- **Where did you journey to?** Can you recognize the location? What kind of physical description of your destination or destinations can you give? How does the landscape appear? Is it in the country or a more populated area? There are many different things that you can note about your surroundings. Are there any landmarks you can describe— mountains, oceans? Perhaps you can get enough information so that you can research the location. Just note anything that comes to mind. You can sort it out later.

  You may recognize the country that you went to but not the specific location. Any information that you can recall such as street signs, names of businesses, house numbers, or other researchable clues can help solve your case. It's important to remember that your information right after you come back from your past life experience may not be totally accurate. Write it down anyway. The more you investigate in the future, the more defined and accurate your information will become.

SOUL STORIES

Robin went back to a biblical time when she was a devout follower of Jesus. She was able to experience that lifetime with all of her image senses, including the taste of their food. She brought back with her a deeper meaning of her faith.

You may have heard and remembered conversations or other sounds that can help you identify where you went. Again, it's possible to recall only part of what you heard. You may have nearly the right sound but not defined enough to recognize it yet. Your unconscious mind will continue to work on the information after you have turned your attention to something else. Don't be surprised if you wake up one morning with a clearer perspective of what you had been trying to piece together.

You can also use your pendulum to dowse a map to help narrow down the location that you visited (see Chapter 12). Ask the pendulum to show you the direction of "yes." When that has been defined, ask which direction is "no." Next, ask your unconscious mind for permission to ask for the location and wait for the answer from the pendulum. Permission is usually asked for as a way of respecting the power of the unconscious mind and its connection to your soul memories. Not everyone follows that step in dowsing. When you are ready, hold the pendulum over the map of the general location where you think you traveled to and narrow down the area until your unconscious mind has found the correct spot.

- **Why did you go back to this specific past life?** Could you find a theme in your past life that relates to your life now? If you think you know what it may be, make a note of it. Can you understand the connection you currently have to your past? Is there any information from your experience that can make a positive difference to you as you go forward in your life? Jot down any ideas relating to the purpose of your visit to the past that you might have when you come back to the surface of your conscious mind.

Keeping a Journal

Do you have enough information to start keeping a journal yet? If you were able to answer all the questions in the last section, you may already have a lot of material to start with. Now you have the challenge of organizing the material you've collected. Your next goal is to develop a way to manage and add to your growing quantity of past life information.

You may already have started a journal relating to your past lives as suggested when you were learning about the connections you have to the past without even consciously knowing it. If you have one, you can add your recently gathered information to what you have already started. This may, however, be an excellent time to start a new journal that you can add your previously gathered information to.

Your journal should not only include the notes from past life discovery sessions but also have a provision for daily insights that may surface after you've experienced a past life. You will probably find yourself thinking about your experiences quite often. As you do, your unconscious mind will be comparing the information that has been deposited in it independently from your conscious mind. These insights may surface at any time while you are awake or sleeping. A small note pad or a portable voice recorder can serve to store the information until you can transfer it into your journal.

KARMIC CAUTIONS

So far you probably have material on just one lifetime. Imagine what it will be like when you have several different lifetimes to keep track of at the same time! A journal of past life material will make it easier to organize your information. It's crucial to start out on the right foot so that you won't get confused with additional information as you continue to visit your past lives.

Your journal can serve as a way to develop goals for your next past life discovery session. The more you become comfortable with visiting your past, the easier it will be to decide what you want to learn from your next experience. The next chapter will consider how you can sift through the data you keep in your journal and help you develop future past life discovery goals.

It's a good idea to have a loose-leaf binder if you are producing a hard copy of your journal. That way you can move the information to the appropriate places. If you are making entries into a computer program, make sure you date each entry so that you can keep track of the chronological order in which you gather your material. Always remember to keep copies and back up all your journal information if you're working on a computer.

Keep a record of each past life session you experience. Include what your discovery goals were, and what your first impressions were after you came back to your conscious mind. Leave room to add more insights as they come to you and what you would like to learn from this life in future sessions. Make sure you note any dreams about your past life experiences that you might have, as well as spontaneous insights.

As you add more sessions and more past lives, keep them in chronological order. You may want to construct a flow chart to help you track the movement of your soul through different lifetimes. This could be a simple map to help follow the sequence of events of one or more past lives and might use symbols to depict people, places, occupations, and other details. Make sure you leave plenty of space at first so that you have room to fill in the gaps as you retrieve the information from your unconscious mind.

You should have a place for character profiles from your past and how they may relate to your present life. You may want to have a place to note the theme of that life and any possible karma you may have encountered. If you sketched any of what you saw, keep a copy of it in your journal.

Keep a record of the relationships and themes that span more than one lifetime. Look for past life abilities or strengths that may be utilized in your current lifetime. Also make note of weaknesses that could have carried over into your present. Finally, try to choose a time that's convenient for you to review your journal and possibly write in it on a daily basis.

The Least You Need to Know

- Always take some time to collect your thoughts and readjust after you experience a past life discovery session.
- Don't be surprised if all the past life material you have collected is confusing at first.
- If you didn't go where you expected, you may have gone where you were supposed to go.
- Always keep good notes after your past life discovery session is over.
- An accurate and organized past life discovery journal can help you sort through your clues from the past.

What You've Learned

In This Chapter

- Organizing your past life data
- Did you collect the information you wanted?
- Revisiting past lives
- Filling in the details
- Make a research project out of your past life experience

You may have a mystery to research from your past life discoveries. This chapter will help you organize your data. Now is the time, right after a past life discovery experience, to make plans for your next adventure. You can go back to that life as many times as you want to continue to collect data, or you can begin to search for historical information connected to the clues you uncovered from past sessions.

Sifting Through the Data

Now that you have experienced a past life discovery and collected a whole lot of data, what are you going to do with it? If you are like most people, you will get excited about something for a period of time and then either lose interest or be pulled away to work on something else. When you get involved with a research project such as looking into your past, it would be nice to be able to devote all your time to it. That, however, is usually impossible to do. Once you get away from it, it's harder to get motivated to begin again. Every time you get back to something you haven't touched in a while, you have to spend quite a bit of time trying to remember what you did before. The further away you get, the harder it is to begin again. At the same time, though, it's good to take a break every so often.

But even when you're unable to devote yourself to researching your past lives as much as you would like, you really are doing something. That something is what your unconscious mind continues to work on while you're consciously occupied with other things. In other words, you can continue to research your past lives while it seems as if you are doing nothing about them. Remembering this will help you not to get discouraged when your time is otherwise occupied. Your unconscious mind can send up information at any time and will help you keep a mental focus on the history of your soul and how it may impact your current life.

As I mentioned in the previous chapter, the benefit of keeping a journal is that you will have a good record of what you've researched so far. When you have a moment to review your past life material or jot down more thoughts and insights, a well-organized journal can make it much easier. You might find a few minutes each day to reflect on your past life discovery project. Establishing a routine in your daily activities can help keep you on track.

The first step in sifting through your past life data is to determine how you want to continue researching your project. What part of your experience do you want to focus on? When you have answered that question, you can select just the data gathered so far on that portion of your past life. It might be a character that you want to learn more about. It could be a geographic location or a certain time period. You may want to further examine a relationship, a fear, or a talent.

That doesn't mean you should discard the rest of the data that you're not using at the moment. They are all pieces of the puzzle of the journey of your soul. Just like putting together a jigsaw puzzle, you may want to put the pieces that are the sky or the border together first. Once you have done that, you go to work on another section until the key pieces that link the whole thing together are found.

KARMIC CAUTIONS

If for some reason you didn't get much data from your past life discovery experience, that is actually material in itself. Keep a record in your journal even when the session didn't reveal much of what you think is past life material. Noting what went wrong will help you come up with a different strategy for the next time. It could be that your nonexperience will make more sense to you as you continue researching your past.

You may also have a lot of data that looks unusable. Just keep it filed in your journal in a place where you can review it from time to time. You are the detective, and every clue could be the one that breaks the case. Hopefully you are having fun with your past life project and feel like a detective! The more you mull the data over in your conscious mind, the more active you keep the investigation into your past lives.

If you have your information recorded, you or someone else will want to get much of the material down in your journal. That way you can review it, make notes on what you want to do next, and then re-listen to the whole recording to help refresh your memory. You may even want to use some imagery to suggest to yourself that when you hear it again, more details of your past lives will become clearer to you. Of course, this will give you more data to record in your journal.

Was One Visit Enough?

Perhaps you got enough information with just one visit to one of your past lives so that you don't feel the need to go there again. If this is the case, you can move on to a different lifetime if you want. You can always revisit a specific past life any time in the future. You may want to follow a theme or karma through more than one lifetime.

Even if it takes you a while to get back to your past life research, you will be prepared to start right in again. You may have a whole binder full of information before you finish your project. At the same time, just as in researching your family genealogy—the study of family history—the genealogy of your soul will always have something more to be learned.

It is very possible that you will want to get to know yourself in a past life better than you did on your first visit. Now is the time to begin to plan to return. Make notes on what you would like to learn next about your soul's memory. Your reasons could include focusing in on the theme of the life, studying either yourself in the past or other characters in the story, visiting a specific location to gather as much historical information as possible, or digging deeper into a past life situation.

> **AGELESS INSIGHTS**
>
> You may discover all kinds of relatives from your past lives when you experience going back. Your family tree may recycle itself and look pretty confusing when you try to chart it out. You may find that your mother in this life was your daughter in a past life, or that a good friend in this life was a brother in the past.

Check your session notes when you are making your return travel plans. Were you happy with the method you used last time? If you were, you can certainly use it again. Even if it was successful, you might want a different experience next time just to compare which method works best. You might want to go to the movies (see Chapter 14), or you may also want to make up a past life discovery technique for yourself.

Whatever method works best for you, it's a good idea to wait a couple of days before you revisit a past life. One reason is that you may not have processed all the information you gathered on your previous visit yet. Some of the material in your unconscious mind will take a while to work its way to the surface. Unless you are clear on the images you've already received, it could cloud the picture even more if you go back too soon.

Another reason to wait is that a past life discovery experience can use up a lot of your energy. Even though you're in a relaxing image trance, there is still a lot that's coming through you. It is good to re-energize your mind, body, and spirit before you take off again. You may sleep a little restlessly the first night or two after a past life discovery experience. That is because there is a lot of processing going on in your unconscious mind, and your dream state is one of the ways it works its way into your conscious.

Were there things that you would do differently this time? Make two lists. The first should include everything you liked about your first session, including the induction, the past life discovery itself, and the quality of images you experienced during the process. Make note of all that went well so you can include them in your next past life session. The second list should include what you did *not* like about your session. Try to break the information down so that you can focus in on the things that didn't work.

Now consider what you would do to change it this time. It could be that your physical location was uncomfortable and made it hard to enter a trance. You may be working with a partner who is not quite fitting into your discovery plan. If that's the case, you might want to change partners or go it alone. Perhaps you tried to go back by yourself and it didn't work out, so you may want to look for someone to assist you during your next past life discovery session. (See Chapter 12 for tips on working alone or with a partner.)

AGELESS INSIGHTS

When you revisit a past life, you take the things you liked that worked for you and add the ideas you think will help you better focus your imagery trance the next time. Don't include the things that didn't work for you the last time. Keep a record of this in your journal. You will find that it may take a few different sessions before you finally develop the method that works best for you. Even after doing all that, each journey into the past will take its own route.

After you have put together your approach to your next past life discovery experience, let yourself relax and try the concept out in your mind. Remember, it's good to allow yourself a few days to process all the information you have collected. You can imagine what it would be like so that you can look for potential glitches in your plan before you actually go. If you find something that doesn't seem to fit, you can readjust it. Now try that out in your mind. Once you are comfortable with the way you'll approach your next past life session, make plans in a few days to get ready to go again.

Going Back Again

You may find that the more you go back, the easier it will be to get there. A method that could take between 5 and 10 minutes can probably be reduced to at least half that time. Eventually you may be able to get comfortable, take a deep breath, exhale, focus on your third eye, and go directly into a past life image. Be patient. If you keep practicing, it will happen for you.

If you are ready, find your comfortable place. Prepare your partner if you have one, and have all your recording equipment ready to go. Have your past life discovery script with your goals clearly thought out, and any other material that will help you gather your past life information. It's still a good idea to take your time going into your trance. At the end of your session, suggest to yourself that on your next visit you will enter your imagery trance state at a faster rate.

SOUL STORIES

"I think that past life regression can be a path to better understanding of humankind. Most of my clients have experienced regressions where they were a different sex, a different race, a different economic background, a different social standing, or in a different part of the world than what they currently experience in this life. It's a great equalizer for people to realize that they may have 'been' of a different sex, race, or religion, or they may have been wealthy or poor, powerful, or powerless."

—Dr. Lisa Halpin, consulting hypnotist, speaker, and educator

If you have chosen to go to a different past life, one that you haven't visited before, proceed with your discovery by focusing in on the first images that come into your unconscious mind. If they are unpleasant, you can change your screen either backward or forward and turn down your sensitivity of the experience. Remember that you can always open your eyes and come back to your conscious mind, relaxed and refreshed, any time you want or need to. Proceed through your past life discovery with the plan that you've developed and gather your information to record in your journal when you return.

Filling in the Blanks

If you are revisiting a lifetime, you will already be familiar with some of the details there. Now you can begin to focus in on the details you may have missed before. Give yourself the suggestion that you can count backward from five to zero any time you want during your past life discovery session, and while you are doing so, the images you are experiencing will become clearer and clearer. It is like adjusting the lens on a camera so that you can bring it more into focus.

You may experience the same situation a little differently this time, or you may replay it exactly the same. Either way can be productive. You may be able to clear up some of the details with this visit. Every new piece of information can help you fill in the blanks. Don't worry if it's different. All you need to do is record the results in your journal afterward, where you can compare this experience with information you gathered earlier.

On the other hand, if you experience the same images over and over, especially if you can approach them from different viewpoints, it's a good indication that you have a clear concept of what happened in your past life. This may give you confidence and perhaps validation that your past life experiences were real and not imagined. If you are seriously trying to prove something about your past lives to yourself, the more consistent your story becomes, the easier it is to believe.

The blanks in your past life story will begin to fill in a little more with each visit. You should be able to develop a good *time line* where you can trace your main character from birth to death. You can go right to different points in the story and start to collect your information. You can study not only your character but also others to learn how their lives intertwined with yours.

DEFINITION

A **time line** is a system for recording events in the order that they took place. It could be similar to a flow chart mentioned in Chapter 16 that uses symbols.

You can study the geography of where you traveled in your past life and experience what it was like to live during that time. You can try out the food and smell the aromas that were there. You can feel the emotions and watch karmic situations develop and resolve. You can study many aspects about your life in the past.

If you are journeying to a new past life, you can look for relationships that spilled over into other past lives. Look for similarities of themes and characters. Is there any karma that might be continued from lifetime to lifetime? Are there any characters that appear together in more than one life? If so, how did their roles differ or stay the same?

Every time you experience a past life discovery, you fill in more of the blanks in the journey of your soul. On your way back to your conscious mind, suggest to yourself that the information will continue to surface from your soul's memory even after you have come out of trance. Suggest that every time you study your journal, more insights about your past will be revealed. Remind yourself that the images of your past will come to you at a rate that is positive and comfortable, and you will only get the ones that are right for you at the time. Also suggest that every time you use an imagery trance to travel back in the past, you will be able to do so at an easier and faster rate. You will begin your journey the moment you start your countdown.

When you are ready, come back to the surface of your mind feeling relaxed, refreshed, and comfortable. Take a little time to readjust and make notes in your journal about your latest past life discovery experience. Fill in any missing details.

Research the Story

Now that you have experienced more than one past life discovery session, you may find that you have a unique story emerging from the memories of your soul. You may want to take your research further and write it down, not only for yourself but for others like your family, friends, or other people who might find it interesting reading. In fact, a lot of great writers wrote best-sellers while in a trance state. They reached back into their soul's memory to provide the research material for their books. One such writer is Taylor Caldwell, who wrote *Dear and Glorious Physician* (Doubleday, 1959) and *Great Lion of God* (Doubleday, 1970) while in an imagination trance state.

SOUL STORIES

Jenny Cockell was haunted by an early childhood memory that she had lived before as Mary Sutton, a young Irish mother who died while she was raising eight children. Jenny was able to use image trances to help her research the information in her soul's memory. She eventually found her children again, now much older than she. Her book *Across Time and Death* (Simon & Schuster, 1994) tells the story of her search.

I'll tell you more about putting talents from your past lives to use in Chapter 21. Even if you aren't interested in writing your past life story, you may want to research as many facts as you can find when you journey back in time. There are many types of information that can help you prove your case that you lived before. The best way to begin is to get as many researchable details from your past life discovery experience as possible:

- **Names of people.** Note in your journal as many names as you can. Try to get the whole name. Then find as many names as you can that are related to the person. Parents, children, other relatives, and people in the same geographic location are very important. Note any name that you can find in your past life sessions. There are several ways to get names. You can ask the character to write them down through you. You can hear someone call a person by name. You can look for something that the person's name has been written on, such as an envelope. Remember that some of the characters in your past may not be literate.

- **Names of locations.** Note the names of countries, towns, states, and streets. Record the names of streets, buildings, boats, trains, etc., as well as any written information you locate in your past. You may have names that you don't even know where they go. That's okay. Just make a note of them in your journal.

- **Dates.** You will want to know the dates of your past life. When were you born and when did you die? What are the dates of other characters in your story? What were the dates when significant events took place during your past life experience? You can get dates from the past by looking for someplace where they are written down, such as a calendar. You might hear someone mention a date. You can also get a general idea of a date by observing clothing styles, hairstyles, modes of transportation, household furnishings, and even physical locations. Or you may know the date, and dowse to help determine the time period that your past life took place.

- **Good descriptions.** Record the best descriptions you can of the characters. Look at their dress from head to foot. Describe the scenery, the buildings, the temperatures, the feelings, the music, the smells, and what the food is like. Make sketches of what you see, if possible. Make sure you note anything that will help you research your past life story.

- **Get other facts.** Note what activities are taking place either up close or in the background. These could include war, social situations, childhood games, and even the lifestyle that the characters live. Don't leave any stone unturned when you research your past. It can be both fun and educational. The more you research, the more complete the story of your soul's journey will become. You may have a book in your hands when you finish.

The Least You Need to Know

- What you have learned during a past life discovery session will help you set your goals for your next return.
- As you experience past life discovery sessions, you will have the opportunity to develop and refine your own unique method.
- Going back again will help you learn more about your past.
- The more you go back to the same life, the more blanks of your soul's story you will be able to fill in.
- Your past life makes an excellent research project!

Updating Your Past

Now that you are an experienced mind detective of your own past lives, it's time to update your old abilities and put them to use again. Were you a writer, a poet, an artist, or someone with great psychic skills in a past life? You may want to look into what your potential will be in a future life. Then there is another intriguing place to go. What happens in between lifetimes?

Finally, it's time to take a look at your past life abilities and decide how they might be useful to you. You now have the tools to learn from your past and can use them to build on your future. Your past will always be a part of your present and your future. That past includes your many past lives.

Was That Really My Past Life?

In This Chapter

- Were you really *you?*
- Could you have more than one life at the same time?
- Tapping into the collective unconscious
- Channeling and communicating with spirits

Just when you have begun to think that this past life stuff is not too complicated, this chapter might change your mind. You will look at several different examples of other things that might be taking place during the time you are experiencing a journey into your past.

As you read about the theories in this chapter, remember that you should make up your own mind as to what you believe. You have a good guidance system already in place inside yourself and looking over you. Always rely on your faith and your intuitive mind to help you bring clarity and balance to your life.

How Do I Know That Was Me?

One of the best ways to decide for yourself whether you are the character you met in your past life discovery session is to ask yourself, "How does what I have discovered relate to how I live my life now? Can I identify with the character in my image?" You might imagine what it would be like to live in that time period. You also could imagine what it would be like for the character in your past life to live as you do now. Of course, you may not have been able to relate to anyone when you journeyed into your past.

Did you feel one of the characters you visited from the past was you in a different life? If so, how do you make the connection? What are your intuitive feelings? Can you explain the bond that you may feel bridges the gap between lifetimes?

What similarities did you have? Do you have the same emotions? Do you have the same interests? These could include music, food, locations, and professions. Make a note in your journal of anything that you can think of that links the memories of your soul with yourself in this life.

Do you share the same fears or phobias? Do you exhibit the same wounds from your past life? Do you have the same interests in relationship types? Do you share any of the same skills, athletic abilities, or artistic talents? Do you dream about the character you were in a past life? Do you have déjà vu experiences that you think may relate to your past life experiences?

AGELESS INSIGHTS

Do you long for something in this lifetime that your character had or did in a past life? Perhaps you have not yet found a family member from the past whom you parted company with before you were ready to separate. It could have been a child, a spouse, another family member, or a close friend. You may have the continuation of the emotions you had in your past life when you died.

Would you rather live now or in the era of your previous life? Do you resent some of the modern conveniences of today and try whenever possible to live a much simpler lifestyle? Since you have met the character of your past, do you often think of how he or she would feel or act as you go about your daily life?

Were you your own relative? Did you go back and experience the life of someone you're related to? Are there still people alive who would have known this relative? If so, can you compare notes on this character and obtain pictures of the person? Do her pictures look anything like you do now or did at a different age in your life?

What is different about you now and you before? Were there things that your character did in a past life that you cannot stand to do in this lifetime? Are you trying to make up for something you failed at or were deprived of in a past life? Perhaps you have a fear of being poor from a time when you were poor. You may hoard items of food because you didn't have enough before.

What other things can you compare about your different lifetimes? What can you research from the past that you can prove was a part of your other lifetime? When you have collected all the evidence both for and against the case of you being you before, let yourself be the judge and mediator. Let the answer be one that both you and your soul can live with.

Two or More Lives at the Same Time

It may be possible to actually experience more than one life during the same time period. Now that can really confuse the picture! How do you explain that you could be more than one person during the same time period? The answer is, you weren't. You may have a psychic ability that lets you connect with the energies imprinted by several people on a specific time and place in history. Therefore, you may be able to experience the imagery from more than one view.

> **SOUL STORIES**
>
> "I always tell my past life regression clients and groups that it doesn't really matter if they personally *believe* in reincarnation or not. Besides reincarnation, the experience may also be explained with quantum physics and parallel timeframes, or genetic memory, or even a very creative imagination. What matters is that the experience is often very meaningful to a person, and can provide them with insights and understanding about their current life, relationships, trials and tribulations, likes and dislikes, and even talents and fears."
>
> —Dr. Lisa Halpin, consulting hypnotist, speaker, and educator

Not every one of you will be able to experience other characters besides your own. It's your own mental DNA that will determine how you'll be able to access the characters in your past life. The things you can do in this life you can take back with you when you experience your past lives. The more you trust in your image ability as you journey back in time, the more you will be able to relate to the many different characters you meet along the way.

AGELESS INSIGHTS

"The ahas are profound and can be life-changing. Life patterns, relationships, and emotions are suddenly understood. You'll wonder what took you so long to experience the regression journey."

—Dr. Georgina Cannon, Ontario Hypnosis Centre School and Clinic

In the case of Bridey Murphy, researcher Morey Bernstein was able to have Virginia Tighe demonstrate Irish dances in a hypnotic trance that she knew from her past life. Was this actually the memory of her soul, or something that she may have observed in her current lifetime? Again, the question will probably remain unanswered, at least for the skeptics who need scientific proof. However, there is another question: how did her muscles "know" how to do a dance she had apparently never physically attempted before, at least in this lifetime?

One word of caution: if you decide you would like to involve yourself in physical acts that you were able to do in another life, it's advisable that you work with a professional past life specialist. You want to make sure you don't do anything that could result in injury. Someone trained in past life discovery can carefully monitor and control physical demonstrations, while someone who is inexperienced and unprepared may forget what to do and leave you at risk.

With this said, you might try out other past life abilities with a partner and some by yourself. These activities include artistic abilities of several types, such as music, painting, or writing. You can even bring forward a psychic or healing gift from before. There will be much more on this subject in Chapter 21.

You can also work with your unconscious mind to help you get to the truth about who you were in your past life. The pendulum is a good way to do that (see Chapter 12). After you have determined yes and no and have requested permission from your soul, you can ask whether or not a character from your past life was you. You may find your answer this way.

There are many more theories on what you are communicating with during a past life discovery session. One interesting concept is *soul fragmentation*. Under this theory you could be communicating with several parts of yourself through the various characters in your past.

DEFINITION

Soul fragmentation is the belief that your soul can divide when it comes back for another lifetime. This means that there could be two or more parts of yourself wandering around the world seeking to reunite. Imagine how that would compound over different lifetimes. Under this theory you could be communicating with several parts of yourself through the various characters in your past.

Make sure you keep records of whom you can communicate with and whom you cannot. You will not be able to step into the soul memories of some characters. Some of the soul energies have been pulled back to the other side and aren't able to communicate with you, at least not at the present time.

The Collective Unconscious: Meeting All Kinds of People

Swiss psychologist Carl Gustav Jung (1875–1961) advanced the theory of the collective unconscious. He believed that beyond one's own unconscious mind, which contained personal repressed memories, was a greater consciousness that contained the memory of the mental energy of the universe. The universal mind is often considered to be the same as the collective unconscious. In other words, all knowledge is accessible to almost anyone who desires to open oneself to it.

Under this theory, when you visit a past life, you are absorbing the knowledge of what was there when the actual experience happened. All the actions and thoughts represented in the energy of each character in your past life may be accessible to you when you open yourself to them. This may create confusion when you try to determine which person you were.

When Edgar Cayce visited the Akashic Records, he was able to peer into the history of any soul that he wanted. He could see the pitfalls and hindrances that potentially lay ahead because of the knowledge of the soul's past. You may have that same ability. If you can go to the Akashic Records through your imagery trance, you may want to look up the record of your soul and compare it to the different characters you have met in your past lives.

SOUL STORIES

You may have heard the story of the hundredth monkey. It goes something like this: There was an island where a colony of monkeys lived. One of the monkeys decided that he would wash his food in the water before he ate it. The other monkeys on the island all decided that they would do the same. Before long, all the monkeys on the island were washing their food before they ate. Soon, on another island halfway across the world, a monkey began to wash *his* food in the water before he ate it. Was this an act of coincidence or universal communication?

Regardless of whose past lives they were, the energy of the collective unconscious could be a great benefit to you. Just imagine what it would be like to consult the masters of knowledge who have gone on to the other side. Perhaps you would like to understand the secrets of the universe or the painting technique of a famous artist. The collective unconscious has the record of all knowledge, thoughts, and actions. All you have to do is connect to it.

There are many other benefits of contacting others during a past life discovery session. One is that you have a greater chance of gaining better insights into your own past life by observing through the eyes of others. You can study relationships and perhaps gain a better perspective of those who have been carried over into your current lifetime. The more you learn about the story of your past, the better you will be prepared to be in tune with your soul's journey into the future.

AGELESS INSIGHTS

You don't necessarily need to go into a deep image trance to experience the collective unconscious. You can tap into the energy through the feeling of déjà vu. You may sense the energy from a different time period from a location that is rich in history, such as a Civil War battleground or a disaster site. Places where many people congregated during a time in history can contain the energy of their souls.

The next time you experience a past life discovery session, you may wish to try visiting the collective unconscious. After you have counted yourself down and traveled back to the lifetime that you want to visit, see how many different characters in your story you can communicate with. Can you directly have a conversation with them? Can you hear what they are telling you? Can you move them around in their lifetime? Can you feel their emotions and image through their eyes? See how well you do communicating with the collective unconscious.

Channeling and Spirit Communication

To compound your past life research even further, consider that you may have opened yourself up to be a channel for another entity. It may be a friendly voice that speaks through you with words of wisdom from the collective unconscious. You could become a medium for an entity who wants to get a message out through you.

Channeling is a different type of image trance experience. The subject enters an altered state, and another personality comes through. During the time that the altered state is in effect, the subject is consciously unaware of what is being said through her. This can also happen through automatic writing and other artistic forms. Two of the most noted channels in the second half of the twentieth century were Jane Roberts, who brought through an entity known as Seth, and Arthur Ford, through whom an entity named Fletcher spoke. Roberts chronicled her experiences in a book called *Seth Speaks* (see Appendix B).

It's possible to confuse a channeling experience with a past life experience. This can easily happen when the entity identifies the time when he lived, especially if it is coincidentally in the time you experienced a past life. The difference between a channeling and a past life experience can in part be determined by the language the subject used. The past life focus is on another time period while a channel often focuses on the present and future.

Do you remember Stephanie's past life in Chapter 8 when she visited Atlantis? As her past life experience continued, she began to speak differently and started to channel information from a higher being who was called Ashar. After the session ended, Stephanie decided to continue with the channeling in future sessions. This ability may not have been identified if she hadn't decided to have a past life discovery session.

You may also run into ghosts and other spirits when you experience a past life discovery session. Image trances can be an excellent method for *spirit communication*. This can be accomplished by giving yourself the suggestion that you'll be open to the energies connected to the location where you are when you are experiencing a trance state. At the same time, you may be open to these energies without realizing it. Remember to ask your faith for protection from unwanted spirit visitors when you are focusing on your imagery trance.

DEFINITION

Spirit communication is the ability to speak to the soul of someone who has died, usually in thought form. People who have this ability will each do it a little differently, using imagery from their five senses.

Some people can actually visualize a ghost and then communicate with him while in an image trance. The purpose is usually to help a spirit who is trapped within the earth plane to move on to the other side. A good way to accomplish that is to ask the ghost to ask someone close to him who has died to help guide him over to the other side.

Do you think you can talk with space aliens while you are in a hypnotic trance? It's possible that you might channel an entity who claims she is from another planet. Her message might be for the entire world as either encouragement or as a warning about the future. This book doesn't make a judgment on what may be speaking through you. The important thing to remember is that all communication should be positive and nonthreatening. If you have continuous negative voices in your head, then you should stop experiencing image trances and seek professional counseling immediately.

As I stressed in Chapter 11, it's very important for you to be grounded in your faith. If you ask that your inner and outer guidance systems help guide and protect you as you experience your past life discoveries, you will have a much better chance of having a positive past life experience. The more you are comfortable with your past life plan, the better you will be able to understand something that might pop up unexpectedly. You know that any time you want to, you can always take a deep breath, exhale, and open your eyes, feeling relaxed and positive.

Delving into the history of your soul can be a very positive, educational, and life-changing experience. Once you are prepared to go beyond a possible negative experience, you'll be able to go about your past life research with confidence. Always keep track of the different types of past life discovery experiences you have. You may want to continue to work with something you discovered from your past.

The Least You Need to Know

- The character you identify with in a past life can be insightful to you in this life, regardless of whether it was you or not.
- You can experience more than one life during a past life discovery session.

- The collective unconscious is also there for you to communicate with.
- Your image trances may also be an excellent way to channel spirit communication.

Relationships from the Past

In This Chapter

- A connection from your past
- Lives that intertwine
- Old enemies from other lifetimes
- More than soul mates

In this chapter, you will learn how to use imagery to give you insights into situations in this life that may possibly relate to past life connections. This process can help you get a different perspective on elements of your life that may be out of balance. It's a way to set aside your conscious mind so you can get more of an objective view of what is actually taking place.

I Know You from Somewhere

Have you ever met someone for the first time that you know you have met before? Perhaps you have asked the person if she knows you. There's just something about her that is so familiar. You may spend a period of time, even days, trying to figure out where you have met her before.

It's very possible that you do know her, but it may not be from this current lifetime. So many of us have been connected before. If this is true, why can't you just remember? Actually you may be recalling much more than you think. Besides, if you didn't somehow remember someone, why would you be trying to figure out where you knew her from?

Every thought you have may be telling you something relating to your past lives. That something may not make any sense when you try to figure it out using our traditional western standards of belief. When you begin to examine your thoughts and feelings from the reality of your past, the present, and the future, you may get some very interesting perspectives.

SOUL STORIES

"So many of our health and relationship problems have roots in our unresolved past lives; from unexplained illnesses to phobias, from irrational fears to the partners we choose. With past life regression hypnosis sessions, people can transform their lives through understanding their previous existences and enriching their lives."

—Sylvia Browne, spiritual teacher and psychic

Even daily experiences may be the result of actions taken in one or more past lives. We are constantly being influenced by situations that happened in the past. That includes how you respond to people you know and to people you meet for the first time. When you begin to pay closer attention to your thoughts, the words that come out of your mouth, the emotions that you experience, or the way you physically feel toward someone, you will start to focus in on clues—clues that are out of context with other ways you experience life.

This is exactly what a past life specialist does when he looks for clues from your past. The way you physically react in a conversation or to your own thoughts, how your mouth moves, the flow of your words, the direction of your eyes, the type of dress you wear, the style of your hair, or the way your body is positioned, are all clues that an individual may not notice about himself until they are pointed out to him.

Crisscrossing Paths

Are there certain people in your life that you keep running into by chance on either a consistent or infrequent basis? Did you ever wonder how or why they appear in your life when they do? They may be someone who is close to you, or they may be a causal acquaintance. You may have good feelings about them or just the sight of them may rankle your ire.

AGELESS INSIGHTS

A chance meeting with someone may cause a reaction that is out of context with the situation. He may have an adverse reaction to seeing you, or he may greet you with an affection that you didn't know existed. You may be confused or dismayed by the reaction.

You may crisscross paths with someone your entire life or you may have these run-ins over a short period of time. The first time that Mitchell met Tina, it was for a business appointment. Some time went by, and then one night by chance she was in a bar that Mitchell had gone to some 50 miles away. Tina reintroduced herself and made an appointment to see him again for advice. As they talked, she said how she was very aware that they seemed to share some sort of a connection.

These chance meetings happened over and aver again. Once it was at a convenience store where Mitchell was having coffee, and Tina had a sudden thought to stop and go in as she was driving by. Over and over again this happened until they both joined a weekly metaphysical discussion group. They eventually accepted that these chance meetings actually came from connections they had experienced in other lifetimes, and this gave them the confidence to realize that they are working together again in the present to help others find their purpose in life.

When a chance meeting causes you to question if it has a deeper meaning, take a few moments and open to your unconscious mind.

- Image in your own way through your five senses, and ask yourself to show you if this connection has a deeper meaning. Can you create a picture of the connection from other time periods? Perhaps you can hear a conversation taking place in a different time. Ask yourself how it feels to be with the same person in another lifetime.

- Just let your mind wander without trying to analyze what is occurring. Remember, if something is unpleasant or unsettling, you can always take a deep breath, open your eyes, and come back to the surface of your mind. The goal is to experience the images in a way that will give you some positive insights relating to your life now.

- Ask yourself what the connection was back then. How did the two of you work together or against each other in that lifetime? Do you still have emotions connected to them now that began in another lifetime? Are these feelings appropriate for the relationship you have in this lifetime?

- Review your life then and look for the beginning of your connection with the other person and how it proceeded throughout your whole life. What parts did you play together in that lifetime? The roles may have been large parts or small.

- Look for your final thoughts about your experiences in that life. Ask your higher consciousness to reveal to you the purpose of renewing this connection now. Ask how you might move forward and use or resolve this ancient connection with the information you have received from your unconscious mind.

Now take a little time and go over what you have experienced. Perhaps you will want to jot down some notes. This exercise may help you look at someone differently and provide you with a different perspective regarding the connection you feel to someone else. Of course, it's possible that this relationship runs through several lifetimes, and you may want to revisit the process again to gain even more information.

Remember, regardless of the roles you may have played in the past, it's important to always keep yourself firmly grounded in the present to avoid potential hazards that could be ahead in the roles you are both currently playing.

KARMIC CAUTIONS

Just because you have gained some past life insight doesn't mean that others connected to you will accept it. That said, you could ask the other person if she had ever imagined that you might have a past life connection together. She might come up with very similar images from another lifetime.

You may have had a negative experience with someone in a past life and still be feeling the same vibes today. Remember that some people stay the same as they were before, while others have learned to change old negative patterns. Both of you may have a wonderful chance to grow in this lifetime as you examine and resolve any old issues that you had together from the past. Then again, just because one wants to change, the other may not. You can still let yourself go by changing your view and releasing those old emotions that are inside.

Understanding Soul Mate Connections

Many people in life, both believers and disbelievers in the idea that we live more than once, use the term "soul mates." Labeling someone a soul mate often infers that there is a kind of bond between the individuals that is much deeper than an occasional connection. There is an unspoken relationship between the two, supported by similar interests and views about life.

A soul mate is often someone you have had very close connections with over other lifetimes. You have had a lot of experiences traveling together, some good and some not so good. You may have been lovers in one lifetime and adversaries in another. There may be unresolved conflict in this life that you now have the opportunity to resolve as you move along your soul's path.

You may have had a wonderful romantic relationship with your soul mate that brings both of you great joy and happiness in this life as you are together again. Chances are that you learned in other lifetimes how to work together. It's possible that you were kept apart the last time around, and you feel the urge to make up for lost time. A word of caution: it is hard to survive on passion alone. Common sense is needed by at least one of the parties to keep you on track with your soul's purpose.

SOUL STORIES

Some of you may feel that you are shouldering more than your half of the partnership this time around. You may be connected to someone who really needs your help even though he may not realize it himself. Edgar Cayce's soul mate, his wife Gertrude, is a great example of someone who stood by her husband through the trials and tribulations connected with the great seer's work. Much of their life was a constant financial struggle, and yet together, along with their assistant Gladys Davis, they persisted, leaving a body of work that is still helping people today.

You may feel a passion for someone you know, who you had an incredible relationship with in the past but who now, unfortunately, is not free to continue it in this life. One or both of you may have commitments to others in this lifetime and part of your lessons may be to find ways to ease or release the connection you felt in the past. In other words, it may not be in your plan to continue as you were in the past.

It may prove difficult to release those old feelings deep inside your soul. Suppose that in the previous life a traumatic event such as a sudden death pulled the two of you apart, not enabling you to finish the work you were doing together. You may have struggled with the guilt of losing a family member or felt the pain of battle and died far away from your loved one.

You may find that you have a large family of soul mates from life-times before who are not physically related to you now. You may actually have two different families here on Earth, those who are blood relatives and those who may feel as close or closer than your blood relatives. The old bonds from other lifetimes can run very deep.

Here are some hints to help you understand your past soul mate relationships. For a moment, stop, think, and write down those people in your life with whom you have felt a strong connection. Remember that there may be some on this list who are not your favorite people. You may in fact have a difficult relationship with them and even though you would like to be clear and free of them, they seem to always be there. Once you have compiled a list—it may only have one person on it or many—begin to examine them one by one.

Using your senses, imagine a story of another time when this person and you had been connected before.

- When did you first connect and how long did it continue?

- What was the last connection you had in that life?

- At the end of that life, did you have any feelings, good or bad, about this other person?

- Was there any leftover karma that you may now have or are working through in this lifetime?

- Review the theme of that life relating to your soul mate and ask yourself how you can use what you have imaged in your current life to help you move forward on your soul's path in the future.

Once you have completed this exercise, you may want to ask your unconscious mind if there are any other lifetimes when you and this soul mate have been together that can help you understand your current connection. You may find some soul mates who have experienced several lifetimes with you in a variety of different relationships.

Soul Mate Connections to Current Family

It's also very possible that many of your current family members have traveled through other lifetimes with you. A child may have been a parent in one life, a sibling in another, a lover, or an adversary. Children often continue to act the roles they played in a previous life.

This can make life very interesting until a balance between the parent and child is reached. A child can become very demanding, want to assume the role of the parent, or have a great affection for one or the other parent, all influenced by memories from another lifetime.

KARMIC CAUTIONS

A parent can become overly protective of a child because she may have lost them in a previous life. The fear could be projected onto all aspects of the child's life or into something specific, such as fear that the child might drown if allowed to go in the water.

It isn't just a parent and child relationship that can be impacted by past life karma. It could be siblings, and it could encompass more than one or two generations. Age is often not a consideration when one is caught up in a past life trance. It's important to always remember your current life situation so that you don't slip through the veil and get lost in the other reality of the past.

Here are some suggestions to help give you some insights into soul mates that are currently family members. Get comfortable and let yourself go back and image the connection you have in a past life. Just let the first thoughts that come into your head play out in your mind. Look for the start of the relationship, the roles you played then, and identify important events in that lifetime that may influence either of you in this life. Look for the last memories of the relationship and the thoughts that you may have had then. Let yourself imagine what it may have been like to be the other person and how that life may have caused him to relate to you now. It may take more than one life to understand the complete basis for the karma in this life that the two of you experience. If you're working on a connection with a child, when it's appropriate and before you share what you may have imaged, ask her to imagine what it may have been like to know you in a past life. Perhaps she will tell you something similar.

The Twin Soul Connection

Have you ever heard of the terms *twin souls* or *twin flames?* Edgar Cayce and his secretary were twin souls. You may remember that I mentioned earlier in this chapter that Cayce and his wife were soul mates. So what is the difference between the two relationships?

> **DEFINITION**
>
> **Twin souls** or **twin flames** are thought to have started their journey together as one single soul or spark of energy spawned from the core of the universe, perfectly balanced, as both male and female. When this energy evolved into physical matter, it divided into two forms, one as a male and the other a female. Believers in the twin soul theory hold that these souls travel together throughout their journey in the universe.

In the beginning, the soul could travel in a state of energy for an indefinite time. In fact, early in the earth's development there were souls with nonphysical forms living in co-existence with physical forms in the lost world of Lemuria and Atlantis. It was easy for them to return to the source for rejuvenation. They were free to fly through the dimensions of time without the restrictions of gravity. Children and many adults retain memories of what it was like to fly. They may often have these experiences during their dreams.

There comes a time during the course of development when the soul takes on a physical form. That form may or may not be human. There are people who have soul memories of other places in the universe and of existing in other life forms. There are some who have memories of being animals or plants early in their soul's development.

When the soul starts to take on physical form, there is also a division of the male and female energies. In other words, it's possible for two life forms to spawn from one soul. You may have many soul mates throughout your various lifetimes but only one twin soul or twin flame. The twin soul relationship has a different energy or feel than any other you may have experienced.

As a child, Paula was convinced that she had a twin. She consistently asked her mother questions regarding her birth, and as she grew older she wouldn't accept the truth until she saw her birth certificate. At one point she thought she had found her twin, someone who looked almost identical, only to be mistaken. Finally, in her late thirties, she met a woman who she knew was the person she had been looking for her whole life. The two became fast friends, could finish each other's thoughts, and together they shared a sense of completeness. Paula went to a past life specialist where she discovered a past life as a sea captain. She/he had mistreated her twin and left her to sail off in his ship. Unfortunately, the ship sank and his last thoughts were great remorse in his actions toward the woman whom he had mistreated. When Paula was a child in this life, she continued to search for this person again, driven by the memories lodged in her unconscious mind. She has finally balanced the karma from the past, and the two remain close friends as they live their separate lives with a knowing and finally a completeness that is not always understood by their friends and family.

Back to Edgar Cayce for a moment. When Gladys Davis first came to work for the Cayces as a stenographer to take down and write up the readings, she also was reconnecting with her twin soul. She was 27 years younger than he, and yet there was energy between them that took several readings to figure out what was taking place. It turned out that they had been together in many lifetimes and had in fact begun their journey together as one. Over these lifetimes they had remained very close. Edgar, Gertrude, and Gladys all came to an understanding with the help of the readings that, in this life, working together as a team they could further the work that had begun so long ago. This body of work is still having positive effects on many through the organization that furthers his work, the A.R.E. in Virginia Beach.

How do you know if you have a twin soul? Have you ever felt energy with someone like that described in the last paragraph? It's possible that you may not have met your twin in this lifetime. Have you felt that there is someone missing in your life? Does this feeling continue to exist even though family and friends surround you? Perhaps you are experiencing the pain of emptiness after someone whom you did feel a bond with has either passed on to the other side or, for one reason or another, just may not be in your life the way he was before? Do you feel lost if you don't have contact with a certain person in your life on a consistent basis?

It would be nice to think that when twins reconnect with each other, the experience would be of two halves making a whole. Unfortunately, that's not always true. The energy is there, but the life conditions and the roles that each are currently playing may lead to an interesting adventure. Terry found his twin again even though he didn't understand it as such. The twin had moved recently to the area where he lived, and when they met, they felt an instant connection. However, he was coming off a very unpleasant marriage and was not ready to enter into another permanent relationship. They tried to lead their separate lives, but the magnetic connection kept pulling them back together. Finally they decided to plan a life together and, in the process, felt a mutual desire to build a log cabin. They went as far as creating a set of plans for the structure, then things fell apart and the cabin was never built.

Their can't-live-with and can't-live-without situation pulled at their hearts until Terry finally sought answers through a past life session. He found himself back in a time where he and his twin were living in a cabin similar to the one they had designed together. In that life, the couple was separated by illness when she had died much earlier than he. He felt both loss and also being trapped when she had left him with the burden of trying to keep the homestead going alone. On one hand, he was attracted to her again, and on the other, he had a fear of being left alone. This caused him to shy away from the same commitment with her in this lifetime.

If you are trying to determine if one of your past life relationships is in fact your twin soul, use the technique that works best for you described earlier in the book, then find a comfortable place and let your mind flow back to another time when the two of you were together. Just accept the first image that comes to mind and examine it through your five different senses. You may watch this life you had together and experience as much of it as you want or as your senses allow. Remember that if you don't process with visual images, use whatever comes to you to fill in the story. Look at the theme of the life and how you traveled together through it. What took place in your last connection in that life? How did that experience impact your current life? Review other lifetimes in the same way, always using the information gathered to relate to situations in your current life.

Finally, using the feeling of the connection you have with this person, imagine going back to a place that was just pure energy. Go back to the time when your soul was just beginning. Take some time to experience the unconditional love that exists in this place in the center of the universe. Begin to follow the migration of your soul as it starts its travel through time and space. What happens when the soul divides? How did you feel after the separation? Now, as you come back to consciousness, imagine how you can use the images you have experienced to give you new, positive clarity and guidance as you continue to follow your life plan.

 KARMIC CAUTIONS

Not all twin souls choose to work together. If one chooses to work with karma and the other doesn't, they may come together and find that they are incompatible. Even though there is that unseen bond between them, it just may be impossible to balance the energy.

These are some of the ways that past life discovery can give you a new perspective on how you may have been experiencing your life. Always remember that what may be true to you, might not be to others connected to you. Each person experiences her own story, and she may not have as open a mind as you do. One way to begin the past life discovery process with someone who's connected to you through another lifetime is to ask his thoughts of that period of time. If he shows interest, you might ask him if he ever imagined what it might have been like to live back then. You may be able to introduce him to the concept that you were together before without the mention of a past life connection. At the same time, he might be so engaged that you could ask, "Do you think it may be possible we actually were together in a past life back then?"

The Least You Need to Know

- Souls who were connected to you from other lifetimes may be crisscrossing your life path now.
- You may run into former rivals from past lives who spark the same emotions as before.
- You and your family members may have played different roles in your past lifetimes.
- You may have a twin soul trying to connect with you again.

Resolving the Old Karma

In This Chapter

- What goes around comes around
- How your free will may be prolonging your karma
- Finding the source of your problem
- Taking healing energy to the past

You now know that you run into your old karma many times each day. It could be in a thought or a communication with someone else. You may be held captive by an issue that started many lifetimes ago. Up until now you haven't found a way to move beyond its old emotions.

As you may remember, in Chapter 10 you learned how past karma can catch up with you. In this chapter you will discover ways to make a fresh start in your life. You can actually get yourself back in tune with your soul's purpose. There's only one thing that stands in your way: your free will. It's the voice inside you that represents your ego.

Now it is time to put your detective skills to work so that you can discover and crack the case of your past life karma. Once you understand it, you can move forward in your life. You may never view an old karma in the same way again.

Old Karma Dies Hard

What goes around comes around. That old saying can certainly apply to the actions that you took in your past lives. Did you discover anything when you visited your past that could be connected to your current lifetime? You may have been looking for something specific. You may not have had karma on your conscious mind when you went into your past. Either way, it exists around you most of the time. Some of it is so strong that it's impossible not to notice, while some is so subtle that you are only momentarily affected by it. What happened during your past life?

Did you identify any karma when you experienced your past lives? If so, do you have a section in your journal on your discoveries? If not, it might be a good idea to make one. You will want to note anything that seemed to conflict with the positive universal energy flow throughout your body. In other words, did you run into anything that indicated issues that haven't yet been worked out in your actions, your relationships, or your internal communication with yourself? Have you found yourself in conflict with others or yourself? If you have, then you may have karma to resolve.

What lifetime was the karma in? Were you able to follow it back through your past lifetimes until you found the beginning? When you do this, you are actually using the affect-bridge technique to trace a feeling or emotion back through your past life rather than your current one. The goal is to get to its beginning and examine it as you are now so that you can get a different view of an old situation.

If you haven't yet uncovered your karma, here is a way that you can try to identify it through a past life discovery session. This technique will deal with looking for previously undiscovered karma in a past life.

After you have focused on your imagery trance, suggest to yourself that when you discover a past life, your unconscious mind will reveal to you any karma that either began or was continued over into the life you are visiting. When you go back, allow yourself to experience what the suggestion brings out of your soul's memory. Then begin to collect the information that's brought forward from your unconscious mind. Focus on the first images you get and deepen them through all your different senses. Don't forget to zoom in and out so that you can get more than one view, if that works for you.

You may have several options for identifying your karma, depending on what you have learned about it. If it started before this life, you can ask your unconscious mind to take you back to the life that contains the same karmic connection. Then focus on the first images that come to you. Use all your senses to help focus more on your imagery trance. Once you have established a strong image, move the karma back through that life until you come to the point where it first began.

Now go forward until you reach the end of the life and examine the last thoughts and the after-death emotions that may have carried over into the next lifetime. Again, examine the relationships of the characters in that lifetime to learn how they're connected with other lifetimes and to you in your current lifetime. Also look for a theme of that life that may have been carried over into another one.

KARMIC CAUTIONS

You might need to examine several lifetimes before you have identified your karmic relationship with the past. It may take more than one session to follow the karma back to its beginnings. After all, it may have existed for a very long time. After each past life session, make notes in your journal about the karma you encountered and then develop a plan for your return visit.

Did your karma remain the same, or did it follow a theme through several past life plays? Did you have repeat characters sharing your past lives? If so, what was the same and what was different from life to life? Did you have an emotional karma that only involved yourself and not others? What other karma did you uncover in your journey into the memory of your soul?

Free Will: You Don't Have to Change

Okay, now that you have gathered some information about your karma, what do you want to do about it? You don't have to do anything if you don't want to. You can keep on going along the same path that you're on, but you can alter your life plan if you so choose. Of course, if you choose unwisely, you may have to revisit the lessons you are currently working on at a later date.

As you already know, the choice to follow your life plan or not is free will. Your life plan is dictated by how you followed your plan during your previous life. If you chose to stick with your lesson there, you moved forward in your soul's journey. If you didn't, you are now dealing with the leftover karma from your past. You may have a lot to work on or you may have already made improvements.

A younger soul may create a lot of karma, but does so out of desire to satisfy its ego. It is more prone to act without consciously thinking about the results of its actions. Only later does the soul realize that it has followed its will for personal satisfaction rather than staying in tune with its purpose. At this point in its development, it may not be paying attention to its potential.

An old soul, on the other hand, knows that it needs to stay true to its purpose. It may resent that it's not free to make its own decisions like a young soul. It is bound by its conscience or awareness that there is a purpose in life beyond material comfort and ego satisfaction. If you are an old soul, you know what it means to be out of sync with most everyone, and you probably resent that fact.

The old soul will often have many more arguments with itself than a younger soul. These arguments are often over the right to do what one pleases rather than to listen to the inner voice that says to do the right thing. An old soul will observe younger souls who seem to enjoy life without an awareness of the consequences of following their own free will. The old soul knows the consequences, but may choose to ignore them.

AGELESS INSIGHTS

As your soul evolved over many lifetimes, it slowly worked its way through the lessons of the universe. When all the lessons are learned, the "old soul" will return to the place where its journey began. There it will exist as a part of the collective unconscious and the knowledge of all its experiences.

Now that you have identified some of your karma and traced it back into other lifetimes, do you want to do anything about it or do you want to keep it as it is? You may have found that in one life your karma gave you a lot of pleasure, and in another it gave you a lot of pain. The pleasure comes when you are taking self-gratifying actions that do nothing to help you learn the lessons of the universe. That brief respite of self-indulgence can result in a much longer period of karmic payback.

"What goes around comes around" means that your quest for self-gain may require you to serve many of those people you mistreated during the time you misused power. If you are now in a vocation that seems menial and you have to serve many people, you may be able to regress back to a lifetime when you were in power and find that those you serve now, served you then. If you can locate such a lifetime, how did you treat others when you were in a position of power? If you are in a position of power or wealth now, you may want to consider how you are currently treating those who cross your life journey. Remember that every action you take now may result in karma in the future.

The choice is yours. You have the opportunity to create and resolve karma with every thought and action. You can go with your heart and soul, or you can listen to the voice inside that seeks to satisfy your ego. You may want to develop a karmic balance sheet in your journal and consider the actions you have taken and those you are contemplating. (Do you need a bigger journal yet?)

Healing the Past and the Present

Rediscovering your past lives can be a healing experience for your mind, body, and spirit. A visit back just may help you resolve some old karma that has been negatively impacting your life. There is a belief that many situations or conditions in your present life are related to actions taken in one or more past lives. In other words, the situations that affect your current life may be the result of the accumulation of experiences from other lifetimes.

Often an individual is not aware how much she is currently affected by past life experiences. One of the most common indicators is the experiencing of physical symptoms such as pain when doctors find nothing wrong. This condition may be diagnosed as psychosomatic pain or a pain created by the mind. However, to the person experiencing it, this phantom pain is very real and can have a major impact on their life.

> **SOUL STORIES**
>
> Betty found that every time she would make plans to travel, especially to new places, she would get sick to her stomach as the time for the trip approached. It impacted her ability to travel, and now that she was near retirement age, she wanted to find a way to overcome this annoying condition. It turned out that in a past life she was the daughter of a prosperous sea captain who traveled the world in search of his fortune. The young girl looked forward to the day she could sail with him, but when it finally came, she was violently ill from the moment they set sail. Her condition was so bad that her father was forced to return to shore and sail on alone.

Past life memories can manifest themselves through any one or more of the five senses. It could be a physical feeling like Betty's or it may be an emotion. It may be a visual image that comes to your mind in a light trance, a wakened state, or a dream. Images could be triggered when visiting a location that you may never have been to before. Some of them may be unpleasant and could be of a violent nature, such as war or other types of conflict. They could be of sickness or of an accidental death. They can often appear suddenly without warning and be so real that it can be disorienting to the one that experiences them.

Every year when summer began to wane and the early hints of fall could be felt in the air, Fran's usually upbeat mood changed to melancholy. It was often a bright sunny but cool day that caused the downturn of her spirits. She had no explanation for why, but just like clockwork, every year the same thing happened. She finally decided to look into the history of her soul for a possible reason.

She went to a past life specialist who used her memory of the heavy heart as a focus to lead her back into the images of her unconscious mind. What she saw was a young girl on a similar day playing alone near the edge of a lake. She had a feeling that someone was behind her. When she turned around, she saw a friend of her father's whom she had never trusted. This figure confused her as it was a memory from Fran's current life, and it had appeared in what she thought was a past life.

The specialist asked her to look for someone in the past life who was connected to this man. She instantly saw an image of a man riding an old-fashioned bicycle from the beginning of the twentieth century. It turned out that he was in love with Fran's widowed mother in that lifetime, and he was very jealous of the attention she gave to her daughter. He hatched a plan to dispose of her, sneaked up behind the child, dragged her into the water, and drowned her. The child was filled with a deep sadness as she made the transition into spirit, filled with remorse that it was ending in this manner.

Both Fran and Betty were able to find ways to resolve the karma from these past life traumas and to heal the physical and emotional effects they had suffered in their current lives. This was accomplished by creating a bridge to help them rediscover healthy and positive memories from before the negative experiences. You may find that this technique helps you heal not only your past but also your current mental, spiritual, or physical components.

- To establish a bridge to the past, find a comfortable place and, using the image technique that works best for you, allow your conscious mind to open to the images of a past life that may be negatively impacting your current life. Remember that at any time you want or need, you can always take a deep breath and come back to a state of consciousness, feeling positive and relaxed.

- Look for a scene that occurs a little before the traumatic event that may be impacting your current life. Watch this event unfold as if you are watching a movie so that you don't experience the emotions connected to the experience.

- After you have done this once or more, let yourself understand the feelings that you felt during that situation. You only need to experience just enough to give you the whole picture. Remember, you can use any of the five senses that work for you.

- Examine the death scene and let yourself become aware of your thoughts before and after your transition.

- Pull back for a moment and consider how this past life experience may be impacting your life now.

- Once you have done this, go back into the life and travel back to an earlier time when the conditions of that life were different and there are pleasant memories. It may be when you were a younger person in that life and had dreams of a positive future.

- When you have found this image, allow yourself to look through your eyes of that lifetime and be aware of your thoughts, emotions, and even how your physical body feels. This is a time with no thoughts of the trauma you will face later in that lifetime.

- Allow yourself to come back to the present, and in your mind, reach back and connect your present self to your self from that positive time in the other life.

- Allow your present self to show your past self that you are whole again and offer an unconditional universal healing energy to the area in that life that experienced the trauma.

- Suggest to yourself that you are now together again with the part of your soul memory that had somehow been disconnected from your unconscious mind and that you no longer need to experience the old karma that had affected you in your current lifetime.

- Let your body, mind, and spirit feel this positive connection to your past. Let yourself imagine moving forward in the future using the memories from your past that you have rediscovered.

- Now when you are ready, come back to the surface of your conscious mind, feeling positive and with a new connection to your past.

It may be that nothing was positive about that particular early life. If this is the case, it may be necessary to continue backward to an even earlier lifetime to find the connection to your unresolved karma. If you are aware that this might happen, you may continue back in your relaxed imagery state to the right images or you can choose to revisit the process later. Just remember to ask your unconscious mind to show you the images that are right and good for you at that moment.

Just allow yourself to go at a pace that is in sync with your soul's memories. Once you have gotten back to the source of this unresolved karma, go back to an early memory that isn't affected by what happened later. Connect to that positive early memory, experience it as it was in that lifetime through your five senses, and bring the experience forward into your conscious mind and your current life, merging the past and present together. Send back unconditional loving energy to the places in your soul's memory that were filled with trauma and allow yourself to feel the healing of your soul mentally, physically, and spiritually.

Soul Memory Healing Exercise

It's important to thoroughly understand how your unique mental imagery processes in your conscious mind. In other words, knowing how you create and remember images in your five senses of seeing, hearing, feeling, smelling, and tasting may help create better and more effective imagery for healing elements of your past lives. To help facilitate this, I am going to ask you some questions that can help you define how to better use your natural healing tools to heal your past life memories.

KARMIC CAUTIONS

This exercise would not be considered a healing, but more a resolution of old karma using imagery techniques. The object of this exercise or any others in this book is not to treat, diagnose, or cure any conditions of the mind, body, or spirit but to provide new ideas that can be incorporated with the wisdom of conventional medicine.

If you have the ability to create and receive images that are visual, think of a color that has a healing quality to it. This color could be the same every time or you can change it any time you want. Can you think of a color that means negativity to you? Perhaps you have the ability to see auras or energies connected to people, places, or events. If so, can you define the colors of a healing aura and a negative aura?

Do you have the ability to hear a sound in your mind that you define as a healing sound? It might be music, the ocean, water flowing, birds, or any other sound that is right for you. Can you turn up or soften this sound? Is there a color associated with this sound? Can you imagine a negative sound?

Can you imagine the texture of a healing color or a negative color? Can you imagine the feel of positive and negative energies? Are you trained in any healing modalities such as Reiki? Can you place yourself inside yourself in a past life memory and see, hear, feel, smell, and taste as you did before?

Can you create an image of a healing smell or taste as well as a negative smell or taste? Are there any other healing images that you can experience through your five senses? Remember, some of these images may not work for you, or some that do work may not be applicable to use when healing past life trauma.

It may be hard for you to define what unconditional loving energy is. For some people it's their love for an animal or a child, or doing good for others, or a connection to a spiritual source or power. Imagine taking in a breath of air that is filled with healing energy and full of unconditional love. You may find this imagery helpful to you as you send back healing energy over the negative parts of your soul memories.

Now you may find a comfortable place and, using the past life imagery technique that works best for you, ask your unconscious mind to take you back to the point in a past life that relates to something you wish to resolve or heal related to a condition in your current life. Remember that you can always take a deep breath and come back to your conscious mind, feeling relaxed and positive. Once you have reviewed the lifetime and have determined the point or points when you experienced a trauma that imprinted your soul's memory, let yourself create in your mind an image of what the negativity is like through your five senses.

Next, go to a point in the life where the energy was positive and connect that to your current life. Then send unconditional love back over all your images of healing. Let yourself feel this positive flow as it washes over the negative memories in your unconscious mind and feel them being cleared away by the positive healing images.

Now imagine yourself moving forward in your current life with this new view. Let yourself feel connected again to the part of your soul that was covered up by the old karma. When you are ready, come back to your conscious mind feeling positive and relaxed.

You may find that there is more than one lifetime related to the same trauma. If that is the case, then use this technique to review them. You could do more than one life in a single session or you could do it over several sessions. It's a good idea to make notes after each past life session. This can help you in planning for the next time you want to discover memories of a past life.

The Least You Need to Know

- You may currently be affected by the actions you took in your past lives.
- You have the right to choose if you want to resolve your karma or not.
- Resolving your karma can help get you back on track with your soul's purpose and move forward in your life.
- Once you are aware of karma, you always have the opportunity to change and resolve it.

Putting Past Talents to Use

In This Chapter

- Learning about your past life skills
- Revisiting artistic talents from a past life
- Rediscovering the writer in your past
- Using your psychic gifts from another lifetime
- How past fame can help you in this life

Have you discovered any past life talents yet on your journeys back in time? If so, what are they? Perhaps you were an artist, a writer, a great athlete, highly intuitive, or a famous person. If you were any of these, wouldn't it be nice to pick up where you left off during your other lives?

You may be able to do just that. This chapter will help you to identify and update the talents you had during a past life. You might think about reconnecting with your past life talents, as a Kellogg's cereal commercial suggests. To get you to retry the product, the commercial invites you to "discover it again for the first time."

You may already be drawn to and even excel in a past life ability. You just may not be aware that you were born already knowing how to use it. At the same time, you may have a special gift that's so natural that you dismiss it and don't use it in this life. Finally, it's possible that you don't want to have anything to do with a past life talent in this lifetime because of the unfinished karma attached to it. This chapter will help you to identify and understand how you can use your abilities from the past if you so desire.

Rediscovering Your Skills

Have you identified any abilities in a past life that you would like to put to use again? Perhaps you discovered that you did something you haven't remembered yet in your current life. If you excelled at a profession, you might want to try it again during this lifetime. You may have already made note in your journal of the occupations you had before. How do you suppose a prospective employer would react to your resumé if it listed your past life occupations as well as those in your current life? Do you think he would be ready for such a claim? Of course, it might be a little difficult to get any references for your past life abilities.

Knowing that you did something well in a past life might give you encouragement and confidence to redevelop what you were able to do before. The goal is for you to reacquaint yourself with your past life skills. To accomplish this, you will want to go back and experience again what you could do before.

SOUL STORIES

Cecilia was never a good student and had trouble concentrating in the classroom. She decided to study massage but was fearful she wouldn't be able to pass the course because of the homework. She was amazed by how she naturally was able to understand the human body and easily finished her studies. She discovered why when she visited a past life where she was a physician.

Remember that each of you will image your past life differently. If you can project yourself into your character, you will be able to feel what it was like when you first developed your abilities. The goal is for you to bring these old feelings of success back with you so that you can update them for your current life.

If you know the life you want to visit, prepare to return to it. Once you have entered your image trance and counted backward to zero, suggest to yourself that when you go back you will feel what it was like to have and use your skill from before. Now go back to that lifetime.

When you have arrived, let yourself experience the past life skill again. Project yourself into the mind of the character. How did she think? Feel the movements of the character in your past. Suggest to yourself that your muscles will remember these movements after you come back to your conscious mind.

Is there anything you know in your mind you can do very well but you have a resistance to even giving it a try? If you do, you may want to understand where you learned it in the first place, and where you learned *not* to want to do it. Maybe you have karma that has prevented you from using a past life skill or natural ability in this lifetime. Maybe it is being blocked by a *suppressed memory* because of a traumatic situation connected to it.

> **DEFINITION**
>
> A **suppressed memory** is one that is buried in your unconscious mind and is only remembered when a situation jogs it. Then it may come flooding back to the surface and cause you to replay the original experience in your mind. Once you resolve the negative part of the memory, you can reconnect with the ability you had before, as you would use it now.

You can bridge yourself back through this life into the past life or lives that relate to your gift and your karma attached to it. Note where you first developed it and where and how you learned to either mistrust or hate it. When you have finished, reunite your past life skills with yourself in this life and give yourself permission to use your ability in a positive way for yourself and others.

Were You an Artist?

Artistic abilities surface in many different ways. You may have been such a natural as a child that you eventually lost interest because it wasn't challenging enough for you. You may still use your creative talent but wish you could develop it further. You may not think that you have ability, but others tell you that you do.

Do you have a natural creative talent? It may be arranging flowers, redecorating your house or apartment, designing and building your own furniture, or putting colors together in ways that bring many compliments. It may be so easy for you that you think everyone else has the same ability. If you get a lot of positive feedback about something creative that you do, then it's a talent that others probably do not have. If that's the case, perhaps you would like to develop it even further.

AGELESS INSIGHTS

Did you ever wonder why some people excel at art while others can't draw a straight line? Maybe they have developed their talent over several lifetimes. Remember that everyone has creative gifts. Your gift is directly linked to your mental DNA. You will use your strongest senses to produce your best work. If you have no pictures in your mind, you will paint differently than someone who has strong visual imagery.

The goal of this chapter is to help you identify where you first learned your "natural" talent and to help you update your abilities from previous lifetimes to the present. To accomplish this, you may first identify what artistic interest you would like to investigate from your past. It may be something you already do or did at one time in your life. It may be something you've always had a great interest in and want to learn where it came from. It may be a time period when great artists lived that you would like to visit to see if you have some sort of a connection with it. Put your travel plan together.

If you have a specific artistic medium that you would like to try or perfect, you will want to have some material ready to practice with. It could be paper and pencils, or paint, brushes, canvas, clay, or some other material. You may already have the right equipment, or you may want to purchase or borrow some. If you are able to put yourself in the mind and body of the character in your past life, you can try to let yourself be taught by who you were then.

You may want to work with a partner at first to assist you when you try out your artistic talent in an image trance state. He can help hand you your supplies and guide you through your project. This will help you focus on the artistic experience you had in a past life. It may take a few attempts before you're able to put yourself in the artistic trance zone. Once you are used to the procedure, you should be able to accomplish your creative trance without the help of someone else.

When you are ready, get comfortable and count yourself backward from five to zero using the induction that works best for you. Once you have entered a comfortable and relaxing image trance, suggest to yourself that when you journey back to the lifetime where you were an accomplished artist, you will allow yourself to experience the skills of the person you were in the past. Also suggest that you will feel your muscles moving the same way and that you will understand how you thought in the past. Suggest that you will remember this when you come back to your conscious mind and will be able to continue developing your artistic gifts from your past.

KARMIC CAUTIONS

If there was karma attached to your artistic talent, suggest to yourself that you only need to feel just enough of the emotion so that you will be able to experience your old gift. If the feelings are too intense, you can always take a deep breath, exhale, open your eyes, and come back to your conscious mind.

Now go to the life where you first developed your artistic skills. Before your experience, go through the lifetime and learn as much about the artist as possible. First be the observer, and when you're ready, step into the experience. Now work with the material and let the artist of old create again. Once you have completed your experience, suggest that you will continue to open your unconscious mind to your soul's artistic gifts after you have returned to your conscious state. Count yourself back up to five.

Were you able to bring your artistic talent from a past life forward to where you are now? The more you practice what you already know, the more you will hone your soul's skills again. Be patient with yourself now and with who you were in the past. If you work together, you will again find yourself in tune with your abilities of old.

Were You a Writer?

Some authors use past life memories to write stories from their pasts. The writer may have developed the skills to produce beautiful and powerful written words some time ago. She may have captured the memories of her soul and is now able to write them for others to benefit from. Taylor Caldwell's books are a great example of how her memories from past lives surfaced when she wrote novels about specific time periods. She was able to write descriptions imaged through her unconscious mind that actually proved to be historically accurate. You may be able to have the same past life recall that provides stories of your own soul's memories.

Do you have an interest in writing? Do you write now or do you have a deep feeling that you want to be a writer? You may be hearing the whispers of a memory locked deep in your unconscious mind. Did you tell stories from different times when you were a child? Do you have an imagination that is rich in memories from the past? If you do, perhaps you were a writer in another life. Do you use this talent in your present lifetime? If not, perhaps you would like to give it a try.

Do you keep a journal? If you do, you may already have the seeds that will help your ideas grow into a novel. You may have had stories come to you in your dreams or just pop out of your unconscious mind with such clarity that they seem to be already written. Perhaps they were, and by you. Now you may be able to reconnect with the writer within.

There are two ways to work with the writer in your past. One is to go back through image trance and connect with your soul's experience. Just as with other art forms, you can feel what it was like to be the writer of old. You can study that lifetime and understand how the ability to write was first developed. You can also resolve any old karma that may be hindering your ability to write in this lifetime.

To go back, follow a normal focus procedure, counting backward and then suggesting to yourself to journey to the time when you were a writer before. Make sure you have something to write with and plenty of paper for your adventure. If you have a partner for the first few times, it may help you focus on your past life session. Review the life first, and then if you are able, let yourself experience how the writer thought and what it felt like to write during that time. Try holding a pen or pencil over a piece of paper and see what happens. Suggest to yourself that you will bring forward your writer soul memory to your conscious mind and update your old skills into your current lifetime.

You may also access your past life memories through automatic writing. Automatic writing happens while you are in an image trance. You can focus your conscious mind on many different things while you write down your unconscious thoughts and images. You don't even need to know what your hand is writing.

SOUL STORIES

Rich knew he had a story he wanted to write, but every time he sat down to put his thoughts on paper, nothing came through. The more he tried, the more frustrated he became. He felt as if something was clamping down on his head and squeezing his brain. He discovered in a past life where he had been killed by a severe blow to the head for writing documents that were unacceptable to the powers that ruled the land. He was able to go back and reconnect with his ability to write before he was persecuted.

To try automatic writing, choose the way you want to set the words of your soul down on paper. It may be with pencil, pen, typewriter, or computer. You can sit at a desk or in a chair, whatever is best for you. Start out with focusing on your image trance. Suggest to yourself that when you're ready, your unconscious mind will connect you with your soul memories and you will let the writer in your past come through your fingers. You may or may not be consciously aware of what you are writing. It may take a little practice to find the best technique for you, but you could have a great story of the past waiting to be told again.

Did You Have a Psychic Gift?

Are you psychic? Actually, everyone is psychic to some degree. Many times a psychic gift is more like a curse. You may know things that you don't want to know. If you have this ability, then you probably live in constant dread that you will suddenly get images of something that will have a negative outcome in the future. It may be a premonition of a death of a family member or friend or a world disaster.

This type of psychic experience often starts during your teen years at a time when you are very open to the images of your unconscious mind. You actually enter a light trance such as a daydream, and all of a sudden you focus on what your unconscious mind is projecting up to you. The images may be of things that you don't understand. You may even become aware that you're leaving your body and are floating up into the universe. That experience can be very scary to anyone who experiences it for the first time, especially to a teenager who is totally unprepared. After the first time, people often live in constant fear of it happening again.

The word *psychic* means "from the human soul." It is the belief that your intuitive abilities in this life are a direct result of past life experiences. This could be true for you. You may be directly influenced by your soul's memories of past life psychic talents. The more you developed your gifts in the past, the stronger their images may be in your unconscious mind today.

Do you have a psychic ability that you would like to understand? Perhaps it's something you would like to use more or just understand more about. It's experienced through the senses that are strongest for you. If you are visual, you may get pictures of events that have not yet happened. If you have a strong sense of hearing, you may have a voice in your head give you information about the future or the past. The same goes for feelings, smell, and taste. These senses have all been developed in a past life to the point that they now work for you. Understanding how you developed them can help you put them to use again in your current lifetime.

Psychic ability and karma can go hand in hand. As I've said, many intuitive people do not enjoy having their gift at all. The experiences you have had before may have been related to survival or overcoming extreme circumstances that gave you great strength. When those abilities are triggered now, the situations are probably a lot different.

An old adversary from your past may have a much different role to play in this lifetime, but your unconscious mind may not know about the change. It is still involved with the conflict from before. Your old survival skills surface without warning. If this is the case for you, you may want to go back and resolve the karma related to your psychic talent from the past.

To go back and investigate a past life when you developed and used psychic abilities, let yourself go into an image trance and count yourself backward from five to zero. Suggest to yourself that you will go back to a lifetime where you learned and developed your psychic talents. Now let yourself travel back to that time. Review the entire life and look for any resulting karma that might have begun because of your abilities. Look for any characters that may also be a part of your life now and note the relationship. Let yourself resolve any karma that may have resulted from your psychic power from the past. Suggest that when you come back to consciousness, you will again be able to reunite your psychic gifts of the past with where you are at the moment.

Now let yourself experience what it was like to be psychic in that lifetime. Bring forward how the different senses imaged so that you will be able to use them again. Feel yourself reuniting with your psychic gifts of the past as they update to your current life. Suggest that you will remember how to use this ability when you come back to the surface of your conscious mind. When you are ready, count yourself back from zero up to five and open your eyes, feeling relaxed, positive, and filled with the peaceful and loving energy of the universe.

Were You Famous?

Perhaps you really were a person of great stature and fame in the past. Do you think you might have been? If this is the case, you may be able to bring your leadership qualities or other qualities forward to help you and others in this lifetime. Of course, just because you were famous doesn't mean you were on the right side of the law. You might have been a powerful scoundrel or controlling ruler.

You may have brought some of these issues with you into your current lifetime. The difference here is that your role in the play is not the same as it was before. This life may be one of service or humility. You may be dealing with the karma you created back then.

KARMIC CAUTIONS

Edgar Cayce cautioned about the dangers of finding out you were a famous person in a past life. It can be a problem if the individual expects to be pampered and have all the wealth and power she may have had before. Of course, the scene of the play has changed, and her role is different now. Trying to live in the past can keep you from addressing the lessons of this lifetime.

Knowing your past can be helpful to you as you journey through your current life. It can help you avoid the pitfalls that are always waiting to pull you off track. The key is to work toward updating the power you held from before in a way that keeps you in tune with your soul's journey. The famous person you were before can lend expertise to help you work to find the balance for the character you are now.

To go back and visit the famous person you once were, let yourself go into your focus imagery trance and count yourself backward from five to zero. When you get to zero, suggest that you will go back to a lifetime when you were famous. You may already have an idea of when that might be, or you might not have a clue at all. Use the past life discovery technique that you're the most comfortable with. Let yourself travel back in time.

The Least You Need to Know

- You can bring your talents from another life with you.
- You can draw upon your past artistic ability in this lifetime.
- You may have some stories from the past to write.
- Psychic abilities don't have to be a burden if you learn from your past how to use them again.
- If you were famous before, it may be a help in your current life.

Future and Parallel Lives

In This Chapter

- Finding out about future lifetimes
- How to create a future life discovery plan
- What's it like to go forward in time?
- Between-lifetime experiences
- Living in parallel lifetimes

Many of you may invest a lot of money visiting psychics who can predict your future. You want to know about your relationships, your prosperity, and your health. You may spend a lot of time and energy worrying about a day that hasn't yet come.

Just imagine what it would be like to know the future in this lifetime as well as the next lifetime. What would you do with the knowledge? Would it be a help or a hindrance to you in your current situation?

You might also want to know what happens to your soul when it is between lifetimes. Where does it go? What does it do? Besides questions about your past, these questions may also be addressed with the help of a relaxing image trance.

A Peek into the Future

By now you have plenty of experience discovering your past lives. What do you think about discovering future lifetimes? You might ask what that is. The concept is similar to discovering your past lives except that you are going ahead in time to the future instead. Do you think this is a good idea or even possible?

Have you ever imagined what the future will be like? If this is of interest to you, you will get your chance to find out before this chapter is over. Perhaps you are already in the habit of visiting psychics who can help you anticipate and plan your future in this lifetime. Discovering a future life may take you one step further down the path of your soul's journey.

> **KARMIC CAUTIONS**
>
> You should not attempt to do a future life discovery alone. Always work with a qualified past life specialist or a psychic who has a recognized ability to see into your future lives. Having someone else there can assist you in processing what you may experience.

Is a future lifetime experience real or imagined? You'll have to decide that for yourself, just as you did when you imagined a past life session. It may be just your imagination, or you may be able to tap into the universal knowledge that knows all facets of time—the past, the present, and the future. The theory of *quantum mechanics* states that everything in the universe is related. Psychiatrist Carl Jung believed that all time is accessible on the unconscious level. Therefore, the collective unconscious contains not only the knowledge of the past but of the future as well. If you believe this theory, you may be able to go to the Akashic Book of Records and look up your future lives.

> **DEFINITION**
>
> **Quantum mechanics** is the theory that every particle or cell contains energy and exists independently of each other. On the metaphysical level, every cell contains the universal life energy that holds the keys to the knowledge of the universal mind.

To take the quantum mechanics theory a little further, there are those who believe that all time exists at once. In other words, the past, present, and future all are happening together. There are even organizations that attempt to go back in time and heal some of the events that happened in the past, such as wars and other oppression. There are also those who put great faith in the predictions of Edgar Cayce, Nostradamus, and the Bible. They live their lives preparing for events that have not yet happened.

There are both pros and cons about going forward in time. Just as Edgar Cayce warned about letting the knowledge of a past life interrupt your current lessons, so could the knowledge of a future lifetime. If you develop a clear objective in your travel plan, it can help clarify your goals when you journey into your future. Your reason for discovering a future life may influence the type of information you receive when you get there.

What about free will? What will you do with the information you receive about your future lives? Will you use it for self-gain, or will you use it to help find a better balance in your life now? You may not know how you will react until you have experienced a future life. It is your free will to do as you want or should. Your faith plays an important role in the outcome of your travels into the future.

SOUL STORIES

When Adam wanted to visit a future life, he could see the life ahead of him, but he was unable to focus on it. After trying unsuccessfully to make a connection, he concluded that the future was not for him to know at this time. He realized he needed to focus on the now.

Establish a Travel Plan

Why do you want to see into the future? It's important to establish clear objectives as a part of your travel plan. As you consider some of the reasons for traveling into the future, make notes in your journal to help you define your goals. Part of your plan should be the flexibility to just go with the experience.

Your reasons for visiting a future life could come from a combination of your experiences in past lives and your present lifetime. You may wish to find out how a karmic relationship may get resolved. Or you may have an affliction that has no cure at the moment. Perhaps you could find an answer in the future that you could bring back with you, just as memories and talents from the past have been brought forward into the present.

You may just be curious to find out what it will be like in a future time. You may want to write about the future and would like to research it with a future life discovery experience. You may want to find out if your struggle in this lifetime will be rewarded the next time around. You might be looking for motivation and encouragement to continue on in the direction you are headed. There are many different reasons why you would want to know what your future lifetimes could be like.

For example, one young man who was suffering from a serious debilitating disease wanted to know what his next life would be like if he chose to end the pain and suffering he was currently experiencing. What do you think? Would he have karma? Is his situation caused by past karma? Even if his body is deteriorating, he could use his mind in a positive way to inspire others. If he did this, would he advance his soul's journey? If he doesn't address his lessons now, will they come back again next time?

When you create your future life discovery plan, you may find it helpful to work with a partner the first few times to help guide you. Much of the preparation will be the same as when you experienced a past life discovery session. You can write it out and record it, or have your partner read it to you, or you could memorize it and repeat it to yourself as you focus on your future life discovery. You will want to have materials available for making notes about your journey, and it would be helpful to record or videotape the session.

You should be in a comfortable place where you won't be interrupted during your future life session. Have a warm blanket ready in case you get a chill on your journey. If you're a veteran of past life discovery, then this is all something that you are familiar with. However, it doesn't hurt to review the process from time to time. You can choose the technique you feel will work the best for you (see Chapter 14).

Remember to use the who, what, when, where, and why observation technique for a future life discovery experience (see Chapter 13).

If you aren't familiar with your mental DNA, you will also want to review Chapter 6 so that you'll be prepared to use all five of your sensory image abilities. The better the flight checklist you develop and use before each travel into time, either backward or forward, the greater the chance is that you will have an informative and productive experience.

- WHO do you want to visit in a future lifetime? Would you like to know what kind of a relationship you would have in the next life with someone you're connected to in this life? It could be a relative, a friend, or even someone you have a conflict with. You may have more than one person whom you want to do future research on.

- WHAT do you want to learn when you go forward in time? The better the definition, the clearer your information may be. There are many different questions that you could ask in a future life. Try to focus on just one or a few at a time so that you won't receive more information than you can remember.

- WHEN is the time period that you want to journey to? Do you want to go just to your next life or to several future lives? You may have a certain time period that you want to investigate, such as the twenty-fifth century. You may want to go forward in time and check out what it's like 100 years from now. If you know when you want to visit, write it into your travel plan.

- WHERE would you like to go when you progress into the future? Do you have a particular location in mind? You may want to know what the area where you live will look like, or you may have an interest in a certain country or geographical location. Of course, your soul may be assigned there in lives to come.

- WHY do you want to progress? The better you can define your reasons, the greater the possibility that you won't be disappointed when you get there. This goal will also address why you want to have this information and how you will use it once you have returned from your experience into a future lifetime.

Karl wanted to know if the work he has been doing in this life to create environmental awareness would help the earth in the future. He progressed forward to a time when the earth was much more energy efficient, and the quality of life was much better. Now he can go about this life believing that his work is actually helping to shape the future.

Create a Future Life Discovery Technique

If you're ready to travel into the future, find a place where you won't be interrupted, and get comfortable. To begin your image relaxation trance, take a comfortable breath of air, exhale slowly, and continue to do so. Let yourself focus on your third eye and begin to feel the peaceful and loving energy of the universe start to flow into your body. Feel the golden protective light of the universe surrounding your body as you continue to breathe slowly in and out. You may allow the muscles in your body to begin to relax as you prepare to count backward from five to zero. Let yourself feel in tune with your faith and your inner and outer guidance systems that are always with you to watch over you.

You may suggest to yourself that if you want or need to end your image trance, you can always take a comfortable relaxing breath, exhale, open your eyes, and come back to your conscious mind. You will always feel relaxed and positive after a trip into the future. You will always feel the peaceful and loving energy of the universe protecting you.

When you are ready, begin to focus on your imagery trance by counting slowly backward from five to zero. With each count you may feel yourself going deeper and deeper into an image trance. With each count you will feel more and more relaxed as you prepare to journey into a future lifetime.

When you get to zero, you may enjoy the peaceful and loving energy of the universe as it flows from your unconscious mind. You may ask permission of your soul to go forward in time by asking a finger to rise when your unconscious mind is ready. If for some reason this isn't the right time for you to visit your future, ask that one of your thumbs rise to indicate it would be better to wait until another time. Once you have gotten permission and you are ready, you may follow your travel plan ahead in time to the life you want to visit.

AGELESS INSIGHTS

You may repeat positive words to yourself during your future life discovery session, such as *relaxing, peaceful, loving, focus,* and you will feel their meaning every time you say them. With each count you will focus more and more on your imagery trance.

If you want to go to the Akashic Records, you may feel yourself gently floating upward until you come to the place where they are stored. Once there, you may begin to look up your future lifetimes in the book of your soul. You may find a computer waiting for you, or even a video center. In whatever form the Akashic Records appear, just let yourself go with the experience. Look for the potential advances in your soul's journey and karmic hazards that may be ahead of you. Once you have gathered your information, you may come back to your body and count yourself back up from zero to five, open your eyes, and come back to consciousness feeling relaxed, positive, and full of peaceful loving energy.

If you are using a movie or library technique, you may focus on your future life discovery trance just as you did your past life ones and follow your travel plans. Focus on the first images you receive with the strongest of your senses. First review the life and look for the theme and the relationships to any of the characters there and compare it to your current life.

Once you have done this, put yourself into the image and experience what it's like to live in a future time. Make as many notes as you can, and when you're ready, count yourself back up from zero to five and return to your conscious mind. Take some time and review your experience. Make notes in your journal so that you can sift through the data whenever you want to.

Can Future Knowledge Help You Right Now?

What will you do with the information you got from a visit into the future? Will you use it for self-gain to avoid your soul's lessons, or will you use it in a way that helps you stay in tune with your current purpose? You have the free will to do with it as you choose. The question is, "Will you create or resolve your karma?"

KARMIC CAUTIONS

Is the future cast in stone? Will it come true as you imaged it? It may be similar to getting a psychic reading. When you are told about something that will happen in the future, what if you take action now to change the outcome? Imagine that you were told that if you drove on a certain road at a certain time, you would have an accident. Would you drive on that road at that time? Probably not. So what about the prediction? Why didn't it come true?

The question brings you back to the concept of quantum mechanics. At the time of the prediction, the outcome is just a probability that will result if the current life pattern continues to be followed. The future is constantly changing, depending on the actions taken in every moment. You can take a chance that your next lifetime will be what you want it to be, or you can work with your current one to prepare for the next one in the best way you can.

What if a future lifetime doesn't look very promising? Remember Mr. Scrooge? The character in Charles Dickens's story *The Christmas Carol* dreamed of what the future held in store for him. He didn't like it, and he changed the outcome, not only for himself, but also for other characters in the story. You may want to make some positive changes in your current life that will be good for you as well as for others as you prepare for the future.

What do you do now if you think you'll have a fabulous life next time? The answer is the same. Concentrate on your current lifetime, regardless of what you see in the future. If you stay in tune with your soul's purpose in this lifetime, you may advance beyond the lessons that your soul needed to learn. That decision is yours; it is also part of your free will and can have a positive effect on your future lives.

Can future knowledge help you right now? The answer is yes if you use it in a way that helps you stay in tune with your soul's purpose. The answer may not have been exactly what you wanted to know, but it may be what is currently right for you. It is up to you to decide.

In-Between Lives: Life Reviews and Sacred Contracts

Many people have had near-death experiences where they were aware that they had left their bodies and found themselves going back over their life to review the advances or setbacks they may have encountered during their current lifetime. Some recalled that a being or an angel was guiding them to show them the gains and losses that were a part of their life experience. These post-death reports can be used to review the goals the soul established before it entered the earth plane in its current incarnation. These goals are often called "sacred contracts," and indicate that a soul draws up a plan or blueprint for each lifetime based on the experiences from the most recent lifetime.

SOUL STORIES

June's routine operation turned out to be anything but routine. In the middle of it her heart stopped beating, and while the operating team worked on her to get her pulse back, June took a little journey with a kindly being who showed her back through her life map. The review was a nonjudgmental examination of how she had gone about honoring her pre-birth contract. At one point in the journey a voice came to her stating, "It's not your time yet." Then she felt what she later described as a "body slam" when she was returned to the living. It was an experience that changed her life and her perception of what happens on the other side.

There is a belief that we actually choose the experiences we have in each life. It seems hard to believe that we might choose to be poor or have a handicap. Even some of those unpleasant relationships we've experienced may have been part of our contract. The argument for this philosophy is that we need to experience all kinds of different life situations to balance our soul as it makes its way back to the core of the universe.

How can reviewing your sacred contract help you now? Going back to before this life may help you gain some answers as to why your life has gone the way it has. If you have an idea of what experiences you chose and why you chose them, it may give you some insights to help you work with situations you may be dealing with and actually help you to continue to gain and grow in this life. It's our ego or free will that can get us out of sync with our purpose. When we search for self-fulfillment, it often gets us out of sync with our contract's purpose. Awareness can always help us get back on course.

Here is an exercise that may help you connect your previous life review and the formation of your contract for this life.

- Find a comfortable place and let your mind drift back to your last lifetime, using the method that works best for you. Remember, you can always come back to the surface of your conscious mind, feeling positive and relaxed any time you want to.

- Allow yourself to watch the end of that life and then feel what it's like to drift outside the body in soul form.

- Let yourself go to a place in your mind where there is someone to help you review the lessons of this lifetime.

- Use all the imagery senses that work for you to examine these lessons and learn why they happened and what you may gain from them.

- After you have completed this review, follow your soul as it rests and prepares to return to Earth for your current lifetime.

- Ask your unconscious mind to access the memory of how and why you chose the lessons in this life that you've been experiencing. Ask to know the reasons for these lessons. It's possible that the karma you have chosen to work on involves more than one of your lifetimes.

- Let your images come to you in all of your five senses. It may be that you will just have a knowing or an awareness of the purpose of this life that you didn't have before you tried this exercise.

- Once you have completed this experience, let yourself come back to consciousness and ask yourself how you can use the information you have discovered in a positive way as you go forward in your life.

If you don't image a lot of information, don't worry about it. What you receive may be just what is needed at the time you discover it. After all, you are part of your soul and the answers are within you.

SOUL STORIES

Jan had an unusual experience while she was traveling to a past lifetime. She was describing a house that she had lived in before, when she began to see two different images of it. One was a small building and the other had been enlarged. As the past life experience continued, she discovered that after she had died in that lifetime, her soul continued to exist on the earth plane for a period of time. As a ghost she lived in the house while it was expanded to its later size. This was the explanation for her two different views of the same location.

Parallel Lifetimes

What would you think if someone told you that we live in the past, the moment, and the future, all at the same time? That is a theory embraced by experts in the field of past life research, including Dick Sutphen, the author of *Past Lives, Future Loves*. Sutphen uses a three-dimensional chessboard to explain this concept. Could you imagine a game that was played on three different levels and the participants were free to make moves on any level they wanted to? In other words, a situation that you're experiencing in this life could also be having an effect on a past or future life at the same time. Imagine one part of you living in the moment while another part of you may be living in the past or the future concurrently.

Dr. Lisa Halpin uses the illustration of an old 33⅓ LP record to illustrate parallel lifetimes. She explains that on a record having a dozen songs all recorded by the same artist, it is possible to place the needle on the third selection or the fifth and hear the song you have chosen. Each song represents a different lifetime. When the needle is moved to a different track, you hear a different song. Each song on the album may affect your mood in the same or different way. A sad song may make you sad, a happy song may make you happy, a slow song may relax you, or a fast song may ramp up your energy. In the same way, whenever you are connected to a sad past life, you may feel sad when there is no reason to be sad.

AGELESS INSIGHTS

The question is, "Are all these different past or even future lifetimes playing at the same time or are you remembering your past lives?" Only you know the answer to that question deep within your soul.

These different theories may be confusing. You can become bogged down trying to figure out which one to accept. Are we living our lives all at once or do we follow a progression from the first lifetime to the last lifetime? Whatever theory you subscribe to, if you have positive results from your past life discovery experiences, then it is right for you. At least you know that someone else may approach the subject a little differently.

The Least You Need to Know

- It's important to establish clear future life goals.
- Use the knowledge of future lives to help you stay in tune with your soul's lessons in your current life.
- You can encounter in-between lifetime experiences when you have either a past or future life discovery session.
- You may experience living more than one of your lives at the same time.

Balancing Your Lives

In This Chapter

- Putting your past experiences to use
- Getting in touch with your soul's purpose
- Rediscovering lost talents and other abilities
- Using past life discoveries in the future
- Creating goals for the future

The evidence has been gathered and examined. Now it's time to present it to the judge and jury—you! What is your verdict on the case for past lives? Did you find enough evidence to support it? Do you need further research? Is it really necessary to believe?

If you have found that doing the exercises in this book has helped you, regardless of whether or not you believe in past lives, now is the time to make your plans for the future. You can use your newfound knowledge from the past to help you as you move forward. Now is the time to put your rediscovered abilities to use.

Using Past Positive and Negative Experiences in the Present

Have you ever had a perfect experience in your life? It could have been something that you made or a place you lived or visited. It may have been a relationship or an event such as a holiday. It was a time when everything came together and you were in absolute bliss. Have you ever had an experience that was that perfect?

You are the product of your past. Once you have had a perfect experience, can you ever call anything less a success? A perfectionist couldn't. A perfectionist's experiences are often painful because his standards required to achieve *perfection* are very high. A tiny flaw can be amplified so that it covers up everything else that may be right.

DEFINITION

Perfection is the highest degree of excellence or experience or proficiency at something that one can achieve. Do you try to match a standard that you were able to reach only once before? If you do, where did you learn to recognize that standard in the first place? Did you acquire it during this life, or were you born with it?

The search for perfection can expand beyond one lifetime. You may have been searching for something that you experienced a long time ago in one or more past lives. Up until now, your soul memories have been the responsibility of your unconscious mind. Now you know how to retrieve them.

Perhaps you look at the world through "rose-colored glasses" and never see anything wrong. You might only see the good in someone who would take advantage of you if she were given the slightest opportunity. Your detached view of the world could have been created during a lifetime when the good you saw was good. There was no bad to experience. You may not be able to see the warning signs until it is too late because you have never learned how. This could be karma that started in a past life that you have not yet learned to resolve.

All of the experiences from your past lives, both negative and positive, are a wealth of knowledge that you can learn from. You know this now, but look around you at the many people who are unaware of how they may be influenced by their past. They may be stuck in karmic patterns that you have learned to resolve. At the same time, you may have some more to discover and resolve.

You have probably been told that you learn from your mistakes. You may have made some in your past lives that are still haunting you in this life. Now you have a choice of continuing the same cycle or finally resolving these mistakes. In fact, you have more of an opportunity to do this from negative past life experiences than positive ones. The positive ones are those that often drive you to match them again, and that is nearly impossible. The negative ones give you the chance to change rather than repeat them. When you find something that went wrong in a past life, you now can change its pattern.

> **SOUL STORIES**
>
> Remember Stephanie? She was one of the past life discovery sessions in Chapter 8. Her past life experiences in Atlantis have had a negative impact on her current life. Once she was able to understand the karma of her past, she has been able to silence the critical voices in her head and go beyond the unconscious limitations that had stopped her progress in this life. She also feels that she has healed the negative experiences from the Atlantis lifetime.

You may have heard the saying, "If life hands you a bunch of lemons, make lemonade." Your past life mistakes as well as your accomplishments can help you get in tune with your soul's purpose. It just takes the willingness to look for and practice your lessons that are waiting for you in this lifetime.

Remember, you can resolve the negative karma from your past lives. You can also use the positive experiences even during current situations that may cause you to wish you lived in the past. In other words, a perfect life before can be used as a model to reach toward again. Remember that you need to update the past and readjust it for your present life. If you are open to the memories of your soul, you will constantly learn from all of your past.

Get in Tune with Your Soul's Purpose

You now have had experiences in discovering your past lives, and probably you have a journal filled with notes on your encounters. You have identified your old karma and have taken action to resolve it. Now you have begun to take the steps that will help you get in tune with your soul's purpose.

So how do you know what that purpose is? Did you come into this life with a master plan? There is nothing that could be called tangible evidence, so what really is locked away in your unconscious mind? Does it contain the instructions for your soul's journey?

How can you get to the truth regarding your soul's purpose? Where do you look for the answers? Is it through religion? Can you find it in the many books and workshops that advise you on the way to live your life? Do you listen to your conscience and make decisions as to how you feel inside? Do you live for today and let tomorrow take care of itself? Do you live in fear of tomorrow? Where can you find the answer? Have you consciously been searching for the truth?

Whether you are aware of it or not, your unconscious mind is always searching for the truth. That search, unfortunately, can take many detours along the winding journey of your soul. You may have been trying to live your life in a past life pattern that's not the same now as it was before. There may be positive and negative components to that pattern. You may not have to get rid of the whole, just the part that is holding you back from your life purpose. You can change old behavior patterns; it just takes the willingness to examine them and to communicate with the voice inside you that represents your free will.

An old fault from a past life may actually be a gift or talent in this lifetime if you are willing to resolve the karma attached to it. Where you used your abilities for self-satisfaction and gain in another life, you can use for good in your current life. Of course, you can still use your power for self-gain. The choice is yours.

SOUL STORIES

Pam was convinced that she had been paying the price in this life for using her beauty in the past for self-gain because she is a very short person. She feels she must do all she can to help others without being recognized. Looking into her past, she found that life where she misused her striking appearance and slowly accepted the fact that real beauty is more than skin deep.

You may already be unknowingly working toward getting your soul's purpose back on course. It happens to many people who don't believe in past lives or the nature of karma. They may endure a traumatic experience mentally, physically, or spiritually and suddenly change. They find it impossible to go back to their old lifestyle because the unconscious knowing of their soul's purpose is now influencing them. They cannot explain it, and they still have the free will to fight it, but they are changed. They have been given the opportunity to get in tune with their life map.

It takes patience and practice to develop your ability to communicate with your soul. Just like learning to tune and play a stringed musical instrument, there is a learning period. Many beginners never get beyond that stage because they expect instant success. Success is an ongoing process. To a beginner, an intermediate can sound like a well-trained master. The master, however, is always seeking to improve. She is well aware of what is left to accomplish.

The same is true as you learn to play the music of your soul. The more you practice, the more in tune you will become. There is always more you can learn. You have at your fingertips the masters of the universe and the memories of your soul; all you need to do is to be open to their wisdoms to help you fine-tune your soul's purpose.

Rediscovering Lost Talents and Other Abilities

You can also use this method of examining your past to reconnect with lost abilities. For example, you may have always wanted to sing but have a fear of performing in public. You could be an art lover but not have the confidence to pick up a paintbrush. You may have a psychic gift but stop short of sharing it with others. Most of us have a passion to be creative in one medium or another, and yet for some reason, we never allow ourselves to develop our natural abilities and skills. It's possible that a past life incident could be the cause of your inability to access your ability in this life.

People often expect that they will have a similar experience to what others may have told them or what they have read about. It just doesn't work that way. If you are nonvisual, you are more than likely not going to rediscover your past life memories through visual images. You may not be able to step into the images at all. You may feel as if you're making the whole thing up. It doesn't matter as long as you are open to receiving information that may give you a different perspective on a situation or condition that you are trying to understand. The more you know how your mind forms images, and the more you are consciously aware of them, the easier it becomes to rediscover your soul's memories of your past lives.

KARMIC CAUTIONS

The memories of your soul are always available to you. All you need to do is stay in touch with your unconscious mind. You can do this easily through the use of image trances. You have learned to peek through the veil and open the window to your past.

Judy was a natural artist who enjoyed sketching human figures. She was good at it, but wanted to go into the subject matter with more depth. She went back and rediscovered how she had learned anatomy in another life. She then merged her ability from the past with her conscious mind. She imagined how she would sketch using this information and could see the outcome in her mind. This knowledge helped her establish a new depth to her artistic abilities, one that she had known all along as it waited to be reconnected, just below the surface of her conscious mind.

Continue to Use Your Ability to Discover Past Lives

Now that you have developed the ability to discover and experience your past lives, what do you want to do with it after you finish this book? It's not unusual for someone to get very excited about something new that he has learned and make great plans to continue his study after he has finished his initial experience. Unfortunately, as time goes on, often a person's enthusiasm diminishes, and it's not long until his newfound skills become rusty and unused. Perhaps you can think of similar occurrences in your life.

Once you have learned to experience and interpret a past life discovery session, you don't have to make much of an effort to keep your new skills honed and ready to use. You may have spent a great deal of time during the course of reading this book and doing the exercises. Your investment can really pay off if you continue to use your ability to consult with your past.

AGELESS INSIGHTS

Just being conscious of the fact that every thought and daily encounter can be connected to the past can help you be more aware of life itself. When you consider every action you take in terms of your soul's journey, you are also focusing your mind on your present. You may never look at life the same way again!

You now have the opportunity to examine two different views, the old and the new. The new perspective is actually gained from examining your past. That past, of course, spans many lifetimes. Your knowledge and ability to experience your soul's memories provides you with the opportunity to consider your life differently.

There will be times ahead when the pressures of your current life temporarily block your memory of the lessons in this book, and then, all of a sudden, a flash of insight will pop into your conscious mind. It will be a message from your unconscious that still remembers your links with your past. When that happens, you have the opportunity of listening to the message or not. Before, you would have missed it altogether. Now you have the skills to be aware of the messages from your soul.

When that flash arrives, you can consider what you received on the spot, or you can delve into it more deeply at a more appropriate time. Having a set time every day when you can communicate with your soul can provide many insights for you in the future. It doesn't have to be long. Only a few minutes can do the trick. What the process does is open you to the messages from your unconscious mind. It will make the link back to the memories of your soul and send up the appropriate information for you when you need it.

Your belief can be an important source of support and awareness. When you practice your relaxing image trances, ask for the guidance necessary to help you understand the daily situations in your life. You may also request that your inner and outer guidance systems work with your belief to remind you of the lessons of your past that relate to where your soul's journey has progressed.

The more you are open to this concept, the more you will be aware of your past lives. The flash of insight you receive from your unconscious mind may come in any of the five senses. You may have a picture come into your mind, a voice, a feeling, a smell, or a taste in your mouth. You may just *know*. The insights may come while you are awake or asleep. They may appear as déjà vu. These are all forms of instant past life experiences. They may have been with you before you experienced this book, but now you know how to recognize the memories of your soul.

SOUL STORIES

Jake didn't believe in the concept of past lives until a chance encounter with someone involved in Edgar Cayce's work presented a view that he couldn't shake from his mind. Jake was given a book on the life of Cayce, and when he read of the struggles that this common man had endured as he began to use his psychic gifts, it gave him new insights into his own life situation. Jake began to compare his life to karmic patterns, and by relating his problems to other lifetimes, he discovered he had a new and different view. He was also able to make some positive changes in his life because of his new concept of past lives. He feels he is advancing on the journey of his soul.

Ask yourself what your passion in life really is. If you could help others and yourself with no limitations, how would you do it? How would you satisfy the yearning that you may feel deep in your soul to be in tune with your life purpose? Perhaps, just perhaps, it is a passion you have carried with you from other lifetimes. Perhaps this is the time to discover your soul's purpose from the rich heritage of your soul.

Chances are you have been journeying into your past lives since you were born. Everyone does, but most people don't know or want to understand the importance of connecting themselves to the past. It can make a great difference in your view of life situations if you continue using your ability to experience past life discoveries.

What You Were and What You May Be

You are a work in progress. You can trace your journey from the beginnings of your soul. You can look into the potential of future lives, but the real focus is on your present lifetime. What you do now can greatly influence what you will have to do in the future. What you may be depends on what you are doing with what you have done. You may have some karma to resolve. You may have an ability that needs to be developed and used for the good. Now is your chance to let yourself become in tune with your life map and your soul's current purpose. You even have the opportunity to go beyond your lessons in this life if your free will lets you.

Remember the suggestion that when you encounter images you don't understand during a past life discovery session, you should just go with the experience. You have the opportunity to go with and work with your current life experiences. If you believe that your soul has a great potential, you may find hope where there is little to find.

The more you focus on the love and peace that is waiting to be experienced when you tap into the universe through your unconscious mind, the more you will be open to the wisdoms from your soul to help guide you into the future. You are never alone. Just by changing your focus you have the wisdom and strength of the universe with you. It will help temper the past and provide hope for the future.

Do you know what patina on a gold ring is? When you buy a ring that is brand new and freshly polished, it has no patina. The ring needs to be worn before it acquires it. You see the patina in all the scratches that are created from its wear. Every little scratch causes the gold to reflect the light much more brilliantly than the new ring. You need to use the ring for its true beauty to be revealed. In the same way, you have acquired a lot of patina from your past life experiences.

AGELESS INSIGHTS

"Ultimately, it's the best of nature re-cycling. Our DNA body returns to the earth, and our spiritual body—or soul—returns to the light to reincarnate into another lifetime of learning and growth."

—Dr. Georgina Canon, Ontario Hypnosis Centre School and Clinic

Serving the greater whole is a lofty ambition, and yet many strive for it unknowingly. An unfinished mission started in a past lifetime may drive you to see it through now. You may not even know what that mission was, but you have the overwhelming emotion that you need to get going. Yet at the same time you may be frustrated that you can't find a way to get started. You may feel like you're spinning your wheels, and time is running out.

So get started. Spend some time with your past and get to know who you have been. Spend some time with your faith and guidance systems so that you may begin to move into the future. Your goal is one step at a time. You may think that you take two steps forward and then one back. If you could sit on a high mountain and follow your soul's progress since the beginning, what would the journey look like? Would it be a straight line or a meandering road as it spans the lifetimes of your past?

How do you think the path of your soul will look in the future? Will it still wander back and forth, or will it show a new direction as you work on the lessons of the universe? You can learn from your past and create a new and positive direction to your future.

You are the master of your soul.

The Least You Need to Know

- You can use all the experiences from your past lives to help you in the future.
- You are ready to stay in tune with your soul's purpose.
- There are always new past life insights to discover.
- You can now recognize when you are instantly experiencing a past life memory.
- You can use your knowledge of the past to help you in the moment and on into the future.

Glossary

affect-bridge regression   A hypnosis technique that takes a subject back through her life to events that relate to a specific emotion. As she regresses, she may transfer the emotion to a similar emotion that she experienced earlier.

Akashic Book of Records   Also known as the "Book of Life." It contains a record of every soul who has ever existed. It is believed to hold every deed, word, feeling, thought, and intent of every soul in the universe.

altered state of consciousness   A trance.

anchor   A special word or physical action such as a touch that can help a person recreate a state of heightened focus.

astral projection   When the mental and/or spiritual parts of a person separate from his physical body. It is usually felt as a floating sensation, and it usually happens when the person is in a state of trance.

automatic writing   Writing from images received in a relaxing image trance.

channeling   When another entity comes through one's unconscious mind for the purpose of communicating.

collective unconscious   The place in the universe where it is believed all thoughts and experiences from the past are recorded.

conscious mind   The part of the mind—approximately 10 percent—that thinks, processes information, and makes decisions.

conscious reality   One's awareness of the present and what is taking place in close proximity to that person.

convergent thinking   A thought process that eliminates options rather than examining them. By this method, eventually there will be no options left and the process will be stuck.

déjà vu   A French phrase that means "seen before."

detachment   The ability to observe, or even experience, a potentially upsetting image with little or no emotional feeling.

divergent thinking   A thinking process that examines options, especially when one can't go forward. By trying out options, one can find another route and succeed in reaching one's goal.

DNA   Deoxyribonucleic acid, a chemical found at the center of the cells of living things that controls the structure and purpose of each cell and carries genetic information.

dowsing   Finding information by using a device such as a pendulum controlled by the unconscious and universal minds of the individual holding it.

external guidance system   Angels, spirits, guides, and other unseen elements that are a part of one's daily life and usually are there to help watch over and assist him or her.

facilitator   Someone who can help guide a person into and out of a trance to experience a past life discovery.

false memory   The recall of events in a way that never happened, due to external influences such as the power of suggestion.

fantasy prone personality   Someone who imagines a great deal in his or her mind and easily enters a hypnotic trance.

flow chart   A simple map to help follow the sequence of events of one or more past lives; the map might use symbols to depict people, places, occupations, etc.

free will   The term given to each person's ability to do as he wants rather than following his own soul's life plan. If a person chooses not to follow his purpose, he will have the opportunity to do it over in a future lifetime.

genealogy The record or study of one's family, including ancestors and descendents. A person can develop a past life family tree through the use of past life discovery.

ghost The spirit of a dead person who hasn't yet traveled on to the other side.

hypnosis An altered state of consciousness where the unconscious mind is receptive to suggestions.

hypnosis script The dialogue used by a hypnotist to induce a trance in a subject. It can also be the words that individuals practicing self-hypnosis say to themselves to help them go into a trance, and may contain suggestions for obtaining their desired goals.

imagination The power of the mind to reproduce images or concepts stored in the memory.

internal belief system The set of values that a person was born with.

karma The unfinished lessons created by a person's actions in one or more of her lifetimes. These actions influence some of the situations that person currently faces now and in her future lives.

labyrinth Like a maze, except there are no dead ends. Once a person enters, he continues inward until he reaches the center. If one views the layout of a labyrinth from above, it looks much like the design of a human brain. There is a right sphere and a left sphere. As a person progresses through it, he can actually balance his own energy flow.

library A real place with books, or one that someone imagines in her unconscious mind where she may find a book, or series of books, of her soul's memories, each featuring one of her past lives.

life cycle A theme or situation that keeps coming up or happening over and over again. It's usually connected to unresolved karma.

life map The lesson plan (blueprint) a soul follows during one incarnation.

lucid dreaming The process of continuing a dream in one's waking state.

manifest reality   What can be seen, touched, heard, tasted, and smelled by whoever is in the same vicinity.

mental DNA   The way a person's mind works in the five senses, which may be shaped by past life experiences.

mesmerize   To induce someone into a hypnotic trance. Named for Anton Mesmer (1734–1815).

old souls   People who are further along their soul's lessons and often don't seem to fit in with others. They know more than they can tell anyone. If they try, they may be looked at as odd or a misfit.

operator   The person who is guiding a subject into a hypnotic trance and usually asks questions that will help produce desired information from a regression session.

past life discovery experience   The process of going back into a previous lifetime through your unconscious mind while you are in a relaxed, self-hypnotic state.

past life regression   When a person goes back in his or her mind in a trance state to experience a past life.

past life specialist   Someone who has been trained to conduct and interpret a past life discovery experience. The training may be recognized by acceptance to an organization such as IBRT, the International Board for Regression Therapy.

pendulum   A weight such as a crystal, a pendant, or anything that can dangle from a chain or string so that it will swing freely. A pendulum can be used with your unconscious mind to provide answers to yes and no questions.

perfection   The highest degree of excellence or experience or proficiency at something that one can achieve.

phobia   A fear that becomes so powerful the one who experiences it temporarily loses touch with her surroundings and enters a second reality that is connected to a traumatic moment in her past (that past may not be in this lifetime!). When the phobia starts, the person relives that memory again without realizing it.

progression The use of a relaxing image trance to project oneself forward into a future lifetime. The concept is similar to regression except that one is going ahead in time instead of back.

psychic A person whose soul knowledge is accessible to him through his unconscious mind. This knowledge may come through at unexpected times until the individual learns to access it.

quantum mechanics The theory that every particle or cell contains energy and exists independently of each other. On the metaphysical level, every cell contains the universal life energy that holds the keys to the knowledge of the universal mind.

reincarnation The belief that the soul returns to live in different physical bodies over a series of lifetimes. These lifetimes are a continuation of the lessons that the soul encounters working its way back to being a part of the universal mind.

sacred contract The belief that a soul draws up a plan or blueprint for each lifetime based on the experiences from the most recent lifetime.

self-hypnosis When a person induces herself into a hypnotic trance.

soul The element of life, feeling, thought, and action in humans. Considered to be a separate part of the mental, physical, and spiritual self. The soul is believed to survive beyond death.

soul fragmentation The belief that a soul can divide into more than one part when it reincarnates. This belief makes it possible for a person's soul to also be a part of another person.

soul mate Someone whom a person has been together with before in one or more lifetimes. The connections in the past were often very close.

spirit communication The ability to speak to the soul, usually in thought form, of someone who has died.

spontaneous memory recall A memory that is stored in a person's unconscious mind and suddenly becomes part of his conscious thinking without any effort to remember. This is different than one that the person may have been trying to remember.

subject   The individual experiencing a trance state.

suggestibility test   An exercise to determine how well a subject for hypnosis follows suggestions.

suppressed memory   A memory that is buried in one's unconscious mind and is only recalled when a situation jogs it. Then it may come flooding back to the surface and cause a person to replay the original experience in her mind.

theosophist belief   A belief system that dates back to the third century C.E. and became popular again after Madame Helena Petrovna Blavatsky founded the Theosophical Society in 1875. Its followers strove to learn the secrets of the universe in order to achieve the same perfection as their supreme deity.

third eye   The energy center where a person's "psychic sight" comes into his body from the "source." Located in the center of the forehead at a point that is above and centered between one's two seeing eyes.

time line   A system for recording events in the order that they took place. Similar to a flow chart, which uses symbols.

trance   An altered state of consciousness in which the unconscious mind is open to suggestion and loses its ability to make critical decisions.

transmigration   Means essentially the same as reincarnation. It's a term that was incorporated into the Christian beliefs until it was purged from the church in the early centuries.

tunnel vision   A focus so narrow that it's like looking through a tunnel. All one can see out the other side is the area in front of the opening. The farther away one is, the smaller the actual view is.

twin souls   Also called twin flames. Two people who are thought to have started their journey together as one single spark of energy, perfectly balanced, as both male and female. When the energy moved into physical matter, it divided in two.

unconscious mind   The storage area for all of one's memories up to this point in time. It makes up 90 percent of a person's total mind.

universal mind   A person's connection to the source or the knowledge of the universe that also contains one's own soul's memories.

unmanifest reality   A reality that is usually not recognized by people and yet is believed by some to actually exist in a different form.

vortex   A place where Earth energies converge and create a swirling cylindrical stream that rises upward into the universe. It's a place where souls can be transported to the other side and where the universe can send through reincarnated souls.

zone   A state of hyper-focus where a person is able to mentally change time, distance, and energy.

Resources

The goal of this book has been to open your eyes to the possibility that other realities, such as past lives, exist around you. The resources listed here may be used to help you delve deeper into a subject that may pique your interest and help you continue your journey of enlightenment.

General

AbeBooks Inc.
655 Tyee Road, Suite 500
Victoria BC
Canada V9A6X5
www.abebooks.com
Online marketplace for used books; thousands of booksellers.

Akashic Record Consultants International
843-991-0831
www.askashicrecordconsultantsinternational.org
Consultants, classes, and teachers for people who want to learn more about the Akashic Records.

American Society of Dowsers
PO Box 24
Danville, VT 05828
802-684-3417
www.dowsers.org
A nonprofit educational and scientific society dedicated to preserving an open forum of ideas regarding dowsing.

Association of Research and Enlightenment
215 67th Street
Virginia Beach, VA 23451
1-800-333-4499
www.edgarcayce.org
Information about Edgar Cayce, holistic health, personal spirituality, intuition, and education.

Audacity
www.audacity.sourceforge.net
Free audio editor and recorder.

Cambridge Dictionaries Online
www.dictionary.cambridge.org
A search engine for English vocabulary using the many dictionaries published by Cambridge University Press.

International Association for Regression Research and Therapies
PO Box 20151
Riverside, CA 92516
www.iarrt.org
Nonprofit organization dedicated to increasing the acceptance and use of professional and responsible regression therapy through education, association, and research.

International Association for the Study of Dreams
1672 University Avenue
Berkeley, CA 94703
209-724-0889
www.asdreams.org
Nonprofit multidisciplinary organization dedicated to the study of dreams and dreaming.

Lisa Halpin, DCH, BCH
2723 Crow Canyon Road, Suite 209
San Ramon, CA 94583
1-888-497-8416
www.HypnoCoachCertification.com, www.MindAdept.com
Consulting hypnotist, speaker, and educator. Originator of professional HypnoCoach training and Mind Adept—the Total Mind Concept.

National Guild of Hypnotists
PO Box 308
Merrimack, NH 03054
603-429-9438
www.ngh.net
Information on hypnosis and hypnosis training.

Ontario Hypnosis Centre School and Clinic
Dr. Georgina Cannon
www.georginacannon.com
Author, change catalyst, corporate speaker, international facilitator, consulting hypnotist, and teacher.

Parapsychology Foundation, Inc.
PO Box 1562
New York, NY 10021
212-628-1550
www.parapsychology.org
Worldwide forum supporting the scientific exploration of psychic phenomena.

Sylvia Browne
www.SylviaBrowne.com
World-renowned psychic, spiritual teacher, author, and founder of the Church of Novus Spiritus and the Sylvia Browne Hypnosis Training Center.

White Mountain Hypnosis Center
Michael R. Hathaway
PO Box 276
Madison, NH 03849
603-367-8851
www.whitemountainhypnosiscenter.com, www.michaelhathaway.com
Consulting hypnotist, speaker, and educator. Author of this book.

Books

Ackerman, Diane. *The Natural History of the Senses.* New York: Random House, 1990.

Andrews, Ted. *How to Uncover Your Past Lives.* St. Paul, MN: Llewellyn Publications, 1992.

Bennett, Dean B. *The Forgotten Nature of New England.* Camden, Maine: Down East Books, 1996.

Bernstein, Morey. *The Search for Bridey Murphy.* New York: Doubleday & Co., 1956.

Bolduc, Henry Leo. *The Journey Within: Past-Life Regression and Channeling.* Virginia Beach, VA: Inner Vision Publishing Co., 1988.

Caldwell, Taylor. *Dear and Glorious Physician.* New York: Doubleday, 1959.

———. *Great Lion of God.* New York: Doubleday, 1970.

Fiore, Dr. Edith. *You Have Been Here Before. A Psychologist Looks at Past Lives.* New York: Ballantine Books, 1978.

Freedman, Thelma. *Soul Echoes: The Healing Power of Past Life Therapy.* New York: Citadel Press, 2002.

Goldberg, Dr. Bruce. *Past Lives, Future Lives.* New York: Ballantine Books, 1982.

Grant, Robert J. *The Place We Call Home. Exploring the Soul's Existence After Death.* Virginia Beach, VA: A.R.E. Press, 2000.

Guiley, Rosemary Ellen. *Harper's Encyclopedia of Mystical & Paranormal Experience.* San Francisco, CA: HarperSanFrancisco, 1991.

Hathaway, Michael R. *It's Time to Simplify Your Soul's Code.* West Conshohocken, PA: Infinity Publishing, 2007.

———. *The Everything Hypnosis Book.* Avon, MA: Adamsmedia, 2003.

———. *The Only Psychic Power Book You'll Ever Need.* Avon, MA: Adamsmedia, 2008.

Kirkpatrick, Sidney D. *Edgar Cayce: An American Prophet.* New York: Riverhead Books, 2000.

LaBerge, Stephen, and Howard Rheingold. *Exploring the World of Lucid Dreaming.* New York: Ballantine, 1990.

Langley, Noel, edited by Hugh Lynn Cayce. *Edgar Cayce on Reincarnation.* New York: Warner Books, 1967.

Lenz, Frederick Ph.D. *Lifetimes. True Accounts of Reincarnation.* New York: Fawcett Crest, 1979.

Lethbridge, T. C. *The Power of the Pendulum.* England: Penguin Books, 1976.

Pliskin, Marci, and Shari L. Just. *The Complete Idiot's Guide to Interpreting Your Dreams.* Indianapolis: Alpha Books, 1999.

Roberts, Jane. *Seth Speaks: The Eternal Validity of the Soul.* Englewood Cliffs, New Jersey: Prentice Hall, 1972.

Schlotterbeck, Karl. *Living Your Past Lives: The Psychology of Past-Life Regression.* New York: Ballantine Books, 1987.

Stearn, Jess. *Edgar Cayce—The Sleeping Prophet.* New York: Bantam Books, 1967.

———. *The Search for a Soul. Taylor Caldwell's Past Lives.* New York: Berkley Books, 1994.

Stevenson, Ian. *Where Reincarnation and Biology Intersect.* Praeger Publishers, 1997.

Sugrue, Thomas. *There Is a River.* New York: Henry Holt, 1942. Reprinted by Holt, Dell, A.R.E. Press.

Sutphen, Dick. *Past Lives, Future Loves.* New York: Pocket Books, Simon & Schuster, 1978.

———. *You Were Born Again to Be Together.* New York: Pocket Books, Simon & Schuster, 1976.

Talbot, Michael. *Your Past Lives: A Reincarnation Handbook.* New York: Fawcett Crest, Ballantine Books, 1987.

Washington, Peter. *Madame Blavatsky's Baboon: A History of the Mystics, Mediums, and Misfits Who Brought Spiritualism to America.* New York: Schocken Books, 1995.

Weiss, Brian L. *Many Lives, Many Masters.* New York: Simon & Schuster, 1988.

———. *Through Time into Healing.* New York: Simon & Schuster, 1992.

Woolger, Roger J. *Other Lives, Other Selves: A Jungian Psychotherapist Discovers Past Lives.* New York: Bantam Books, 1988.

Index

A

affect-bridge technique, 86-87, 116, 167-169
after-death emotions, 233
Akashic Records, 16-17, 167, 212
anchor, 47-48
angel, 126-127
artistic ability, 136, 245
automatic writing, 139, 143, 249

B

balance, 121
    angel, 126-127
    escape route, 121
    exercise, 128-129
    faith, 125-126
    guides, 126-127
    manifest reality, 126
    past life specialist, 123
    travel insurance, 122-124
    unmanifest reality, 127
basics. *See* past life basics
Bennett, Dean, 134
birthmark, 118
bliss, 266
body heaviness, 184
breathing, 76-77, 174

Browne, Sylvia, 218
Buddhist religion, karma, 7

C

Caldwell, Taylor, 56, 201, 248
Cayce, Edgar
    Akashic Records, 16, 153, 212
    caution, 252
    guide, 138
    health problems, 142
    karmic attraction, 117
    struggles, 272
    twin souls, 225-226
    warning, 255
    wife of, 222
channeling, 213-214
character development, 122
children, 29
    living past life, 31-33
    mannerisms, 31
    memories, 29-30
    preserving memories, 35-37
    reincarnation of family member, 34
    role reversals, 33-35
    vocabulary, 31
    wisdom, 30-31

collective unconscious, 211-213,
254
comfort zone, 73
   breathing, 76-77
   favorite place, 74-75
   focus, 79
   healing energy flow, 81
   meditation, 74
   nonvisual, 80
   prayer, 81
   return to reality, 79
communication, 212-215
   faith, 125
   imagination, 41
   soul, 19, 269
conscience, 18
conscious mind, 6
   flash of insight, 271
   imagination, 21
   insights, 121
   old trauma, 105
   return to, 45, 103, 185
   spacing out, 51
conscious reality, 33-34
convergent thinking, 151
counting backward, 77-78
   balance, 129
   discovery session, 175,
      179-180

D

Dalai Lama, 29
data collection, 193-195
   blanks, 199-200
   family tree, 196
   need to return, 195-197
   revisiting of past life, 198
   story research, 201-202

data organization, 193
definitions
   affect-bridge technique, 87
   Akashic Records, 17
   anchor, 47
   conscious reality, 34
   convergent thinking, 151
   déjà vu, 55
   divergent thinking, 151
   DNA, 5
   facilitator, 84
   ghost, 24
   hypnosis, 11
   imagination, 11, 107
   karma, 8
   life cycle, 114
   past life specialist, 85
   perfection, 266
   phobia, 40
   quantum mechanics, 254
   soul fragmentation, 211
   spirit communication, 214
   spontaneous memory recall,
      62
   suppressed memory, 245
   time line, 200
   twin flames, 225
   twin souls, 225
   unconscious mind, 64
déjà vu, 55, 213
detective work. *See* evidence
   detection
discovery of past lives, 99
   experience, 99-101
      imagination versus,
         106-108
      lessons, 102
   imagination, 107
   mental DNA, 101
   patience, 106
   post-experience, 104-106

relaxing image trance, 101
stuck in past life, 102-104
discovery session, 171-172, 267
Atlantis, 91-94
benefits of contacting others, 212
counting backward, 179-180
destination, 134
ending, 161
energy, 196
evidence detection, 150
goals, 53, 172
images, 273
impressions, 183-186
journal, 190-191
notes, 187-189
interpreted, 271
involvement, 142
old karma, 232-233
panic attacks, 94-95
past life discovery specialist, 86-91
return to present, 179
script, television method, 174
spirits encountered, 214
steps, 173
stuck in past life, 102
theme, 174
trance, 174-176
travel, 177-179
unconscious mind, 151
video, 173
visited lifetimes, 152
divergent thinking, 151
DNA
body return to earth, 274
mental, 5, 69, 145
physical, 5
dowsing, 140

dreams
flying, 17
lucid, 58
nightmares, 123
precognitive, 58
symbolic, 57
trance and, 57
waking up, 184

E

emotional images, 147, 168
environmental awareness, 258
evidence detection, 145-149
characters, 152-153
convergent thinking, 151
detective work, 149-151
discovery session, 150-152
divergent thinking, 151
karma, principles, 153
relaxation exercise, 155
story theme, 154
unconscious mind, 151
exercises
anchor creation, 47
breathing, 76
imagery trance, 42
imagination, 41
in-between lives, 262
relaxation, 43
return to consciousness, 79
soul memory healing, 239
unconditional loving energy, 241
experiential visual image, 146

F

facilitator, 83-84, 137
faith, 125-126
false memories, 105
family
  genealogy, 195
  memories, 29
  soul mate connections,
    222-224
fatal attraction, 10
fear. *See also* phobia
  death experience, 25
  public performance, 269
  separation, 25
  twin souls, 227
feelings, 147
flashback, 62
flying dreams, 17
Ford, Arthur, 214
free will, 8
  ego, 234
  future life, 255
  rediscovered abilities, 268
  regression, 235
  warning signal, 9
future life
  debilitating disease, 256
  discovery, 253-255, 258-259
  environmental awareness, 258
  information gained from, 260
  investment, 253
  karmic relationship, 255
  quantum mechanics, 260
  trance, 259
  travel plan, 255-257

G

ghosts
  case, 24
  channeling, 214
  fear, 25
  questions, 26
  return to conscious mind, 27
God Kings, reincarnation, 29
Great Lion of God, 201
grounding, 100
guidance systems, 274

H

highway hypnosis, 11, 51
Hinduism, 8
hologram, 85
hundredth monkey story, 212
hyper-focus, 63
hypnosis, 11, 34, 105, 215

I

IBRT. *See* International Board
  for Regression Therapy
identity, 15-17
  fear of separation, 25
  foreboding feeling, 27
  ghosts, 24-27
  heart, 22-23
  reality versus imagination,
    20-21
  soul, 18-20

imagery trances, 42, 109, 184, 270
    artistic talent, 246
    perspective, 112
    spirit communication, 214
imagination, 11, 20-22
    children, 30
    communication, 41
    discovery of past lives, 106
    dual reality, 40
    exercise, 41
    influence, 43
    memories and, 107
    trances, 41, 73
in-between lives, 261-262
International Board for Regression Therapy (IBRT), 85
intuition, 9, 250

creation, 18
cycles, 111, 114-116
description, 112
fears and phobias, 117-118
identification, 232
life cycle, 114-115
medical conditions, 119
negative, 267
opportunity to resolve, 174
principles, 153
psychic ability and, 250
rediscovered abilities, 266
resolved, 268
soul mates, 117
twin souls, 228
types, 112
unfinished, 243
unresolved issues, 112-113
"Kinder Music," 37

J

journal, 248, 190-191
    benefit, 194
    children's memories, 36
    data collection, 195
    discovery session, 187, 190
    dream, 58
    encounters noted, 267
    karma encountered, 233
    karmic balance sheet, 235
Jung, Carl, 211, 254

K

karma, 7-8, 111. *See also* old karma
    aches and pains, 118-119
    artistic talent, 247

L

library, 160
life
    cycle, 114
    map, 18-19, 273
    plan, choice to follow, 234
    purpose, 16
lucid dream, 58

M

manifest reality, 126
medical conditions, 119
meditation, 74
memory
    affect-bridge technique, 169
    analogy, 61

blocked, 271
children, 29, 35
comfort zone, 74
connection, 239
dreams, 57
false, 105
flashback, 62
imagination and, 107
influence, 4
mental energy of the universe,
  211
recall, spontaneous, 62
relationships, 218
repressed, 211
revivification, 108
senses, 6, 70
soul, 117, 147, 196, 241
suppressed, 245
tactile, 68
unconscious mind, 15
visual, 66
mental DNA, 5, 65-67, 101
artistic talent, 246
assessment, 71-72
comfort zone, 74
evidence detection, 145-147
experiential visual image, 146
sensory images, 5
smell, 69
soul memory, 147
sounds, 67, 146
taste, 69
travel insurance, 122
understanding, 66, 70
mental imagery, athletes, 79
mind
child's, 31
confusion, 6
conscious, 6
  flash of insight, 271
  imagination, 21

insights, 121
old trauma, 105
return to, 45, 103
spacing out, 51
ego, 18
focus into future, 63
highway rotary, 111
illustration of operation, 61
information, 64
relaxing place, 75
tenses, 6
unconscious, 6
asking, 239
data, 194
discovery session, 151
emotional experiences, 25
evidence detection, 146,
  151
future life, 259
hologram, 85
information collection, 233
library, 160-161
memories, 15
messages from, 272
movie theater, 163
old karma, 241
past life discovery experience, 4
relationships, 219
search for truth, 268
suppressed memory, 245
television watching, 163
writer, 248
universal, 6, 65, 128
mood changes, 115
movies, 149, 163
Mozart, 37
music, 269

N

Native American culture, 54
natural talent, 246
natural trance, 74
near-death experiences, 261
Neuro-Linguistic Programming
(NLP), 41
nightmares, 123
NLP. *See* Neuro-Linguistic
Programming

O

old karma, 231-233
exercise, 241
free will, 234-235
healing, 236-240
identified, 267
journal, 235
senses, 240
soul memory healing exercise,
239
unconditional loving energy,
241
unconscious mind, 241
visual images, 240
olfactory sense, 69

P

panic attacks, 94
parallel lifetimes, 263
parent relationship, 224
past life basics, 3-6
Buddhist religion, karma, 7
free will, 9
highway hypnosis, 11
Hinduism, 8
hypnotic trance, 11
imagination, 11
intuition, 9
karma, 7-8
play, 7-8
relationships, 8-10
self-image trances, 12
senses, differences in
experiences, 7
trances, 11-12
past life discovery. *See* data
collection
past life discovery session. *See*
discovery session
past life discovery specialist, 83
affect-bridge technique, 87
credentials, 84
disappointment, 85
discovery session, 86-90
Atlantis, 91-94
panic attacks, 94-95
escape route, 123
expectations, 84-86
facilitator, 84
old karma, 237
reality versus imagination, 21
relationships, 218
self-trances, 83
session length, 86
travel insurance, 123
past relationships. *See* relationships
pendulum, 140-141
perfect experience, 266
phobia, 117-118
shared, 208
trances, 104
triggering of, 62

physical DNA, 5
prayer, 81
precognitive dream, 58
psychic gifts, 249

Q-R

quantum mechanics, 254

rediscovered abilities, 269-272
   experiences, 265-267
   present lifetime, 273-274
   soul's purpose, 267-268
regression, 198, 218
Reiki, 105
reincarnation, 29-30
   belief in, 209
   child, 34
   process, 4
relationships, 8-10, 217-219
   children, 35
   crisscrossing paths, 218-220
   family members, 223-224
   karma, 116
   record, 191
   soul mate connections,
      221-223
   travel plan, 137
   twin souls, 225-228
   unexplainable, 113
relaxation, 43, 138
repressed memories, 211
research, 207-208
   belief in reincarnation, 209
   channeling, 213-214
   collective unconscious,
      211-213
   data collection, 194

   ghost, communication with,
      214
   guidance systems, 215
   simultaneous lives, 209-211
   spirit communication, 213-214
Roberts, Jane, 213
romantic relationship, 221
rose-colored glasses, 266

S

sacred contract, 261-262
scripts, 159
   affect-bridge technique,
      167-169
   discovery session, 161, 172
   emotional images, 168
   goals, 198
   going backward in time,
      165-167
   library, 160-161
   movies, 163
   television, 163-164, 174
   trances, 47
self-imagery, benefits, 46
self-relaxing session, 11
self-trances, 83
senses, 61
   comfort zone, 75
   discovery of past lives, 100
   evidence detection, 146-147
   feeling, 68
   hard of hearing, 70
   image recall, absent, 72
   memory, 70
   mental DNA, 65-67
      assessment, 71-72
      smell, 69
      taste, 69

mind, 64-65
old karma, 236, 240
relationships, 219, 223
smell, 70
spontaneous memory recall,
    62
tenses, 62
    differences in
        experiences, 7
    disappointment, 63
    flashback, 62
    future, 63
    hyper-focus, 63
    memories and, 6
    past, 62
    present, 63
    spontaneous memory
        recall, 62
    zone, 63
travel, 177
unconscious mind, 64
visual memory, 66
soul, 18
agenda, 136
communication with, 269
development potential, 19
ego mind, 18
end of journey, 17
equalizers, 19
evolution, 235
fragmentation, 211
history, 215
information, 19
life maps, 18-19
memories, 30, 240, 266, 270
music, 269
old, 17
physical form, 225
purpose, 18, 112, 267-269
resonance, 20
travel, 225

soul mates, 137, 221
experiences, 221
family members, 223
karma, 117
passion, 222
questions, 223
romantic relationship, 221
senses, 223
traumatic event, 222
space aliens, 215
spirit communication, 213
spontaneous memory recall, 62
Stevenson, Ian, 30
suppressed memory, 245

T

tactile memories, 68
talents, 243
    artist, 245-247
    fame, 251-252
    lost, 269
    psychic gifts, 249-251
    rediscovery of skills, 244-245
    television commercial, 243
    unfinished karma, 243
    writer, 248-249
television, 163-164, 174
therapeutic session, goal, 105
third eye, 76
trance
    artistic, 247
    counting backward, 175-176
    creation, 39
        communication, 41
        daily practice schedule,
            46-48
        goal, 40
        imagination, 41, 43

natural experience, 42
phobia, 40
relaxation, 43-45
types, 40
discovery session, 174
future life, 259
getting stuck in, 12
hypnotic, 210, 215
image, 112, 246
inability to enter, 73
life cycle, 114
living in, 51, 55
   closeness to God, 52
   déjà vu, 55
   dreams, 57-58
   highway hypnosis, 51
   old things, 52
   period of time, 53-54
   sleep, 57
muscle relaxation, 174
phobia, 104
relaxing image, 101
self-, 83
universal loving energy, 174
traumatic event, 222
grounding and, 100
keeping grounded, 121
rediscovered abilities, 269
travel
   discouragement, 177
   fast-forward, 178
   important event, 178
   insurance, 122-124
   plan, 133, 137-138
      automatic writing, 139
      destination, 134-135
      discovery session, 142
      duration, 141-143
      music, 141

      pendulum, 140-141
      tools, 139-140
   purpose, 134
   search, 178
   senses, 177
   theme, 179
   unconscious mind, 178
twin souls, 225-228

U–V

unconscious mind, 6
asking, 239
children's memories, 35
data, 194
emotional experiences, 25
evidence detection, 146, 151
faith, 125
future life, 259
hologram, 85
information collection, 233
library, 160-161
memories, 15
messages from, 272
movie theater, 163
old karma, 241
past life discovery
   experience, 4
relationships, 219
search for truth, 268
suppressed memory, 245
television watching, 163
travel, 178
writer, 248
universal energy force, 16
universal mind, 6, 65, 128, 211
universal protective light, 258
unmanifest reality, 127

video, discovery session, 173
visual memory, 66

W–X–Y–Z

willingness to imagine, 112

zone, 63, 79

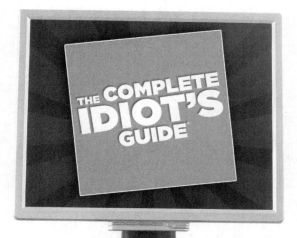

CHECK OUT THESE
BEST-SELLERS

More than 450 titles available at booksellers and online retailers everywhere!

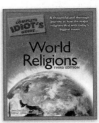

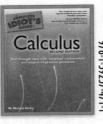

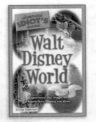